Culture, Conflict and Coexistence

American–Soviet Cultural Relations, 1917–1958

by J. D. Parks

McFarland 1983

Jefferson, North Carolina, and London

Library of Congress Cataloguing-in-Publication Data

Parks, J.D.
  Culture, conflict, and coexistence.

  Bibliography: p.
  Includes index.
  1. United States—Relations—Soviet Union. 2. Soviet
Union—Relations—United States.
E183.8.S65P37 1983   303.4′8273′047   83-42891

ISBN 0-89950-094-3

Manufactured in the United States of America

McFarland & Company, Inc., Publishers
  Box 611, Jefferson, North Carolina 28640

Contents

Culture, Conflict and Coexistence

Preface

Thursday, July 17, 1975, about 140 miles above the Atlantic, off the coast of Portugal. Two tiny craft approach each other across the reaches of space, join, and lock. Three hours later a beaming Soviet cosmonaut pushes open a hatch, and, as hundreds of millions watch on television below, clasps the hand of an equally beaming American astronaut. With that handclasp, American-Soviet cooperation literally and figuratively reaches new heights.

But the space spectacular was only the most visible instance of American-Soviet interaction. As the linked capsules circled overhead, thousands of American and Soviet citizens traveled, studied, performed and competed in the country of the other. Within proscribed limits, books, magazines and newspapers flowed back and forth across their borders, providing objective knowledge and subjective insight to readers on both sides. Though lacking the spontaneity and latitude characterizing America's relations with many other nations, the friendly interaction seemed to indicate that in matters cultural, at least, the American and Soviet people had found the key to coexistence.

But not all was smiles and handshakes between Washington and Moscow. Immediately beneath the surface old fears and suspicions lay waiting, ready to rise at the least prompting. Indeed, on the day that they reported the space extravaganza, a number of publications deemed it wise to run concurrent articles pinpointing the problems dividing the two and detailing the sources of tension on each side. And in so doing, they unwittingly illustrated a basic theme in American-Soviet relations.

While Washington and Moscow have carried on a long-standing ideological feud, American and Soviet cultural representatives have, at the same time, carried on an active, albeit restricted, cultural intercourse. Only at the depths of the cold war did the political conflict become so acute as to almost entirely eliminate cultural connections as well, and then only for a short time. Within three years of the low point of their cultural relationship the two nations were again exchanging delegations,

1

and within six years had signed a formal exchange agreement that propelled cultural contacts far above previous levels.

This study traces the course of those contacts from the Bolshevik Revolution to the signing of that first official agreement in early 1958. In so doing it defines cultural relations in broad terms, including within its scope those activities normally considered "cultural" in nature — art, literature, music, etc. — as well as cooperative and competitive activities in the fields of science, technology, tourism, athletics and other areas in which the American and Soviet people associated as human beings rather than as ideological opponents. For regardless of their specific activities or purposes, the people of both countries who dealt with each other on a human level necessarily reciprocated a degree of knowledge about themselves and the culture that influenced the direction of their development.

The cultural relationship between the two nations divides itself rather naturally into four periods, three of which are treated in this study: the pre-Stalinist, from the 1917 revolution to the mid-thirties; the Stalinist, from the late thirties through the special years of World War II to the dictator's death in early 1953; the post-Stalinist fifties to the signing of the formal exchange pact in 1958; and the period of organized exchanges under official auspices following the latter year. Because both the nature and the scope of the cultural relationship changed so dramatically after 1958 as to deserve special treatment, that period is here dealt with in only an incidental manner.

Cultural contacts during the pre-Stalinist period of the twenties and early thirties were surprisingly full and free; indeed, were maintained on a broader scale than during any time prior to the 1958 agreement. Though Moscow rarely permitted its ordinary citizens to travel abroad, Soviet cultural representatives, technical delegations and artistic exhibits visited American cities throughout the prerecognition years, and American tourists, technicians, businessmen and cultural figures reciprocated the visits in large numbers. But as Stalin consolidated his power, purged the Party and waged an antiforeign campaign during the late thirties, the relatively free and easy contacts began to diminish; by the time of the Nazi-Soviet Pact had dwindled to a trickle. The exigencies of wartime partnership temporarily revived and extended the former friendly intercourse, but even before the fighting was over, Moscow began rejecting American overtures tendered under official auspices, and, in the immediate postwar years, resumed both the internal purges and the antiforeign rhetoric of the prewar period. As the decade of the forties progressed, Stalin, apparently for purposes of maintaining both Party and personal power, increasingly isolated the Soviet people from outside contacts, purged Soviet cultural life of western influences and turned the nation's cultural organs into weapons to attack bourgeois civilization. Perceiving a threat in the Soviet

dictator's treatment of his own people, in his suspected designs in Iran, Greece and Turkey, and in such successive shocks as the Berlin Blockade and the Korean War, Washington responded by erecting its own barriers to contacts with communists and conducting a campaign of national purification, ensuring the estrangement of the American and Soviet people. By the early fifties, the cultural relationship had reached an impasse.

Stalin's death in early 1953 provided the possibility of ending that impasse, but official Washington remained reticent. While Moscow's new rulers broadened Soviet contacts with nations throughout Europe and Asia, a reluctant and suspicious Washington provided little encouragement or support for similar contacts with the United States. But despite the official hesitance, individual Americans responded to the new overtures coming from the Soviet side, and initiated contacts of their own. As the cultural climate slowly thawed, the tentative first steps gradually gave way to more formal exchanges which, despite the failure of the powers to reach accord on the matter of East-West contacts at the Geneva Conference in 1955, continued throughout the middle of the decade and culminated in the official exchange pact signed in 1958.

Throughout the course of their relationship the two nations proceeded from different principles and, to a degree, pursued different aims. From the mid-twenties forward, Moscow organized and controlled its cultural contacts with foreign nations in accordance with state policies and plans. Though individual Soviet citizens may well have relished the human contact and the sharing of common interests on a personal level, Moscow viewed such contacts as assets to serve the interests of the Soviet state, or, if deemed advantageous, to be liquidated in the pursuit of those same interests. Cultural relations constituted a means, not an end, and that fact necessarily limited the extent to which the people of the two nations could enter into the kind of unfettered relationship that characterized the interaction between American citizens and those of nations less subject to state control.

Washington's role was more varied and complicated, and changed considerably over the years. During the twenties and thirties the State Department played an insignificant role in the realm of cultural contacts, exercising its minimal influence through its control over visas and passports. Contacts on the American side during these years were almost entirely matters of private preference, conducted by individuals and organizations whose interests lay in that direction. Prior to 1933, the State Department occasionally frowned on projects that implied recognition of the Soviet government, but its refusal to recognize the Moscow regime proved little handicap to cultural connections. Serving no official policies or purposes, cultural contacts represented to pre-World War II Americans, as they properly should have, ends and not means.

Washington began changing its role with respect to the Soviet Union during World War II. Having discovered the benefits of cultural connections in dealing with the Latin American nations during the late thirties, the State Department vigorously encouraged the same kind of friendly contacts with the Soviets during the war and early postwar years, emphasizing all the while its role of promoter and coordinator of private activities rather than that of purveyor of an "official" American culture. But as the Soviets withdrew from contacts with the West and as international tensions rose to the danger point in the postwar period, both Congress and the State Department took an increasingly narrow and practical view of cultural relations. Congress attacked the same cultural organizations that had only recently won praise and esteem for their wartime contributions to American-Soviet cooperation and created formidable barriers to contacts by passing legislation that practically prohibited any Soviet-bloc citizen entering the United States. The State Department turned its cultural relations program, now grown worldwide and official, into a tool to fight communism. The only contacts with the Soviets that he favored, Secretary of State Dulles made clear during the fifties, were those that allowed the United States to infuse "ideas and information" into the Soviet Union in order to encourage the Soviet people to resist their rulers. Washington, too, had learned to use cultural relations as a means to an end.

But Washington's desire and ability to manipulate cultural contacts for state purposes was limited in relation to Moscow's. Though the State Department had developed its own goals and aims with regard to cultural relations by the late forties, and though it sometimes discouraged private exchanges, particularly if those exchanges involved large numbers, it ordinarily neither prevented individual Americans making overtures on their own nor prohibited them responding to initiatives coming from Moscow. And though legislative barriers and Congressional suspicions posed obstacles to contacts in some instances during the fifties, by the middle of the decade even State Department officials were, at least on occasion, helping to find ways to diminish those difficulties. Americans, in short, usually had the option of engaging in contacts outside the official State Department framework; an option that Soviet citizens, to be sure, did not enjoy.

But to say that Americans and Soviets proceeded from different premises and pursued somewhat different aims is not to argue that Moscow's aims and methods were without merit or necessarily inimical to American interests. Particularly, it is not to argue that Soviet representatives were ordinarily bent on some subversive or otherwise harmful aim. At various times the Kremlin's principal motive may have been to promote recognition, to gain increased access to American technology, to impress

Americans with Soviet cultural achievements, or, as the Soviets themselves claimed, simply to promote mutual understanding and international accord, but whatever the aim the interaction would have been less had not Moscow promoted cultural contacts pursuant to its larger purposes. And it is difficult to believe that the resulting interchange played a negative role in American-Soviet relations, for regardless of the ulterior motives involved, the individuals who dealt with each other on a personal level presumably communicated elements of their common humanity that transcended state aims. Only the certainty that all nonofficial relations between American and Soviet citizens worked to the detriment of American national interests would have justified discouraging and restricting cultural contacts to the point of extinction, for they provided a measure of communication that otherwise would not have existed. The choice, then, was to accept Moscow's methods and to maintain contacts in a restricted and limited manner, or to reject both the method and the contacts, for although Americans could try to influence Washington's policies and principles, they could do little about Moscow's.

The same choice — or lack of choice — prevails today, for despite the biennial exchange agreements signed by the two nations since 1958, Moscow's fundamental approach has not changed. Americans today must still recognize the limited possibilities inherent in the Soviet approach and make the most of them, for the American and Soviet people already know too little about each other to forego any opportunities to speak to each other as human beings. While Americans would prefer speaking more openly and freely to their Soviet counterparts, they must realize that their inability to do so lies at least in part in the Russian past; that the offending Soviet barriers and restrictions reflect centuries of Russian fears and habits as well as decades of communist concerns. And Americans must also realize that their own country has not been entirely blameless; that their own policies and practices have at times been less than conducive to free and easy relations between the two peoples. The task today is not to assess guilt or to assign blame, but to continue and to intensify the effort to close the chasm that still separates the people of the two nations.

The encouragement and assistance of many people made this study possible. University of Oklahoma professors Russell Buhite and Henry Tobias provided their special kind of encouragement, kindness and critical comment, as did professors H. Wayne Morgan, Donald Secrest, Sidney Brown, and, in a less direct but valuable and appreciated manner, professors Ronald Snell and Arrell Morgan Gibson. The librarians and researchers at Rice University, the University of Houston, the Texas State Depository at Austin, the Hoover Institution on War, Revolution and Peace at Stanford University and the Diplomatic Branch of the National

Archives in Washington provided invaluable assistance in locating materials and suggesting sources. Dr. James Leyerzapf of the Eisenhower Library in Abilene, Kansas, was particularly helpful, as were Bernard Koten and Dr. Holland Roberts, who permitted unrestricted access to materials pertaining to the American-Russian Institutes located in, respectively, New York and San Francisco. Roberta Sealy, Geri Davis, Debbie Visage and Dr. John W. Larner deserve special thanks for their comments and assistance, and, above all, my thanks to Kristin, whose chatter lightened long hours of typing, and to my wife, Sharon, without whom this study would not have been completed. The interpretations, conclusions and the shortcomings of the study are, of course, my own.

I
Restoring a Relationship, 1921–1925

The Russian Revolution ruptured an historic friendship.[1]* The United States and Russia never faced each other on a battlefield; suffered no acute confrontations in any area. Statesmen on both sides were aware of this friendly tradition, and spoke of it often. Washington would have felt more comfortable with a less dictatorial regime in St. Petersburg, but it was no real burden to be friendly to a czar. Some late nineteenth century Americans complained about czarist oppression and Siberian prison camps, but their complaints remained rhetoric, and though conflicting ambitions in the Far East caused concern in Washington at the turn of the century, the rivalry never reached the crisis stage. Russian autocracy that posed no immediate threat to the national interest neither aroused the fear nor challenged the pride of most Americans.

Cultural friendship was even older than political amity. Long before the two governments exchanged ambassadors, learned men from both countries noted the achievements of the other, exchanged information of scientific interest and traded memberships in scholarly societies. In the 1750's St. Petersburg newspapers reported Franklin's experiments with electricity, in the 1760's Franklin and Ezra Styles of Yale College communicated with the scientist Michael Lomonosov, and in the 1770's the American Philosophical Society began a regular correspondence with the Russian Academy of Sciences.[2] In 1771, the American Society elected its first Russian member; a few years later the Russian Academy reciprocated by choosing Benjamin Franklin. The practice begun continued throughout the next century: by the time of the Revolution the American Philosophical Society listed 32 Russian members.[3] The American Academy of Arts and Sciences, founded in Boston in 1780 at the suggestion of John Adams, likewise established contacts with the Russian Academy of Sciences and began electing Russians to its membership as early as 1782.[4]

Several future presidents contributed to the developing relationship.

*See Chapter Notes, beginning on page 179.

In the 1780's George Washington and John Adams, responding to Catherine the Great's request for assistance in compiling a dictionary of comparative languages, provided the empress with information concerning native American dialects.[5] Jefferson's correspondence with Alexander I influenced the czar's drafts of proposed constitutions for Russia, and through liberals such as Alexander Radischev the Jeffersonian ideals of American democracy became known to Russian intellectuals.[6] Ambassador John Quincy Adams made extensive personal acquaintances within St. Petersburg learned circles, forwarded books to the Harvard Library and to the American Philosophical Society, and, by transmitting the results of Benjamin Rush's medical investigations to the Russian Academy of Sciences, played an important role in establishing an exchange of medical information that flourished in the nineteenth century and continued in the twentieth.[7]

The near-simultaneous deaths of Jefferson, Adams and Alexander I, along with the accession of Nicholas I, marked an end to the early period of burgeoning cultural interaction: as St. Petersburg intensified its efforts to destroy all manifestations of liberalism a chill crept into the relationship between the two nations.[8] But despite the period of cultural coolness, contacts continued to develop throughout the remainder of the century. The American Philosophical Society and the Russian Academy of Sciences shared information in a number of fields, particularly in astronomy, geology, medicine and the natural sciences, while individual scientists exchanged visits in order to personally observe the investigations and experiments of their peers.[9]

Contacts between scholars and scientists constituted only a part of the cultural communication between the Russian and American people. Books, music and entertainers traveled back and forth throughout the 1800's, and as the nineteenth century turned into the twentieth the increasing influx of Russian immigrants into the United States further broadened the basis for cultural interaction.[10] Beginning in the late 1800's a growing number of Russian entertainers, many of whom made a lasting impression on the world of American music and dance, appeared in the United States. Pyotr Tchaikovsky's works won acclaim more quickly in New York than in Moscow or St. Petersburg, and upon his arrival in America in 1891 the composer was surprised to find himself, as he wrote home, "a far more important person here than in Russia."[11] The great basso Feodor Chaliapin gave performances in several cities prior to World War I, as did the dancers Anna Pavlova, Mikhail Mordkin and Mikhail Fokine.[12] Rachmaninoff performed in several cities in 1910, and in the years 1916 and 1917 the Diaghilev Ballet toured the country, featuring the famed Vaslaw Nijinsky along with other celebrated names from St. Petersburg's Imperial Ballet and Moscow's Bolshoi Ballet.[13]

While Russian artists entertained American audiences, other Russians urged their countrymen to study and emulate American technological efficiency. In 1912, a Moscow University professor urged his country to send a delegation to study the mechanics of American production techniques and the psychology of the American businessman, while a returned Russian school teacher presented lantern slide shows on American industrial development, likewise impressing upon his audiences the importance of looking to America for industrial guidance.[14]

Despite the numerous personal contacts and exchanges carried on by scholarly bodies, each country neglected the academic study of the other. At the turn of the century, Harvard began offering courses in Russian language and literature, the University of California established a Department of Slavic Languages, and Samuel N. Harper tried to interest students in Russian studies at the University of Chicago, but few followed their lead. When World War I erupted only two American universities offered classes in Russian history, and only three taught the language and literature.[15]

Nor were the governments of the two countries concerned in any official capacity with promoting cultural relations. Both Washington and St. Petersburg facilitated travel and other contacts through incidental means, but neither actively encouraged organized exchanges. On the other hand, neither placed insuperable obstacles before private citizens whose interests lay in that direction. And given the increased emphasis on international understanding and cooperation during the early 1900's, plus the rapidly improving means of transportation and communication, there was reason to believe that an increasing number of people would in fact become more interested in the culture of the other.

The Revolution interrupted this agreeable state of affairs. As the momentous events of 1917 swept Russia past liberalism to communism, as Russian armies withdrew from the struggle against Germany and as the Bolsheviks encouraged world revolution, the enthusiasm in the United States turned to alarm. American soldiers occupied Russian soil as did those of England, France and Japan, giving at least the appearance of a willingness to assist any promising counter-revolutionary movement. Washington denied export licenses and clearance papers to ships bound for Soviet controlled ports, issued visas and passports only under certain conditions, and cut off mail service between the two countries.[16] Nor would Washington recognize the legitimacy of the new Soviet rulers. Asserting that the Communist Party did not truly represent the Russian people, that it felt no compulsion to fulfill international obligations and that it was committed to world revolution, President Wilson refused to follow the lead of those nations granting diplomatic recognition to the Soviet regime.[17] For the next sixteen years, official Washington did not speak to Moscow.

Moreover, communist victory in Russia helped ignite a domestic upheaval in the United States. Bolshevik success proved to many that communism was indeed a real and immediate danger; that its adherents were willing and capable of doing more than making speeches and writing pamphlets; that regardless of the conditions in Russia fostering Lenin's victory, the same could happen here. From that perspective the postwar strikes, bombings, and unfortunate utterings of a few anarchists and sympathizers, galvanizing fears and suspicions long lying uneasily in the American mind, assumed a sinister meaning. Democracy had just been defended abroad; it must now be protected at home.

Thus the excesses of the Red Scare. Seized by war mentality and frightened by the cataclysmic events in Russia, the nation temporarily succumbed to its passions; momentarily ignored the contradiction of violating the constitution in the name of defending it. Thousands of alien anarchists, socialists and communists were arrested and hundreds shipped back to Russia, with or without benefit of legal proceedings.[18] By 1921 the nation had largely regained its equilibrium, but not before the arrests, deportations and sporadic outbursts of violence had satisfied all but the most zealous that the nation had secured itself against communism.

Having protected itself against bolshevism on one level, the nation was ready to deal with the Soviets on another. Within a year Americans were conducting a massive campaign of famine relief in the new Soviet state, providing technical assistance to its war-ravaged industries, welcoming its performers and traveling abroad to investigate the new phenomenon for themselves. As individuals and organizations re-established old ties and created new ones, the rupture in the cultural relationship began to heal. Washington and Moscow did not speak, but even in the early twenties the American and Soviet people talked a great deal. And the efforts of Herbert Hoover's American Relief Administration greatly facilitated that conversation.

There is a certain irony in the fact that Herbert Hoover, archproponent of capitalism, did so much to create an early feeling of goodwill between the American and Soviet people. One of the staunchest supporters of the nonrecognition policy, Hoover nonetheless organized and administered the American agency that fed millions of starving Russians between 1921 and 1923, solving thereby gigantic problems for Moscow.[19] At the height of its operation some 180 Americans supervised the feeding of ten million people per day out of eighteen thousand kitchens scattered over 25 provinces.[20] In some instances special efforts were made to assist intellectuals, artists, students and clergy, all of whom the Soviet government assigned a low priority.[21] Students at the University of Kazan were fed at least one hot meal a day, and faculty members provided with supplementary rations. In Odessa some 107,000 meals were served in student dining rooms during a two month period.[22] In addition, the relief agency equipped hospitals, provided shelters for children, built sanitary facilities and prevented epidemic outbreaks through a massive innoculation program.[23]

Other agencies supplemented the work of the American Relief Administration. At least a half-dozen church related organizations concentrated on relief to their Russian counterparts, while the YMCA and the YWCA focused on students and teachers, and the Volga Relief Society, organized by German groups in the United States, extended assistance to the German settlements along the Volga River.[24] In addition to providing immediate relief, the various agencies supplied seed grain, purchased horses and imported tractors for the peasants, and distributed clothing and gift packages sent by their congregations and supporters at home.[25] With the withdrawal of the ARA and its administrative support in 1923, several of the agencies made individual arrangements with the Soviet government that allowed them to continue their activities for several months.[26] The YMCA, for instance, continued its work until Moscow ordered its representatives out of the country in 1926.[27]

The human contacts involved in the famine relief effort necessarily created a number of ties between the American and Soviet people, and, more significantly, fostered a friendly and appreciative attitude toward America within a large segment of the Soviet population. The Director General of the ARA found the people so appreciative as to be embarassing, as did a *New York Times* reporter who noted not so much the intensity of the feeling as its prevalence.[28] Large numbers expressed their gratitude in writing, their compositions ranging from childrens' scrawls to elegant praises, written on odd scraps of paper and typed under company letterheads.[29]

The relief effort contributed directly to cultural contacts that vitally affected the development of the American theatre. Through ARA activities and reports, American entertainers became aware of the desperate plight of their Soviet counterparts; learned of the hunger and the cold that reduced the proud actors and famous names of czarist days to chopping wood and unloading freight in order to survive between the performances that continued despite the conditions. Only those backstage, wrote one ARA official, knew that the actors actually shook from hunger; were weak to the point of collapse.[30]

American artists, many with ties to Russia by birth or acquaintance, responded with a number of fund raising activities. The impresario Morris Gest, himself Russian by birth, personally raised several hundred dollars which the ARA's food remittance program transformed into food parcels and delivered to Moscow, primarily to members of the Bolshoi Ballet. The recipients in turn showered Gest with letters of appreciations, one for each food package received.[31] And when Gest shortly thereafter collab-

orated with a Russian émigré theatrical group to stage a gala benefit performance, the acting community's most noted names contributed to the
cause. Lillian Gish and Irving Berlin early volunteered their services, as
did Al Jolson, Ed Wynn and the movie director D.W. Griffith.[32] On opening night Jolson acted as doorman and Ed Wynn opened car doors for
patrons while a number of other noted entertainers checked hats and
worked as ushers. Those attending proved generous with their money.
When the evening was over, $11,000 had been raised, most of which went
to the Moscow Art Theatre.[33]

The connection thus made between the American theatrical world
and the Moscow Art Theatre had important consequences. In early 1923,
at the invitation of Morris Gest and with the financial backing of the industrialist Otto Kahn, the famed acting company made its first appearance in the United States.[34] In November of the same year it returned for
the 1924 season, and later in the decade portions of its cast gave further
performances in American cities.[35] Those visits, especially the first two,
had a significant impact on the direction of American drama.

Americans interested in the theatre were familiar with the Moscow
company long before it arrived. They readily recognized the names of its
founders, Constantin Stanislavsky and Vladimir Nemorovich-Dantchenko, and were well aware of the organization's impact on the acting profession in Europe. Trade magazines explained the "Stanislavsky method"
of acting and wrote extensively about the company's performances in
Moscow and western European cities. American visitors made a point of
seeing its performances in much the same way that later generations
flocked to the Bolshoi Ballet.[36] The financial assistance rendered during the
famine heightened the feeling of familiarity. The announcement of the
impending visit therefore produced an understandable excitement: all
tickets to its New York performances were sold six weeks before the company reached the United States.[37]

The actors equalled their reputation. During the 1923 and 1924
seasons the company gave 380 performances of thirteen productions in
twelve cities, drawing praise from both critics and audiences who attested
to the actors' virtuosity despite the fact that all performances were given
in the Russian language.[38] New York, Chicago, Boston and Philadelphia
accorded particularly enthusiastic welcomes; in Philadelphia a Quaker
organization started a drive to raise $100,000 for Russian relief with a
dinner given in Stanislavsky's honor.[39] The entire venture was deemed so
successful that Nemorovich-Dantchenko proposed establishing a joint
Russian-American foundation to finance and stage theatrical productions.[40] Even the Russian State Opera and the Russian Kamernay Theatre,
he suggested, might wish to join the foundation.[41]

The performances thoroughly impressed America's leading authority on the Moscow Art Theatre, who, along with Nemorovich-Dantchenko, envisioned an "intimate and intricate comity" between the theatres of America and Russia. "The Russian theatre," Oliver Sayler wrote in 1925, "has found a second home in the United States." But since free aesthetic intercourse presupposes unhampered diplomatic relations, he added in a remark similar to many to be uttered subsequently, the Russians, unfortunately, would be able to visit that home only when chance paved the way.[42] And judging from the reception accorded the company, many Americans undoubtedly agreed with another critic who wrote that "the visit of these players to America will be educational, for they will show that Russians have neither horns nor tails, despite government innuendo. By speaking to America through their art, they may be prophets of a new understanding between their people and ours."[43]

That sentiment was likewise to be oft-repeated, but not all Americans either then or later agreed with it. Weeks before the company first arrived in the United States the American Defense League warned its countrymen of the evils inherent in the visit. The actors, the League implied, were agents of their government; were obliged to turn over their earnings to Moscow; were to receive special favors for propagandizing the red regime. The American Legion and other patriotic organizations, League spokesmen suggested, should protest the actors' presence.[44]

Both American supporters of the Moscow players and Stanislavsky himself vigorously rejected the accusations. The private opinions of the company's members, Stanislavsky retorted, were no one's business; they were artists, not politicians. The only propaganda they indulged in was "art-propaganda"; the only money they turned over to Moscow a stipulated amount for famine relief.[45] To demonstrate their support and friendship the Actors Equity and the Producing Managers associations made honorary members of the theatre's cast.[46] Had it been widely known that the Soviet government considered the Moscow Art Theatre so old fashioned as to be an unworthy representative of Soviet dramatic art, as one critic pointed out at the time, perhaps the League would have been slower to make its accusations.[47]

Despite numerous offers and inducements to remain in the United States, Stanislavsky returned to the Soviet Union at the end of the second tour. Many of his actors, however, joined American companies, established their own schools in America or made their way to Hollywood and the movies.[48] All propagated Stanislavsky's teachings, and those disciples, along with an outpouring of books and articles concerning his life and theories, spread the master's ideas throughout the United States. The Little Theatre, the Group Theatre and the Neighborhood Playhouse School of the Theatre all acknowledged their indebtedness to Stanislavsky's genius as did, at a later date, the Actors Studio headed by Elia Kazan and Lee

Strasberg. It was both "theoretically wise and practically sound" to speak of the work done by the Actors Studio as being an adaptation of the Stanislavsky system, Kazan wrote, noting that "the 'method' is our version of the system."[49] Those Americans who have since employed the techniques of "method" acting, as well as those who have enjoyed the pleasure of those performances, owe a great deal to the early visits of Stanislavsky and the Moscow Art Theatre.

While the Moscow Art Theatre reaped praise and profit, less publicized artists and performers made the same journey during the early twenties. In 1921, Feodor Chaliapin returned for the first of several postwar performances, receiving a friendly welcome that contrasted sharply with the rabid anti-Russian sentiment of a few months earlier.[50] The following year the poet Essinine accompanied his wife Isadora Duncan to America. Essenine largely limited himself to observing, but his outspoken wife, still an American citizen despite having spent most of her adult life outside the United States and having established a dance school in Moscow at the request of the Soviet government, could not restrain her enthusiasm for the Moscow regime. That enthusiasm, along with revealing costumes and uninhibited dancing, annoyed proper Boston, which banned any further performances by the free spirited dancer.[51] Nevertheless, through her acquaintances and contacts in both the United States and the Soviet Union, and through her influence on the development of the dance in both countries, she reduced by at least a small degree the distance separating the two cultures.[52]

In early 1924 a group of Soviet artists opened a massive exhibit of art in New York City's Grand Central Palace. Comprised of approximately one thousand paintings, sculptures and handicraft items, the show was, according to the *New York Times*, the largest exhibition of Russian art ever to appear in a foreign country. American sponsors included Rockefellers, Goulds, Vanderbilts and Harrimans, and the accompanying Soviet delegation, led by the director of Moscow's Tretiakov Gallery, included prominent representatives of Soviet artistic circles.[53]

As in the case of the Moscow Art Theatre, the famine was at least partly responsible for the exhibit. Through the show the artists hoped to raise $100,000, ten per cent of which was to be turned over to the Soviet government for famine relief. Unfortunately for the artists the exhibit never became the financial success anticipated and the entire venture eventually degenerated into a series of recriminations between the artists, Russian émigré groups and Paxton Hibben, director of the Russian Red Cross and the person designated by Moscow to collect its stipulated ten per cent.[54]

Financial difficulties did not lessen the artistic merits of the exhibit; indeed, the opportunity to view such a wide collection of contemporary

Russian and Soviet art was a rare treat for Americans. Although trade magazines made little mention of the show, the *New York Times* gave it extensive and favorable coverage, and the exhibit itself drew large crowds.[55] Not until the late twenties did Americans again have the opportunity to view a similar exhibit from the Soviet Union.[56]

During the summer of 1923 it appeared that one of the famed Russian ballet companies would appear in the United States. In June the director of the State Theatre of Petrograd announced that, under contract with Sol Hurok, the company would tour America with a full cast of 200 members, performing a repertory of ten operas and ten ballets. Chaliapin was to serve as its music director. Moreover, the announcement from Petrograd read, "if America likes our work we propose to establish a permanent ballet in New York with seventy of our best performers. Perhaps in other cities also."[57]

The Petrograd company never arrived, but circumstances seemed more promising when Theodore Dreiser tried to bring the Bolshoi Ballet to America in 1928. Under his direction a committee of prominent Americans raised $70,000, enlisted the support of influential art patrons, and tried to establish a corporation to provide the financial guarantees requisite to the venture.[58] But after months of effort the project lost momentum, Dreiser resigned, and the plan folded.[59] Although many of the famous Russian dancers of imperial days performed in the United States during the twenties and thirties, they were almost without exception émigrés living either in Europe or America.[60] Soviet ballet in the United States was still decades away.

American efforts to ease the professional plight of Soviet scientists likewise led to increasing connections in the scientific realm. These efforts were particularly welcomed, for the years of war, revolution, civil war and famine had hit scientists and scholars particularly hard, isolating them from contact with western scientific thought, destroying their laboratories and forcing them to abandon their researches to struggle for their own existence.

American scientists were well aware of the problems of their Soviet colleagues. The Soviet scholars themselves appealed for help through a number of channels, professional publications publicized their plight, and the relief organizations reported extensively on their conditions.[61] To determine the accuracy of the reports and the realities of the problem, the ARA sent Vernon B. Kellog to the Soviet Union as its special representative in late 1921. Kellog found the personal situation of the scientists improving somewhat, but their professional problems remained the same.[62] Particularly, he determined, the scientists needed recent scientific literature that would allow them to pull abreast of western advances since 1914. Consequently, Kellog and several others formed the American Committee to

Aid Russian Scientists with Literature and appealed, both directly through personal solicitations and indirectly through professional journals, for the donation of books, periodicals, reprints and the findings of government and university laboratories.[63]

The response to the appeal was widespread and generous. During 1922 and 1923 some 360 individuals, institutions and societies contributed 28,000 pounds of scientific literature which the ARA shipped to Moscow on behalf of the Committee, and which a Soviet organization representing the Academy of Sciences distributed to universities and scientific institutions.[64] Yale University provided six copies of 24 of its first class publications, while Doubleday, Page and Company, in an even more generous gesture, instructed the Committee to select whatever titles it desired from its list of scientific works.[65]

Others contributed through alternate channels. The YMCA distributed almost 80,000 books and supplied 300 periodicals in various languages to universities and libraries, though the works were not necessarily of a scientific nature.[66] The American Astronomical Society sent money which the ARA turned into food packages and distributed to 25 institutions and observatories.[67] Some gave to the Gorki Fund for the Relief of Russian Scientists, and others donated directly to acquaintances and professional colleagues.[68] Harvard researcher Walter B. Cannon, for instance, collected and sent $2,000 to the renowned scientist I.P. Pavlov, with whom he was already carrying on a correspondence stemming from the similar nature of their research.[69] Another scientist sent a shipment of birchwood essential to the research being conducted by a Soviet colleague, and received a gratifying reply for his efforts. "The consciousness that somewhere there were people who thought about and cared for me touched me," the Soviet researcher wrote, "and at a moment of the greatest need dispersed to a great extent my darkest thoughts."[70]

The connections thus established both developed from and contributed to a number of personal contacts during the early twenties. As early as 1919 the Russian scientist Nikolai Borodin journeyed to the United States on behalf of the Ministries of Agriculture and Education to arrange for credits to purchase laboratory equipment, and the following year N.I. Vavilov, director of the Russian Bureau of Applied Botany and Plant Breeding, made the same journey at the invitations of the United States Department of Agriculture and the American Society of Phytopathologists in order to collect plant specimens and seed samples.[71] And in 1923, Pavlov visited the Rockefeller Institute for Medical Research and conferred with Harvard researchers in Boston, particularly with Cannon.[72]

At least two American scientists returned the visits. In 1922, Herman J. Muller of the University of Texas, a pioneer in the field of genetics research, spent several weeks visiting various Soviet individuals and agencies and familiarizing them with the fruit fly, *Drosophila Melano-gaster*, a staple of American research in genetics.[73] Having received permission to enter the Soviet Union at least in part because of Borodin's intervention on his behalf, Muller's stay was made more pleasant and productive because of the fact that Vavilov, upon his return to the Soviet Union, had acquainted many of his colleagues with American scientific thought through an extensive series of illustrated lectures.[74] Back in the United States, Muller, who like Kellog found his hosts hungry for American scientific literature, published a lengthy list of Soviet individuals and agencies desiring to receive information in the field of genetics, creating thereby another avenue for scientific interchange.[75]

In 1924, University of Colorado botanist T.D.A. Cockerell, learning of the Siberian discovery of the fossilized remains of a previously unknown insect, applied for permission to investigate for himself. Despite assurances from Washington acquaintances that the "Reds" would not grant the request, the Soviets welcomed him enthusiastically.[76] Like Muller, Cockerell spent several weeks in the Soviet Union, enjoying both the personal and professional hospitality of his hosts. Upon departure the Soviets presented him with several bags of samples and specimens as a gift to the U.S. Department of Agriculture and other scientific agencies in the United States. The Department of Agriculture in turn shipped a collection of cereal seeds to Moscow.[77]

The personal contacts thus established, though limited in number, provided a precedent for continued personal interaction among scientists during the twenties and thirties. Later in the decade, to mention only one example, two Soviet geneticists worked with Muller at the University of Texas, and Muller himself took a leave from the university to become the head of the Department of Mutations of the Soviet Institute of Genetics.[78]

While few Americans traveled to the Soviet Union for strictly artistic and scientific purposes during the early twenties, thousands made the journey for other reasons. Russian immigrants hoping to find revolutionary Russia a better place than the czarist nation they abandoned, Party members and sympathizers eager to aid the cause, and those whose curiosity compelled them, all made the trip. But regardless of the motive, each traveler necessarily carried a bit of America in his luggage; necessarily served as a human link between the two nations and their cultures.[79]

A few Americans made the journey to observe the new wonders in old Russia and to report those observations to the American people. Senator Robert LaFollette led a party in 1923, liked much of what he saw, and so informed his readers in *LaFollette's Magazine*.[80] Lincoln Steffens, traveling in the senator's entourage, had already made the trip once, and returned to utter his oftquoted remark that he had seen the future and it

worked. In 1924, Lillian Wald accepted Moscow's invitation to inspect
Soviet public health facilities, and in the same year Avraham Yarmolin-
sky, head of the Slavonic Division of the New York Public Library, spent
six months studying the new realities in his native land.[81] Will Rogers,
too, decided he must see for himself; he couldn't miss the opportunity,
as he phrased it, to "x-ray" Trotsky. Unfortunately for the humorist, he
never got to see the commissar; or perhaps fortunately, for the occasion
added a popular phrase to American folklore. It would have been nice to
see Trotsky, he reflected, for, after all, "I never met a man I didn't like."[82]

   If few Americans traveled to the Soviet Union specifically for cultural
purposes prior to the mid-twenties, American literature, motion pictures
and music effectively transmitted images of American life to the Soviet
people, and, in so doing, maintained and broadened the popular admiration for America and Americans that the famine relief effort had stimulated.

   Literature played a particularly important role in the process, for
the voracious reading appetite of the Soviet public gave widespread circulation to the ideas of America's great writers, and those writers, as
Robert Magidoff noted, "became the mirror of American life for Russian
readers."[83] Jack London, Upton Sinclair, O. Henry, and Edgar Rice
Burroughs, reported Maurice Hindus in 1924, were raising even higher the
prestige which the American Relief Administration had brought to Americans; were acting as "America's ambassadors to Russia ... destined to
wield a more profound influence over Russian social and intellectual life
than any official America has ever sent from Washington to Petrograd."
No wonder, he concluded in an observation that was to be echoed scores
of times over the following decades, that "America is so highly esteemed
in Russia and every American who comes here is a privileged character."[84]

   Louis Fischer found the same esteem for American writers the following year. On a popularity scale of ten, he computed, Jack London
received a ten along with Tolstoy and Gorki, Upton Sinclair rated an
eight and O. Henry a six, while, by comparison, Turgenev rated a seven,
Dostoevsky a five, Gogol a four and Pushkin only a two.[85] In 1924, Soviet
publishing houses turned out 10,000 copies of 20 of London's works,
quickly selling all.[86] In the same year, Upton Sinclair proposed establishing his own publishing house in Moscow, keeping only enough of the
profits "necessary for the living of a poet."[87] O. Henry's works were both
read and performed on stage in the early twenties, and, according to
Hindus, "anyone who read anything" read the Tarzan stories of Edgar
Rice Burroughs. "I do not recall a single newsstand at any of the railroad
stations," he wrote in 1924, "but had a prominent display of Tarzan
books."[88] By 1928, Soviet publishers were turning out the works of some

fifty Americans. By that year, Jack London had sold 1,300,000 copies; Upton Sinclair, 485,000. Sinclair Lewis's *Main Street* had sold 30,000 copies; Sherwood Anderson's *Triumph of the Egg*, 14,000.[89] Eugene O'Neill was likewise popular with the Soviet public, particularly his "Anna Christie" and "The Hairy Ape."[90]

Hollywood films were almost as popular and widespread as American literature, startling visitors who found them in the most unexpected places. Gloria Swanson played in tiny Caucusus towns; Tom Mix, Corrine Griffith and William Hart starred in Rostov-on-Don. One Moscow theatre devoted itself solely to Clara Kimball Young, while Douglas Fairbanks and Mary Pickford, who traveled to the Soviet Union in 1926 to meet their fans, displayed their screen talents all over the city.[91] American films, Paxton Hibben complained in 1925, "dominate, innundate, glut, overwhelm the Russian motion picture industry today.."[92]

If Hibben was distressed at the abundance of American films in the Soviet Union, the Soviets were not; indeed, the Soviet film agency Amkino urged Hollywood to increase its sales in the USSR. American movies were particularly appealing, and the Soviet Union offered an unparalleled market for their distribution, the director of Amkino write in 1928, because "America ... represents to the Russians a land of incredible efficiency, and in his desire to imitate its ideas the Russian is eager for every bit of news of life in this country." Moreover, the official suggested, Hollywood should consider producing films in the Soviet Union, both independently and in conjunction with Soviet studios. "I have no doubt," he stated, "that we would cooperate with any group which would want to undertake a program of production in Russia working in close interchange of ideas and suggestions with our studios and our directors." The two nations should also consider exchanging films, especially in view of the improvement in Soviet films as exemplified by Sergei Eisenstein's "Potemkin." And, the director was careful to suggest, since the cinema offered a universal medium of interpretation and expression from one people to another, the object of such exchange should be artistic interchange, not propaganda.[93]

The Amkino director's remarks produced no immediate, concrete results, but there is little reason to doubt their validity and sincerity. And even though the kind of extensive cooperation he suggested was still decades in the future, American and Soviet studios did display an increasing interest in each other's activities and techniques as the decade progressed, culminating in a trip to Hollywood by Eisenstein to produce an American film.[94]

America's jazz met an equally favorable reception. When New Orleans saxaphonist Sidney Bechet and his five man band introduced jazz to Soviet audiences in 1925, crowds of frenzied fans cheered the Americans all the way from Odessa to the Soviet capital, prompting pundits to joke about jazz coming up the river to Moscow.[95] Alexander Tsfasman, future jazz king of the USSR, left Moscow Music Conservatory to become Bechet's disciple, and others, such as Odessa singer Lenoid Utesov, formed their own bands to create the kind of music which, prior to Bechet's arrival, had only been rumored.[96] During the mid-twenties jazz became the rage of the Soviet Union, but as the relatively relaxed years of the New Economic Policy gave way to the strictures of Stalin and the production goals of the five year plans, the new music fell into official disrepute. In 1929 the newly formed Association of Proletarian Musicians banned its performance before Soviet audiences, restricting Tsfasman, Utesov and other bands to Intourist hotels and foreign listeners, and thus forcing jazz to make the first jump in its checkered career in the USSR.[97]

By 1925 the temporary rift in cultural relations between the two nations was healing itself as the disorganized and sporadic contacts among actors, artists, scientists and musicians prevented cultural as well as diplomatic alienation. To that point the contacts had largely been matters of individual and private concern on both sides, but that pattern began to change on the Soviet side during the second half of the decade.

II
Organized Contacts, 1925–1933

From the mid-twenties to the early thirties the cultural relations between the United States and the Soviet Union became more purposeful and better organized as cultural agencies on both sides placed contacts on a more systematic and rational basis. On the Soviet side Moscow played the role of organizer and promoter, while in the United States private organizations served a similar function. As the twenties merged into the thirties, thousands of American tourists and delegates flocked to the USSR, and Soviet visitors in lesser numbers journeyed to the United States. Soviet entertainers and cultural exhibits appeared in American cities, Soviet students studied in American universities, and Soviet technical delegations searched the nation for advanced techniques and machinery. Beneath the official estrangement and the recriminations stemming from political differences, the American and Soviet people interacted to a degree not matched again until the decade of the sixties.

Moscow early began organizing and controlling its cultural contacts with foreign countries, first through the Joint Information Bureau, and, after 1925, through the Society for Cultural Relations with Foreign Countries, known to subsequent millions by its initials, VOKS.[1] Headed originally by Olga Kameneva, wife of Kamenev and sister of Trotsky, VOKS coordinated cultural affairs on both an import and export basis. Soviet cultural agencies dealing with other countries did so largely through its offices, as did foreigners in contact with Soviet groups.

In the 1920's, VOKS consisted of a number of bureaus, each serving a specific function. The Contact Bureau exchanged information and reports of a scientific nature, the Book Bureau served its implied function, the Press Bureau supplied articles and notes of cultural interest and the Russ-Photo Bureau furnished pictorial material on Soviet life. The Service Bureau for Foreign Visitors, destined to become familiar to large numbers of Americans, assisted foreign travelers in the USSR. By the end of 1929 VOKS had established contact with most western nations, including the United States.[2]

21

The Soviet Information Bureau, established in Washington in 1923 by Boris Skirvsky, a member of the delegation from the Far Eastern Republic, served as VOKS' initial representative in the United States.[3] In early 1925, Skirvsky's bureau sent letters to various American companies explaining its role and its purpose in promoting scientific and cultural relations. The lack of such contacts prevented peer groups becoming familiar with the activities, trends and discoveries of their counterparts, Skirvsky wrote, but the Soviet Information Bureau, in contact with VOKS and thus with the leading cultural bodies in both the Soviet Union and other countries, could solve the problem by facilitating the exchange of books, periodicals, and persons.[4] In some instances, as in letters to the magazines *Motorship* and *Safety Engineering*, the recipients were asked only to reprint Skirvsky's letter in order to publicize the cause of cultural exchange; in others the recipients were asked to engage in direct exchanges with Soviet agencies.[5]

Undoubtedly, VOKS was more interested in serving Soviet state interests by creating a friendly attitude toward Moscow and forwarding the cause of recognition than in fostering human relationships for their own sake, but it served its ulterior purposes only indirectly. The State Department did not deem its activities to be subversive, nor did it appear particularly concerned about the overtures of Skirvsky's Joint Information Bureau. In response to inquiries, the Department informed recipients of Skirvsky's letters of his background, but made no further comment.[6] Though Americans would have preferred direct and free cultural intercourse with the Soviet people, they had to settle for the reality of working through VOKS or some other state agency. And, considering its official role, VOKS served a worthy purpose. By arranging visits, sponsoring delegations, organizing exhibits and exchanging cultural material it provided a legitimate and useful channel of communication that, even though restricted, would not have existed otherwise. It left the more overt forms of propaganda to noncultural agencies, and conducted its affairs in a straightforward manner. There were many Americans who were interested in the Soviet Union without being the least interested in forwarding the cause of communism in their own country, and it was with these that VOKS largely dealt.

Among these was a group which in 1926 formed the American Society for Cultural Relations with Russia. Holding its first meeting at Lillian Wald's Fourteenth Street Settlement, the Society elected William Smith, president of Smith College, as its first president; chose John Dewey, Lillian Wald, Leopold Stokowski and Stephen P. Duggan as vice-presidents. William Allen White, Arthur Garfield Hays and Jane Addams, to name only a few of the prominent members who originated the Society, sat on its board of directors.[7] By 1929, the organization listed more than one thousand members, representing every state in the Union, and possessed branches in several cities. Paul Douglas headed the branch in Chicago.[8] Its purpose, in its own words, was "to bring together those who are interested in Russian life and culture; to promote cultural intercourse between the two countries, and especially the interchange of students, doctors, scholars, artists, scientists, and teachers; to collect and diffuse information in both countries on developments in science, education, philosophy, art, literature, and social and economic life."[9]

The Society carried on a number of activities and served a variety of purposes during the late twenties. Noted Soviet visitors spoke at its dinners, American authorities on particular aspects of Soviet life lectured at its meetings, and visitors returning from the Soviet Union recounted their experiences before its membership.[10] Through its contacts in the Soviet Union it placed Americans and Soviets with mutual interests in touch with each other, taking advantage of its close working relationship with VOKS in that regard. It sponsored delegations to study specific areas of Soviet society, and, along with others, arranged for Soviet exhibits to appear in the United States.[11]

The Society's library was the center of its activities. Through purchases, donations and direct exchanges with Soviet agencies, it quickly gathered a reputable collection of materials relating to its interests, and employed a professional librarian with a knowledge of the Russian language to manage the collection.[12] A clipping file of current events, drawing on both American and Soviet sources, provided a unique and heavily used source of information, utilized eventually by a number of American newspapers, magazines, businesses and universities.[13]

The library early began a collection of Russian and Soviet music. By 1929 its music committee, which included such musicians as Leopold Stokowski and Fritz Reiner, had gathered and indexed some four hundred manuscripts, including the music of all the great Russian composers. Books and new pieces constantly broadened its holdings and four periodicals regularly received from Moscow kept it abreast of contemporary Soviet music.[14] Members of the committee presented programs of Russian music at the Society's library, at schools and at various civic functions.[15]

From the beginning the Society exhibited a remarkably high degree of professionalism, maintained a low profile and avoided controversy whenever possible. Cultural relations, it believed, should promote knowledge and mutual understanding, not the national interest of any particular country. Its activities reflected that belief.

While the Society for Cultural Relations with Russia took the lead in promoting cultural intercourse during the late twenties, other institutions, organizations and individuals established contacts on their own. The Rockefeller Foundation, the Institute of International Education and California librarian Harriet Eddy played particularly important roles.

As early as 1921 the Rockefeller Foundation began awarding fellowships to promising young Soviet scientists, financing their advanced
studies at universities in the United States, western Europe and the USSR.
A partial listing of the recipients, including only those receiving fellowships and grants in the field of natural science prior to 1930, indicates that
in this area alone the Foundation awarded 21 fellowships between 1921
and 1929.[16] All the recipients held responsible positions in Soviet universities, research institutes and medical establishments prior to receiving the
financial aid, and all returned to the same or similar positions upon com-
pleting their studies. Only the reluctance of the Soviet government to
allow its young scientists to go abroad prevented the Foundation providing even more extensive assistance. In 1928, for example, the Foundation was prepared to grant ten fellowships, but Moscow would not
endorse more than a third that figure.[17] Some that received the grants
studied at Harvard, Princeton, Cornell, Johns Hopkins and the Universities of California, Texas, Michigan and Chicago, some enrolled in the
prestigious universities of England, France and Germany, and still others
studied at Soviet institutions.[18]

In addition, the Rockefeller Foundation provided Soviet scientific
institutions with medical aid and laboratory equipment and helped the
medical faculties of a number of Soviet institutions to obtain foreign medical publications. Between 1923 and 1932 it spent $15,000 supplying medi-
cal literature, and another $50,000 from 1933 to 1937. Then Moscow
began refusing both the fellowships and the equipment assistance, stating
that it could afford to pay for such things itself.[19]

In 1925, Stephen P. Duggan, Columbia University professor, member
of the Society for Cultural Relations with Russia, and recent founder of
the Institute of International Education, traveled to Moscow at the request
of the Soviet government to establish a program of student-professor
exchanges. In Moscow, Duggan had a number of conferences with officials
at the Ministry of Education, during which the Soviets asked the IIE to
extend its student-teacher program and its summer students tours to the
USSR and to provide the opportunity for Soviet students to study in the
United States. As a result, Duggan and the Soviet ministry agreed that six
Soviet students would study in American universities during the second
half of the 1925 academic year, and that a delegation of Soviet specialists
would investigate American educational methods during the 1926 term.[20]
Duggan was optimistic over the results of his efforts. "The restoration of
Russia to more reasonable attitudes toward human affairs," he wrote at
the time, "will be greatly facilitated by the visits of our teachers and students to her institutions and of her students and teachers to our institutions."[21] Whatever our political relations are to be, he concluded, "our
educational relations should be the same as with other countries."[22]

The extent to which Duggan's agreement was carried out cannot be determined, because, as the IIE itself pointed out, no precise records were kept of the Soviet students and teachers who came.[23] American universities enrolled hundreds of "Russian" students each year, but the bulk of these were undoubtedly émigrés. A Soviet professor lectured at Princeton during the second half of the 1925 academic year, at least a dozen Soviet students attended American universities on Rockefeller fellowships, and a group of 64 students from the USSR enrolled in American engineering and technical schools in 1931, but quantification beyond those numbers is impossible.[24] During the summer of 1934 and 1935 the Institute of International Education, in conjunction with several Soviet agencies, undertook a much more ambitious project but both sides became disenchanted and the venture collapsed.[25]

American and Soviet libraries likewise cooperated during the late twenties, and, largely through the efforts of librarian Harriet Eddy, the United States made a significant contribution to the development of a rationalized and systematized Soviet library system.

During the postrevolutionary years the number of Soviet libraries grew enormously as Moscow waged a campaign to eliminate illiteracy. Schools, universities, factories, villages and clubs established their own libraries, creating problems as well as promises in the process. By 1926 the system had become so cumbersome as to be unmanageable, at which point the Soviet Ministry of Education invited Mrs. Eddy, formerly a University of California librarian who at the time was in charge of the state's free county library system, to analyze the problem and suggest solutions. Accepting the challenge, Mrs. Eddy spent six months in the Soviet Union, examining more than 50 libraries ranging from the largest to the smallest, and finding herself amazed at both the gigantic effort undertaken by Moscow and the chaotic conditions within the system.[26]

Upon Eddy's return to the United States, and at her suggestion, the Soviet government sent librarian Anna Kravtchenko to study the California system. After observing its operation for several months, Kravtchenko returned to the USSR to adapt its procedures to Soviet conditions. By 1930, implementation of the system had progressed to the point that the Soviets needed additional advice and assistance, whereupon Eddy, again at Moscow's request, returned to provide the necessary help. In 1931, a model library which served both as a prototype and a training school was completed outside Moscow. Librarians from across the Soviet Union studied its operations, as did students from the newly organized University Library School attached to the Lenin Library.[27] And even the University Library School, which trained librarians for the Soviet state, had a strong influence, for its director was an American, a graduate of Simmons College Library School and a former employee of the Library of Congress.[28]

The Library of Congress had itself earlier contributed to library development in the Soviet Union. In 1925, the library donated a complete collection of its publications to the Lenin Library, along with a sample dictionary catalogue of several thousand printed cards. The gift was particularly welcome, a Lenin Library official wrote in the *Bulletin of the American Library Association*, for it greatly improved the Soviet method of cataloging, allowing it to develop a system based largely on the rules of the American Library Association.[29]

American-Soviet cultural relations during the late twenties and early thirties consisted in large part of the personal interaction between citizens of the two countries, the extent of which increased dramatically as scores of American delegations and thousands of American tourists traveled the length and breadth of the USSR. Many went at Moscow's invitation. Almost all, judging from their accounts and comments, were well received.

That Moscow welcomed the various delegations represented a change attitude on its part. When Washington intimated in 1922 that an American mission should investigate conditions in the Soviet Union, Moscow indignantly refused, stating that to accept such a mission without some reciprocal arrangement would place it in an inferior position. Only if it could send a similar delegation to the United States, Moscow answered in a response immediately dismissed by Washington, would it consider the proposal.[30] But when Columbia professor E.A. Seligman made a similar suggestion in 1928, the Soviets accepted the idea. "Accurate information about ... life in the USSR will clear up many of the points which at present stand in the way of establishing normal economic relations between the two countries," the head of the legal department of the Soviet Commissariat of Trade wrote in the *New York Times*, and therefore "the suggestion of professor Seligman that information be obtained by a delegation of nonpartisan American experts is perfectly in accord with the expressed desire of Soviet public opinion to welcome such a delegation."[31]

No official nonpartisan delegation made the trip to Moscow, but a variety of others did. Students groups were particularly numerous. As a result of Duggan's visit in 1925, VOKS invited several student groups to spend the summer of 1926 in the Soviet Union. A number of Yale students accepted the invitation, as did students and teachers from the City College of New York, Pennsylvania's Pocona College and a number of others.[32] By 1928, newsman Walter Duranty reported from Moscow, the Soviet capital was flooded with visitors, a large proportion of whom were American students.[33]

Dozens of business and technical groups, representing America's leading corporations, traveled extensively throughout the Soviet Union, as did delegates representing labor unions.[34] In 1927 a labor delegation that included Rexford Guy Tugwell of Columbia University and Paul

Douglas of the University of Chicago exchanged views with top level Soviet officials, including Stalin.[35] Others examined Soviet beliefs and practices regarding morals, manners, marriage, family, religion, health education and other areas of social life.[36] A committee of women, representing in part the NAACP and in part the Society for Cultural Relations with Russia, undoubtedly upset many by remarking upon its return that the status of women was higher in the Soviet Union than in the United States.[37]

Most delegations neither attracted attention nor created controversy, but in 1928 a group of educators did both. Invited by VOKS, sponsored by the Society for Cultural Relations with Russia and led by John Dewey, the 25 member delegation, including among its numbers the presidents of Amherst and the Universities of Pennsylvania plus professors from various other universities, spent some 30 days in the USSR, traveling freely, visiting the places in which they expressed an interest and exchanging views with their Soviet colleagues.[38] The entire stay was warm and friendly, and Dewey, whose ideas were already known and in some instances implemented in the USSR, was a particular favorite.[39]

The high point of the visit came at a VOKS dinner which Moscow observers, according to Walter Duranty, considered the most significant manifestation of American-Soviet rapprochement since the departure of the American Relief Administration. There was, the veteran reporter wrote, a noticeable lack of "hoakum propaganda" at the affair hosted by Kameneva and Commissar of Education A.V. Lunacharsky. And given the entire tenor of the trip, it is easy to believe that Kameneva spoke sincerely and Duranty reported accurately her closing words. "We do not ask your praise when you reach home, nor fear your blame," she told her American guests, rather just "tell your people the facts and let them judge. But it is my hope that your visit may contribute toward sweeping away the cloud of prejudice that has long hidden this country from the American people and convince them that with all our faults we are genuinely striving to transform our backward nation into one of citizens of progressive and enlightened humanity."[40]

If the Dewey delegation was highly popular in the Soviet Union, it was less so in some quarters in the United States. The president of Northwestern University cancelled his place in the delegation before departure, charging that he was expected to write a report favorable to the Soviets upon his return. Both the Society for Cultural Relations with Russia and the individual delegates denied the charge, and even voted to make no collective report, but the disgruntled member still refused to go.[41] Another delegate expressed his reservations concerning the venture to the State Department, and found his reservations shared.[42] The leadership of the American Federation of Labor was particularly upset about the Dewey trip, refusing to allow union newspapers to carry any account of the matter.[43] The *New York Times*, however, was more generous in its estimate of the value of the tour and the gullibility of those involved. It did not believe, the paper editorialized, that men the caliber of Dewey and President Olds of Amherst would "mortgage their opinions of sympathies in advance."[44]

More numerous than delegates were tourists who represented no interests other than their own; whose aim was primarily to enjoy themselves and to satisfy their curiosity. For during the late twenties Moscow discovered the benefits of the tourist trade; discovered that tourists spent money, and, if well treated, left friendlier than they arrived.

To a generation only recently acquainted with the possibility of travelling to the Soviet Union without explanations and complications it is somewhat surprising to discover the multiplicity of advertisements featuring tours of the Soviet Union during the twenties and thirties.[45] Tours came in all sizes and shapes; long, short and medium; emphasized study, pleasure or both; featured the modern sites of European Russia or the ancient cities of historical interest, Leningrad or Samarkand. One company featured a trip across Siberia; another advertised a visit to the Arctic aboard an icebreaker.[46] World Tourists, Open Road, Amalgamated Bank Tours, Cunard Lines and American Express were only a few of the companies arranging tours.[47] Open Road tours became so common that, as Joseph Barnes wrote, Americans in the USSR were commonly referred to as "Open Roadovski" tourists regardless how they traveled.[48] As the twenties turned into the thirties the numbers involved increased enormously. In 1927 approximately one hundred and fifty Americans made the journey; in 1932 the figure reached upward toward ten thousand.[49]

The Soviets actively promoted this burgeoning business, largely by simplifying the administrative procedures involved. Moscow authorized certain agencies to issue entry permits, thus reducing the complexities of visa applications, and, after 1928, Intourist provided guides, made travel arrangements and reserved rooms, the quality of which depended upon the class and price of the tour.[50] In 1931, Intourist even purchased a fleet of Lincoln automobiles to move travelers around at the "Amerikansky tempo."[51] Particularly elaborate arrangements were made when the occasion warranted the effort. A 1929 business delegation traveling under the auspices of American Express and the American-Russian Chamber of Commerce rated, for example, a special luxury train dating from czarist days, complete with plentiful quantities of champagne and caviar.[52]

The increase in tourism produced a wave of books and articles in the United States. Seventeen of the 21 books pertaining to the Soviet Union during 1928 and 1929 were, as Peter G. Filene pointed out, written by tourists.[53] At the same time the number of articles relating to some aspect of Soviet life increased sharply, as a quick survey of the *Reader's Guide to Periodical Literature* attests. The value and validity of the articles varied greatly, ranging from observations by judicious commentators to paeans and diatribes written by the convinced. Some presumed an unwarranted authority based on a few days of sightseeing, while others like Oswald Garrison Villard cautioned his readers that his comments were based strictly upon his view of "Russia from a car window."[54] Some like Theodore Dreiser made a serious attempt to view Soviet reality objectively and to distill some essential truth from that reality, but the contradictions inherent in Soviet life during the twenties rendered the task impossible. At one moment Dreiser, who found it difficult to decide if he approved or disapproved of what he saw, felt only contempt for the backwardness and lack of creature comforts; at the next only admiration for the massive effort undertaken to relieve those hardships.[55] But regardless of the fact that most visitors viewed the Soviets through the spectrum of their own prejudices and expectations, the essential consideration is that they made the journey, and in so doing helped reduce by at least a small degree the barrier of unfamiliarity separating the two nations. As Joseph Barnes wrote at the time, "with every tourist who goes to Russia our cultural recognition of the regime becomes more complete."[56]

There was no corresponding flow of Soviet tourists to the United States, but noted individuals, performing groups, delegations and cultural exhibits did enter the country. In 1926 the celebrated poet Vladimir Mayakovsky toured the nation, finding much to both praise and scorn, and finding a pithy phrase to capture the contradictions he perceived. "You look like a million dollars," he told Americans, "you look like two cents."[57] In the same year two Soviet directors visited Hollywood, a company of 120 cossacks performed in Philadelphia, the Musical Studio of the Moscow Art Theatre captured audiences in much the same way its parent body had done two years earlier, the Jewish Habima Theatre traveled from Moscow to entertain in several American cities, and Chaliapin returned to perform in New York City.[58] In 1930, the writer Boris Pilnyak traveled across the country recording his impressions for readers at home, and the film producer Sergei Eisenstein, already acclaimed in the United States for his "Potemkin," arrived to direct a film for Paramount Studios.[59] From the first, however, the director and the studio disagreed on the nature of the film to be produced. Paramount considered Eisenstein's version of Dreiser's *American Tragedy* too artistic, Eisenstein considered Paramount's version to be too commercial, and patriotic groups considered any version produced by a Soviet director to be unacceptable.[60] The proposed film was never made, even though Eisenstein and Upton Sinclair subsequently collaborated in an attempt to produce a movie.[61]

Soviet technical delegations toured the country by the dozens, usually in conjunction with technical assistance agreements negotiated with American companies.[62] Some came primarily to attend technical and scientific conferences. In 1927 the scientist K.D. Glinka headed a 20 member delegation attending the first International Conference on Soil Sciences, held in the nation's capital, and afterward led the delegation on a lengthy trip across the country. The "pleasant contacts thus established," a delegation spokesman remarked optimistically upon departure, were only the beginning of "a firm bond of both professional and personal relations with American scientists."[63] In 1929, Pavlov returned to the United States as a guest of Walter B. Cannon to attend the thirteenth International Physiological Conference, held in Boston, and three years later the American Philosophical Society elected the famed physiologist to its membership.[64] A number of other eminent scientists, including the directors of the Soviet Geological Committee and the Soviet Institute of Botany, also visited colleagues in America.[65]

More publicized than these visits was a series of exhibitions that displayed various facets of Soviet life to the American people. In 1927 an exhibit of architectural sketches, photographs and plans, shipped directly from Moscow and assembled by the Society for Cultural Relations with Russia, appeared at New York's Machine Age Exhibition, to be followed by a more comprehensive exhibit in 1928.[66] Sponsored by the Society for Cultural Relations with Russia and the American-Russian Chamber of Commerce, and designed to show all phases of Soviet life, the 1928 exhibit was divided into segments depicting education, health, agriculture, industry, transportation, theatre, art, and other aspects of Soviet culture. The first exhibit of its kind to leave the Soviet Union, it had already appeared in Berlin, Paris and Brussels, and was headed for Japan upon its departure from the United States. Both American and Soviet speakers, including Columbia professors George S. Counts, authority on Soviet education, and Geroid T. Robinson, a noted historian, gave accompanying lectures.[67]

Still another exhibition, sponsored by Amtorg and the Society for Cultural Relations, appeared in 1929.[68] Drawing heavily on the annual fair at Nizhni-Novgorod, which had been attended by a number of Americans in the Soviet Union, the exhibit featured displays of both traditional Russian handicrafts and contemporary Soviet paintings.[69] The Musical Studio of the Moscow Art Theatre and the Kiev State Opera staged performances at the show, which was heavily attended.[70] "Just as this exposition will interpret Russia to America," Amtorg president Saul G. Bron commented, he hoped to arrange a similar exhibition in the USSR "which will interpret the American arts to the Russian people."[71]

In addition, the Society for Cultural Relations with Russia sponsored a number of smaller, traveling exhibitions. In the early thirties it arranged through its contacts with Soviet museum authorities, for the showing of valued Russian ikons in America's principal art galleries. Trade magazines and museum bulletins gave the traveling exhibit wide publicity and critics gave it high praise, though in at least one instance it drew protests as well.[72] In 1930 the Society collaborated with Columbia University to feature an exhibit of American school work at Leningrad's All-Union Pedagogical Exhibition, and two years later the Soviets reciprocated by sending an exhibit illustrating Soviet school life.[73]

Other examples of cultural interaction could be cited, such as the appearance of an exhibit of Soviet woodcuts in 1932, and the participation of Americans in drawing the architectural designs for the proposed Palace of Soviets to be located in Moscow, but it is not the purpose here to enumerate every instance of cultural contact.[74] Suffice it to say that Frederic Barghoorn was altogether correct when he wrote that cultural relations between the two nations "were, in many respects, freer and more spontaneous during the 1920's ... than during any other period."[75]

Washington was a silent partner in the process. While Moscow used such agencies as VOKS and Intourist to encourage and facilitate cultural contacts pursuant to its own purposes, Washington only acquiesced in the growing cultural intercourse, and in a limited manner at that. The State Department firmly rejected projects involving the nation in any official capacity, obviously fearing, though not directly stating, that such participation might imply an unwarranted approval of the Soviet regime. In contrast to Moscow, Washington neither engaged in rhetoric concerning the benefits of cultural exchange, nor promoted contacts as a means toward international understanding. Cultural relations as an instrument of foreign policy was still alien to Washington's thinking in the decade of the twenties.

While it granted the necessary passports, the State Department was not enthusiastic about either the numerous excursions to the USSR or the assumed Soviet motive in encouraging those excursions. Moscow's presumable purpose in promoting and arranging visits by prominent Americans, a Department spokesman replied to an inquiry from a member of the Dewey delegation, was the fostering of opinions favorable to the Soviet Union, and consequently the enhancement of the possibility of diplomatic recognition. And, the official added, given Moscow's ability to control the itinerary, along with the usual inability of the visitors to speak the language, it always had a good chance of impressing Americans to a greater extent than reality warranted. Moreover, the spokesman concluded in a statement indicating the Department's position vis-à-vis the Society for Cultural Relations with Russia, it was doubtful that any tour arranged by the Society could be considered "private" in nature, since it "presumably" was a branch of VOKS.[76]

On at least two occasions the State Department vetoed projects by Soviet agencies. though in each instance it indicated a willingness to permit a lesser degree of cooperation on a more informal basis. In early 1930, the Soviet State Institute of Microbiology and Epidemiology, located at Saratov, proposed a reciprocal exchange of researchers with the Hygenic Laboratory of the United States Public Health Service.[77] The Hygenic Laboratory, noting that its cooperation with the Soviet Sanitary Bacteriological Laboratory at Sverdlovsk had helped establish the presence of a particular type of bacteria in the USSR during the previous winter, forwarded the request to the State Department.[78] The latter rejected the proposal. "While this Department is desirous of facilitating, insofar as it appropriately may, collaboration between scientific institutions in the United States and those in Russia," it stated, it could not do so on the reciprocal basis specified in the Soviet offer.[79] However, the Department reply added, it did not object to the informal exchanges of information as had transpired between the Hygenic Laboratory and the Soviet laboratory at Sverdlovsk.[80] But to enter into a reciprocal arrangement with an agency of the Soviet government, the Department's answer clearly implied, was to deal too fully with a government that did not officially exist.

In a somewhat similar instance occurring during the same year, the Department rejected a Moscow proposal to establish a Soviet scientific agency in the United States. But, it assured the Department of Agriculture, it objected neither to the presence of Soviet scientists in the United States nor to the Agriculture Department providing those scientists with whatever facilities it deemed proper.[81] And when the American consul in Berlin refused to grant visas to 64 Soviet students because he believed them to be either Party members or sympathizers, Washington reversed his ruling and allowed the students, who had already arranged for enrollment in American colleges, to enter the country.[82] Washington may not have been enthusiastic about cultural intercourse, but it was not altogether unwilling.

By 1933, contacts between the American and Soviet artistic, scientific and intellectual worlds were established and growing despite the absence of official relations between the two nations. But in yet another way the people of the two countries interacted on a large scale, and in a manner that caused the United States to have a significant impact on Soviet development and thinking. And that impact, building on the favorable image created by the American Relief Administration and by American jazz, literature and movies, raised even higher the esteem in which the Soviet people held America and Americans.

III

The USSR and American Technology

The heralded successes of the Soviet five year plans were in large part the successes of American engineering and technology. Americans designed the factories, supplied the machinery and trained the workers of Soviet industry; instructed the farmers in the mysteries of mechanized agriculture. American help and technical assistance, Stalin told United States Chamber of Commerce president Eric Johnston in 1944, helped build about two-thirds of the large industrial enterprises in the Soviet Union.[1] And in the process the Soviets absorbed more than technical skills: the attitudes and values that made the United States the world's leading producer penetrated deeply into Soviet society as well.

That Americans contributed so much to the economic development of the USSR was no accident. Soviet leaders may have castigated America's social and political values, but they had long admired its industrial efficiency and technological know-how. They were neither hesitant to seek its assistance nor, until the late thirties, acknowledge its contributions. Increasingly during the twenties and thirties the Soviets admired and emulated the American emphasis on speed, efficiency and rational production. To be credited with running an "Amerikanski office" or working at the "Amerikanski tempo" was a coveted form of praise. Americans became national heroes in the Soviet Union: Marx and Engels might have understood the secret of historical evolution, but Henry Ford understood the secret of the factory. "If Lenin is Russia's God today," as Bernard Knollenberg precisely penned it in 1930, "Ford is its St. Peter."[2]

The Soviet government early turned to Americans for assistance, offering a variety of incentives to attract their capital and their skills.[3] The earliest incentives usually came in the form of concessions, under the terms of which foreigners developed and marketed Soviet raw materials on a profit basis while Moscow retained possession of those resources. Concessions attracted a large number of Americans, many of whom were Party members or sympathizers, during the early twenties. Some four hundred Americans helped develop the coal, iron ore, timber and other

33

resources of the Kuznets Basin, using "American" methods to turn the defunct operations in the area into a productive enterprise. Within a short time the Kuzbas colonists were exploiting the regions's iron ore and coal deposits; operating brick kilns, sawmills and shoe factories; building new railroads and re-equipping the mines, and, in the process, amazing the local population which assured them of the impossibility of their undertaking.[4]

American farming techniques were early valued and sought. Lenin wanted to establish a model American farm on each of the 250 farming districts, and 25 to 30 were actually created, often assuming the names of the American cities from which the settlers were recruited. These communes established "circles" which taught American methods, instructing Soviet farmers in horticulture, seed selection and other wonders of scientific farming.[5] As in the case of the Kuzbas colony, many of these Ameri cans, a portion of whom were sympathetic to the communist cause, were recruited by the Society for Technical Aid to Russia, an organization with some thirty branches in the United States.[6]

Ideological affinity likewise influenced the early assistance that Americans gave the Soviet textile industry. American workers entering the Soviet Union — both those who traveled voluntarily and those who made the trip via the compliments of Attorney General Palmer — established model textile plants in Leningrad and Moscow and worked to create a "genuinely American attitude" toward production in those plants.[7] More importantly, Sidney Hillman and the American Clothing Workers' Union helped modernize the clothing and textile industry in the USSR, supplying much of the capital and technical skills while the Soviets supplied the labor and raw materials.[8]

A number of concessions were devoid of ideological overtones. The industrialist Armand Hammer produced the pens, pencils and drawing equipment used by the Soviets in the early twenties, and American concessionaires repaired homes in Moscow as early as 1922.[9] International Barnsdall of New Jersey supplied much of the technical expertise to reopen the devastated Caucusus oil fields, employing American drilling, pumping and pipeline construction techniques to accomplish the task, while a Los Angeles firm trained the Soviet pipeline welders and supervised them on the job.[10] And the Caucusus refineries, though largely built by British and German companies, employed the American cracking process.[11]

These early efforts were insignificant compared to those that followed. As the twenties progressed, concessions increasingly gave way to technical assistance contracts under which the Soviets simply purchased the knowledge, skills and machinery of the more advanced nations. Several nations sold in this market, but the United States did so to a disproportionate degree. Henry Ford played perhaps the most visible and dramatic role. Before 1933, Stalin later remarked, the Soviet Union had no automobile industry.[12] Ford created that industry.

Ford was a name familiar to the Soviets years before the company began its massive technical assistance program. Between 1920 and 1926 the Soviet government purchased some 25,000 Fordson tractors from Detroit; by 1927, 80 per cent of the trucks and tractors in the USSR were Ford models.[13] Maintenance on these machines was erratic and Soviet-made parts inadequate, prompting Moscow in 1926 to invite Ford to send a delegation to design a maintenance system patterned on Ford lines and, more importantly, to examine the possibility of erecting a plant on Soviet soil. A group of Ford officials subsequently traveled throughout the Soviet Union studying the prospects but ultimately rejecting the offer because of a lack of Soviet managerial talent, the possibility of government expropriation and the likelihood of political decisions over-ruling economic considerations.[14] Similarly, General Motors sent a delegation to study the merits of a plant on Soviet soil, and likewise decided that the disadvantages outweighed the advantages.[15]

If Detroit was not willing to go to the Soviets, the Soviets were willing to come to Detroit. In mid-1928 four delegates arrived from Moscow and, after complicated negotiations, Ford agreed to provide the technical knowledge and plant designs necessary to erect two automobile plants in the Soviet Union. These plants were designed to produce some 100,000 trucks and Model A automobiles per year.[16] "Henry Ford manifestly took a generous position," Allan Nevins wrote of the agreement, for

> his company agreed to give Russia the full rights to make, sell and use Ford units throughout the USSR, to make and use Ford machinery and other equipment, and to use all Ford inventions and technical advances patented or unpatented. Ford would furnish detailed drawings of all the departments of a complete factory, specifications, and schedules of machinery and operation sheets. The company would supply two or more detailed sets of drawings of all tools, jigs, fixtures, and other special equipment at the Rouge plant. Ford would permit access to American plants by Russian engineers and other employees, to learn by actual floor work the methods in use. Finally, the company would send to Russia its own skilled engineers and foremen to help plan the new work, install the equipment and train the working force.[17]

Having contracted with Ford for the necessary designs, patents, and technical assistance to start its automobile industry, the Soviets then engaged two American firms to construct the physical plants. The Albert Kahn Company built one plant in Moscow; the Austin Company a larger one at Nizhni-Novgorod.[18] As the work progressed the human traffic between Detroit and the plants increased; at Nizhni-Novgorod an American community sprang up, complete with tennis courts and other artifacts of

American culture. Eventually a body of 150 Soviet workers arrived in Detroit for final training, a contingent of seventeen Americans left to initiate start-up procedures, and the magic day of production began. "Townspeople wild with elation entered in droves to look," Ford offiicial Frank Bennett wrote of the occasion, "and grave professional men begged to help on the assembly line to see how it produced its wonders."[19] From Nizhni-Novgorod, Bennett went to Moscow to open the smaller plant. Having accomplished that task he succumbed to the hospitable but insistent urging of his hosts to take a Black Sea vacation, only later realizing that his gracious hosts wanted to make sure that they could operate the plant by themselves before allowing him to leave the country.[20]

Measured in terms of immediate gain, the Soviets undoubtedly received the better end of the Ford bargain. The arrangement assured them a supply of automobiles, trucks, well-equipped factories and careful tutoring, while Ford lost some $578,000 in the process.[21] Still, Ford was proud of what he had done to advance Soviet development, and believed the Soviets were wise in looking to the United States for assistance. The greater the balance among the world's economies, he wrote, the better for all concerned.[22]

While the Ford-designed plants turned out trucks and automobiles, other American-engineered plants produced farm equipment. Failing in their efforts to produce a copy of the Fordson by studying Ford designs and by dismantling a number of the machines to measure the actual parts, the Soviets contracted with a number of American firms to build a series of tractor plants.[23] The Albert Kahn Company built some of the factories; McClintock and Marshall built others.[24] Caterpillar, which had been selling its equipment in the USSR for some time, agreed to bring Soviet engineers to its American plants and to send its technicians to the Soviet Union to instruct in the use and maintenance of its machines.[25] And in 1929 a number of American companies, working with Soviet engineers, designed a plant to produce approximately fifty thousand Caterpillar-type tractors per year on Soviet soil. American workers built and completely assembled the plant in the United States, then disassembled it and sent it to Stalingrad, where 570 Americans and 50 Germans reassembled the entire structure. The resulting Stalingrad Tractor Works was the largest plant of its type in Europe.[26] By the 1930's the various plants on Soviet soil were turning out machinery patterned on Ford, Caterpillar, International Harvester, Holt and Farmall models.[27]

While Ford's role was most visible and publicized, other American firms contributed in large measure to Soviet development. The Albert Kahn Company, America's leading industrial architectural firm and designer of many of the nation's most noted industrial facilities, played an extremely important role. Undoubtedly its reputation prompted the unprecedented offer which Moscow proffered. In 1928, a company official wrote, "the most extraordinary commission ever given an architect came in the door unannounced. In that year a group of engineers from the USSR came to the Kahn office with an order for a $40,000,000 tractor plant, and an outline program for an additional two billion dollars worth of buildings."[28] The order, Anthony Sutton wrote in his remarkable study of western technology and Soviet economic growth, "was nothing less than the First and Second Five Year Plans of socialist reconstruction."[29] About a dozen of the buildings were designed in Detroit; the rest handled in a special office housing fifteen hundred draftsmen in Moscow.[30]

The Soviet iron and steel industry also benefited from American technology, largely that of the Freyn Engineering Company of Chicago, leading designer of steel mills. In the late twenties Freyn agreed not only to build eighteen new iron and steel mills and rebuild some forty outdated metallurgical plants, but also to permit Soviet engineers access to its archives, and thus to its design technology. The Freyn agreement was, according to Sutton, "the first milestone in the transfer of western metallurgical technology" to the Soviet Union, and the plants it helped design and build formed "the basic structure of the Five-Year Plan."[31]

The Arthur McKee Company contributed its share to the Soviet steel industry through its assistance in designing and building the gigantic steel works at Magnitogorsk. Basing their design on the United States Steel plant at Gary, Indiana—at the time the largest integrated iron and steel plant in the world—some 450 American draftsmen worked day and night to accomplish the unprecedented feat of reducing every detail of the Magnitogorsk plant to paper, complete to the last nut and bolt, before construction ever started.[32] Once designed, American engineers, along with some from Germany, supervised the actual construction of the various Freyn and McKee plants, for which General Electric supplied the electrical technology.[33] Even the Soviet state trust in charge of iron and steel production was heavily Americanized, with Freyn and McKee personnel serving as advisers and filling key positions.[34] The objective, Henry I. Freyn wrote in 1930, was to provide American training, knowledge and practical experience to the end that the new iron and steel works would "be predominantly of American design and standards."[35]

American techniques also helped mine the raw materials that fed the steel mills, particularly the coal. In 1925 the Soviets, after comparing the coal mining methods of England, France, Germany and the United States, opted for the latter.[36] Thereafter, leading American firms designed and built mines in the USSR, supplied supervising engineers and trained Soviet mining engineers in their American facilities. The firm of Allen and Garcia, builders of the world's largest mine at Peoria, Illinois, constructed mines for the Soviets in the Donetz Basin, provided engineers to run the mines and brought Soviet engineers to the United States.[37] Stewart, James and Cooke carried out similar contracts, as did other companies and individual consultants.[38] Still other American firms helped develop the non-ferrous mining and smelting industry, so that by the end of the twenties over 200 American engineers and specialists were engaged in the production of lead, zinc, copper and silver.[39] The Aluminum Company of America signed an agreement in 1926 permitting it to explore for bauxite, and the Allied Dye and Chemical Company received a concession for the mining of asbestos.[40] Even the Soviet gold mines relied heavily on American engineers, reportedly as many as four or five for each mine.[41]

American companies supplied the machinery that American mining technology utilized. Allis-Chalmers, Westinghouse and other firms began selling equipment to Moscow early in the decade, and Soviet purchasing commissions scoured the United States for ever-improving designs.[42] Along with this equipment went even more Americans to install, train and supervise, and even more Soviet specialists came to America to familiarize themselves with the technology of the new tools.

Just as electrification was fundamentally important to Soviet modernization, American engineering was fundamentally important to Soviet electrification. American engineers under the direction of Colonel Hugh Cooper supervised the construction of the massive dam at Dneiprovstroi, largest in the world, and American firms helped supply the complex equipment that rested inside. General Electric and RCA turned the electrical current produced inside the dam into a useful commodity.

Beginning in the late twenties, General Electric supplied the Soviets with vast quantities of equipment and technology, sent company personnel to Soviet sites, and trained Soviet engineers in American plants. To handle the flow of business and information, General Electric opened an office in Moscow; the Soviets one in Schenectady.[43] A 1929 agreement calling for a "broad exchange of patents as well as exchange of designing, engineering and manufacturing information," Sutton wrote, was "by far the most important single agreement in the development of the Soviet electrical equipment industries."[44]

What General Electric did for Soviet electrical development, RCA did for its electronic technology. By the terms of an agreement signed in 1929, RCA agreed to "grant exclusive right to the (Soviet) Trust to manufacture, use and sell all patents, applications for patents and inventions, owned and/or controlled by the Radio Corporation of America and/or General Electric and Wastinghouse...."[45] Under this arrangement and a similar one signed in 1935, Soviet engineers visited a number of radio stations in the United States, and RCA engineers worked throughout the Soviet Union.[46]

Soviet transportation, too, looked to the United States for help. In 1930, a 34 man delegation made an extensive and detailed examination of America's railroad network, and found much to praise. The Soviets, announced the vice-commissar who led the delegation, must adopt the advanced techniques of American equipment and management. Subsequently Ralph Budd, president of the Great Northern Railroad, traveled to the USSR with the returning delegation, and, after inspecting the Soviet system, hired a large number of American specialists to assist him in the task of reorganizing the Soviet railroads, appointing a Reading Railroad official as chief consulting engineer for the project. The Baldwin Locomotive Works brought a number of Soviet workers, firemen and engineers to its shops for training, and General Electric began turning out the first electric locomotives for the USSR; locomotives which formed the basis for later Soviet designs.[47]

During the 1930's Soviet avaiation benefited from American aircraft technology as a number of American companies, including Douglas, Sikorski and Glenn Martin, signed technical-assistance agreements with Soviet agencies. Those contracts supplied aircraft, parts and design technology, and frequently stipulated that Soviet aircraft designers be allowed to spend a certain amount of time in American facilities. Likewise, American designers and technicians worked in the USSR under the agreements.[48]

Soviet agriculture also continued to draw on American experience throughout the twenties, as the limited lessons of the communes gave way to the technology of specialists in later years. As early as 1924 the Soviet government placed an American named Harold M. Ware in charge of several thousand acres near Piatagorok with a specific assignment to "train Russian agriculturists in American methods and organize model agricultural enterprises," which Ware attempted to do with the help of fifteen American subordinates and a number of tractors given him by the Ford Motor Company.[49] In 1929 the Soviets, noting that Thomas Campbell farmed 95,000 Montana acres with only 200 workmen and 109 tractors, invited the American farmer to advise them in the development of 10,000,000 acres of wheat land, and Campbell accepted.[50] Even the vast irrigation efforts depended upon American personnel and technology. Prior to World War II, Arthur P. Davis, construction consultant for the Panama Canal, Director of the U.S. Reclamation Service and one of the nation's best known irrigation engineers, conducted a feasibility study for the Russian government in the Steppes of Central Asia, but heard nothing further until the Soviets contacted him in 1929 and requested that he direct the development of irrigation projects in the area. Davis signed a technical-assistance agreement with Moscow, set up an office in Tashkent, hired a number of American engineers and began the task.[51]

The list of technical-assistance contracts and the myriad ways in which Americans contributed to Soviet development could be extended at length. Standard Oil, for example, built a kerosene plant for the Soviets at

Batum, the Seiberling Rubber Company of Akron, Ohio, built a tire factory on Soviet soil, and Soviet representatives of the glass-making industry studied American techniques in several cities.[52] Other Soviet representatives examined American bridge building methods and harbor designs, while still others studied the operations of American cash registers and business machines.[53] But to enumerate further is to obscure the essential point: contracts meant contacts, meant extensive and prolonged interaction between Americans and Soviets, and consequently meant penetrating to at least a degree the barriers of cultural differences.

By the early thirties at least a thousand American engineers and several times that number of skilled workers and technicians were working on Soviet soil.[54] Some of the engineers became national heroes; one even gained a reputation as "Russia's miracle man."[55] Their portrayal in Soviet literature as "efficient matter-of-fact technicians who knew how to give and receive sarcastic remarks about theirs and the Soviet social order," as Ina Telberg wrote, enhanced their image, and Nikolai Pogodin's dramatization using the "miracle man" as the model for his American engineer raised even higher the esteem in which the Soviet public held these practitioners of technology.[56] Frictions and differences existed of course, and on occasion flared openly, but the overwhelming evidence is that the American technical assistance, following so closely the ministrations of the American Relief Administration, produced among the Soviet people a genuinely friendly and affectionate attitude toward America and Americans—an attitude that never completely disappeared even when official relations later strained toward the breaking point.

Even before the Revolution some Russians urged their countrymen to look to America for inspiration and guidance, for the vision and vigor necessary to develop Russia and shape its future. "We must wake from our sleep which has been lasting for centuries," a Moscow University professor wrote in 1912, "we must take a good dose of Americanism." Russians must look to America, where a new race of men was boldly writing its name across the pages of history, asserted the professor in trying to persuade a technical delegation to visit the United States, in order to observe the initiative and energy of the businessman; to learn the value of time and work; to "imbibe the American culture and to bring the principles of the same over to Russia." Like America, Russia possessed vast spaces and resources, but its people lacked "that certain psychology ... necessary for a rapid and successful development of the productive powers of the country." Americans on the other hand had learned how to conquer distances and harness energies. "It is these principles of American life," the professor concluded, "that we must study and ... put to use in our own country."[57]

The following year a Siberian school teacher, just returned from a three year stay in the United States, spread a similar message. The zemstvos, he urged in presentations featuring magic lantern slides portraying American life, should send entire groups of idealistic Russian youth to learn the practical ways of America, for there "the question of happiness and meaning in life are not solved by theory, but by practice." In America there were no "unhealthy diversions into the spheres of excessive reasoning, ruining the nerves; muscles are working, and one voluntarily ceases to be a pessimist."[58]

Despite the urgings and the encouragement of the American consul-general in Moscow, the proposed technical delegation never came to the United States nor did the zemstvos organize excursions of Russian youth to America. But it mattered little, for within a few years America was taking its technology to Russia.

The transition from czarism to communism did nothing to diminish the admiration of American technique; indeed, it heightened it, for communists and capitalists shared a belief in the virtues of progress. And progress, as Lenin remarked to American concessionaire Armand Hammer, meant "buildings, inventions, machines, development of mechanical aids to human hands."[59] Lenin sounded as though he had just read the Moscow professor's article when he further remarked to Hammer that "Russia today is like your country was in the pioneering stage. We need the knowledge and the spirit that have made America what it is today."[60] For the Bolsheviks, a German historian wrote in 1926,

> Industrialized America became the promised land. At an earlier period the "intelligentsia" still looked for their models in Europe; but immediately after the Revolution, a wild enthusiasm for America started; the magnificent industrial works of Germany and the highly perfected plant of France and England all at once appeared paltry to Soviet Russia; they began to dream of Chicago and to direct their efforts toward making Russia a new and more splendid America.[61]

In the country of wasted time and apathetic men like Goncharov's Oblomov, the German writer concluded, "Lenin decided to create a superhuman American system of labor organization in which not a grain of energy should be wasted."[62]

Throughout the twenties and part of the thirties, Soviet officials openly admired and praised the technological aspects of American culture. The two proper elements of state and party work, Stalin wrote in 1924, were "the wide outlook of the Russian revolutionist" on the one hand and "American practicality" on the other. Only a combination of the two produced "a finished type of Leninist worker, the Leninist style of work."[63] A few years later, in an interview with Emil Ludwig, Stalin again lauded Americans for their "business-like cooperation in industry, literature and life."[64] Trotsky praised American mass production methods, and Rykov,

speaking before the Fifth Congress of Soviets in 1931, expressed appreciation for the technical aid rendered by Americans to Soviet construction.[65]
According to Frederic Barghoorn, Soviet Ambassador Alexander Troyanovsky remarked to President Roosevelt upon presenting his credentials
that there existed among his countrymen "a most natural feeling of sympathy, respect and admiration for your country, which they associate with
high technical and scientific progress and which they regard as an immense
creative force."[66] Making due allowances for the element of diplomatic
courtesy reflected in the statement, Barghoorn concluded in what seems to
be an altogether accurate observation, it "summed up the favorable aspects of Soviet reactions to acquaintances with American engineers,
technicians and scientists."[67] Shortly after assuming his duties, Troyanovsky spoke in a similar vein to an audience at the American-Russian
Institute, as the Society for Cultural Relations with Russia had begun
calling itself.[68] The thousands of Soviet youths preparing themselves for
technical careers, he remarked, were "students of American scientific
achievements and techniques." Since his country stressed science, and
since 144 Soviet scientists were members of American scientific organizations, "a scientific rapprochement with the most advanced western nation
is of greatest interest to us."[69]

Soviet delegations arriving in the United States likewise voiced their
esteem for American achievements. His country greatly admired America's technical accomplishments, a vice-commissar accompanying the railroad delegation touring the nation in 1930 commented, and could hardly
complete its railroad reorganization plan without availing itself of the
knowledge which Americans possessed.[70] The director of Amkino, as
noted above, attributed much of the popularity of American films in the
Soviet Union to the fact that his countrymen viewed America as a land of
"incredible efficiency," and even though the Soviet display at New York's
Machine Age Exhibition was designed to in turn impress Americans with
Soviet achievements, accompanying spokesmen were not hesitant to express a desire for more American know-how. Should American engineers
and architects forward some of their technical knowledge to the USSR, "it
would be a great contribution toward better cultural relations."[71]

P.A. Bogdanov, for five years director of Amtorg in the United
States, stated in full what many expressed in fragmentary form. Upon
returning to the USSR in 1935, Bogdanov became, Ambassador Bullitt informed the State Department, the leader of "those forces isn the Soviet
Union which are emphasizing the importance of Soviet industry looking to
the United States for technical guidance."[72] In a series of speeches, newspaper articles and personal comments to Embassy personnel, Bogdanov
explained at length why many in the Soviet Union considered it necessary
to look to America. Since Comrade Stalin "teaches us to combine the wide

revolutionary elan with American efficiency," he wrote in *Pravda*, the USSR should "seek American guidance even more than it has done hitherto"; should apply even more fully the American principles of simplicity, expediency, specialization, scientific research and willingness to discard conservative ways.[73] While it was true that "capitalist anarchy and private ownership" kept America from reaching its full potential, he continued in a disclaimer that sounded more obligatory than real, that fact posed no problem for Soviet socialism. "America," he concluded, "must serve as the measure by which we constantly check our technical achievements ... we must adapt American methods of work to our conditions; this being one of the chief prerequisites for the mastery of American technic."[74]

Moreover, Bogdanov wrote a few days later in the *Moscow Daily News*, it was not enough simply to import and copy American equipment and techniques; more important was the study of *"the technic itself, its progress, its improvement,"* for the rate of development in American technology was so fast that "whatever we had taken from America a few years ago seems already to have become obsolete."[75] The Soviets must maintain "constant and systematic connections with American engineering," otherwise they would lag in development. To accomplish this, Bogdanov suggested, Moscow should stop sending commissions and delegations to the United States, for these merely looked and inspected when the situation demanded study and application; rather it should stay abreast through establishing "an efficient information system, exchanging experience between scientific research institutions, and by organizing production methods similar to those in the Ford and other plants."[76]

A few weeks later Bogdanov returned to the same theme in yet another *Pravda* article. Noting that the "tens of commissions and hundreds of engineers" who had examined various European enterprises "found only in America what could best be applied to the Soviet Union," the former Amtorg director again urged closer and more permanent technical ties with the United States."[77] The American research institutions and societies, he wrote, were glad to exchange their research and literary works; the American Society of Mechanical Engineers had in fact already proposed permanent relations which Moscow, unfortunately, had failed to act upon.[78] The solution, Bogdanov suggested, was to maintain "bases of production" in the United States, from which American methods could be constantly studied. These bases of production should be secured through contracts such as that earlier signed with Ford, for that contract had afforded the opportunity of putting through the Ford plant "hundreds of our engineers and technicians who mastered the organization of production and the technological processes of the modern American plant." Such bases of production, Bogdanov concluded, should become "schools for our workers who would master American technique in practice."[79]

One of the "fundamental though somewhat abtruse" reasons for the Soviet desire to establish economic connections with the United States, Joan Hoff Wilson wrote in a study of American-Soviet economic relations during the prerecognition period, was the desire to come into contact with the material and pragmatic achievements of the American experiment in the new world.[80] The remarks of Bogdanov and other Soviet spokesmen leave no doubt as to the accuracy of that assertion. Nor can there be any doubt that the admiration of American technique implicit in the assertion affected the Soviet attitude toward America and Americans in areas beyond those of economics and technology.

During the late thirties, as the technical-assistance contracts expired, as Soviet internal troubles grew and as the international situation worsened, the Soviets grew increasingly reluctant to praise American technique or to acknowledge its contributions to their development; even occasionally refused to allow Americans to enter the plants that they had helped design and build.[81] But even then there were scattered expressions of gratitude and occasional indications of a continuing desire to reap the benefits of American technology. Speaking before the Eighteenth Party Congress in 1939, Anastas Mikoyan, recently returned from inspecting America's bottling and canning industry, noted that although the USSR had learned much from the United States, it still was not employing its technique on a sufficiently large scale.[82] And as late as 1939, Moscow made a determined effort to keep a number of American engineers working in the fuel industry in the USSR so as to take advantage of their knowledge.[83]

During World War II the Soviets again became fulsome in their recognition of America's technical contributions and in their gratitude for that assistance. The president of the USSR Academy of Sciences acknowledged that his country had assimilated American technology "on a grand scale" during its years of "technical reconstruction," and academician A.M. Frumkin referred to the United States as a "country of mighty technology."[84] The chief administrator of the Federal Works Administration, inspecting Soviet war damage at the special request of President Roosevelt, found America admired throughout the USSR. "Everywhere," he informed an American-Russian Institute audience in 1945, there was "a burning desire to lift up Russian technology to the level of American efficiency."[85] Soviet officials in the Soviet Central Institute for Building Research, addressing ARI members as delegates of the Soviet Purchasing Commission in the United States, spoke at length about the Soviet admiration of American technique and the necessity of emulating American technology in the building industry.[86] And, as noted above, Stalin himself acknowledged the tremendous contribution of the United States to Soviet industrial development.[87] Frederic Barghoorn, whose Embassy duties during the war years included working with cultural matters, noted that the flood of Lend-Lease products confirmed the Soviet impression of the United States as a technological wonderland. The jeep, which the Soviets knew only as a "Willys," he wrote, "was a wide-spread advertisement for American know-how."[88] But perhaps the ultimate tribute came in a remark made to Barghoorn by an American G.I who worked with Red Army troops. The Soviet soldiers, the G.I. noted, used the term "Studebaker" as the superlative form of praise in all matters — even to describe ladies of their choice.[89]

Admiration of America's technology translated itself into an interest in and friendliness toward the American people. As early as 1924, International Barnsdall employees in the Soviet Union expressed surprise and pleasure at their reception and treatment. "We have been received," a Barnsdall official told Anna Louise Strong, "with the most unexplained cooperation from the managers of the oil fields down to the oil workers."[90] Famine relief accounted in part for the friendly attitude, Strong concluded from her observations and interviews in the area of Barnsdall operations, but overwhelmingly it stemmed from admiration of American skill and efficiency. They gave the name "American" to almost any method that was quick and time saving, she wrote, and every official wanted an "American office" like Trotsky's.[91] Eugene Lyons, soon to oppose the red regime even more adamantly that Strong supported it, found the same attitude. "Americans," he wrote of his arrival in 1928, "were infinitely fascinating to Russians. For the older generations nurtured on democratic hopes, America was the land of vast freedom and individual opportunity. For the younger people, thrilling to the vision of an industrial future, it was the land of marvelous technique."[92] Two years later Bernard Knollenberg, assessing financial conditions and investment possibilities for a New York banking consortium, observed that although western clothes might attract unfavorable attention in the USSR, "say the magic word 'Amerikansky' and the atmosphere immediately changes to that of friendly interest."[93] Famine relief, the traditional Russian-American friendship and, above all, the "canonization of American industrial efficiency," he deduced, all contributed to the atmosphere of goodwill.[94] Frederic Barghoorn discovered the same attitude during the war years. Admiration of American technology, the extensive personal contacts of the preceding decades, and, most importantly, the legacy of the engineers, he wrote, accounted for the goodwill of the Soviet public.[95] Scores of others, including tourists, delegates, ambassadors and visiting officials commented on the Soviet friendliness toward Americans, and in 1943 Stalin himself confirmed the fact of that friendliness during a conversation with Donald M. Nelson, chairman of the American War Production Board.[96]

If ordinary Soviet citizens treated Americans with friendliness and respect, they looked upon Henry Ford with awe, for Ford represented the epitome of the American ideal. "It is really extraordinary," Maurice Hindus wrote in 1927, "how popular Ford has become in Russia. Incredible as it may seem, more people have heard of him than Stalin ... next to Lenin, Stalin and Trotsky, Ford is possibly the widest known personage in Russia."[97] "Fordisimus" and "Fordizitsia" became terms synonomous with orderly, rational production and progress. Ford's My Life and Work sold in large numbers and some Soviet universities and technical schools used it as a text.[98] Workers emblazoned Ford's name on processional banners, agricultural communes adopted the name "Fordson," and Soviet officials accorded fulsome tribute to the American capitalist.[99] "Trotsky praised the Ford production methods," Allen Nevins wrote, "and Pravda chronicled the progress of 'Fordization' in Russian factories."[100] And it is easy to appreciate the surprise of U.S. Chamber of Commerce President Eric Johnston when during a conversation, Stalin, after acknowledging Ford's contributions to Soviet development, suddenly remarked, "may God preserve him."[101] For the chief communist to praise the chief capitalist was not unusual, but to invoke the name of the Deity in doing so was sufficient to surprise any listener not familiar with Stalin's past as a seminary student.

It was a popularity neither sought nor promoted. "Ford just happens to be," Hindus wrote in trying to explain it, "the symbol of something which the Russian craves with all the flaming fervor that is in his soul."[102] Nevins agreed with that assessment, adding that the Soviets viewed Ford not as a capitalist but as a revolutionary in the art of production, "the chief economic innovator of the age, the leader who had scrapped established methods and hewed-out direct roads to well being."[103] Perhaps there was something symbolic about a wedding in a Soviet village which Hindus attended in the late twenties. The bridal cart was pulled to the ceremony by a Fordson, around which the guests gathered and proudly discussed as an example of Soviet progress. The bride, it seems, was ignored.[104]

In late 1933, at the height of the traffic in technology and tourism, the United States granted diplomatic recognition to the Soviet regime. Though Washington's motives stemmed from concerns other than cultural, for many Americans the new relationship promised the heightened level of cultural interaction to which they aspired.

IV
Recognition and Cultural Relations:
A Disappointing Decade

Understanding between peoples, newly appointed Ambassador Alexander Troyanovsky told an appreciative American-Russian Institute audience in early 1934, was basic to all international relationships; cultural rapprochement as important to cordial Soviet-American relations as the diplomatic ties only recently established. Ambassadors came and went, but peoples endured and the various harmonies and discords of international life remained. "Each of our countries," he emphasized, "must have a broader understanding of such wholly vital matters as the cultural aspirations and ambitions of the other." As for his country, he assured his hosts, it would respond with a "hearty reciprocity" to any American efforts toward "those cultural interchanges on which real understanding between peoples must rest."[1]

Troyanovsky's remarks could hardly have pleased his listeners more, for they seemed to go far toward turning their hopes into reality. With diplomatic relations established and the Soviet ambassador promising to support the cause of increased exchanges that they espoused, Institute members left the dinner honoring Troyanovsky and William C. Bullitt, America's new ambassador to the USSR, feeling their past efforts vindicated and their optimism about the future justified.

The optimism was misplaced. Recognition did not bring the anticipated increase in cultural intercourse. Until 1937, tourist travel to the USSR continued unabated, the American-Russian Institute continued its efforts toward organized exchanges, and some artists and scientists maintained connections with their counterparts, but there was no increase in the level of interaction. Washington's passive attitude toward cultural matters and the Embassy's irritation over official difficulties in Moscow did little to encourage contacts, but the real problem lay in Stalin's growing campaign of internal repression and antiforeign rhetoric. As the decade progressed the contacts between the two peoples became increasingly irregular and infrequent; by the time of the Nazi-Soviet Pact almost nonexistent. Russian ballet and theatrical groups continued to perform in the United States throughout the decade, but almost without exception the performers were émigrés, not Soviet citizens.[2] The broadened, systematic exchanges to which Troyanovsky alluded and for which his listeners hoped did not materialize during the thirties.

American tourists continued to travel to the Soviet Union through the middle of the decade. Some went strictly to see the sights, traveling either singly or in packaged tours, but an increasing number joined small study groups led by persons with specialized knowledge. The study tours covered almost every aspect of Soviet society. Travelers interested in art, drama, economics, education, sociology, psychology, criminology and a number of other subjects joined tours focusing on their particular areas of interest, often led by Americans eminent in their fields. They traveled with theatre authorities H.W.L. Dana and Oliver Saylor to the annual Moscow Theatre festivals, joined Harvard professors Samuel Cross and Merle Fainsod in traveling Soviet seminars, investigated sociological trends with University of Wisconsin sociologist Edward A. Ross, studied economics with professors from the Wharton School of Finance and pondered the educational implications of Soviet practices with faculty members from Teachers College, Columbia.[3] Prominent representatives of scholarly, religious, journalistic, literary and educational circles joined Sherwood Eddy's annual vacation pilgrimages, which in 1934 added the Soviet Union to their itinerary.[4] Those interested in more varied and general topics accompanied *Nation* correspondent Louis Fischer or CBS news editor H.V. Kaltenborn.[5] In both 1934 and 1935, Intourist expected over one hundred such tours; in 1936 anticipated a total of seven to eight thousand American visitors.[6]

Until the late thirties Moscow encouraged and facilitated the influx of of Americans. Intourist advertised widely in magazines and newspapers, as did the agencies that delivered the travelers to Intourist's care.[7] In 1936 the Soviets opened their borders to foreign automobiles at three points, prompting American Express to advertise motor tours of the USSR[8] In the same year Moscow added airline routes to move travelers between distant points; provided hydroplane service to facilitate travel between resort areas along the Black Sea coast.[9] Though they wrote less about their experiences than did the travelers of the late twenties, Americans in general seemed well satisfied with both Intourist and the general treatment accorded them in the USSR, though some found cause to complain and others ridiculed both the Soviets and their fellow tourists.[10] Judging from what they wrote upon their return, most would have emphatically agreed with Walter Duranty's assertion that individual visitors were "invariably treated with kindness."[11]

If Moscow encouraged Americans to come to the USSR, it remained reluctant to allow its ordinary citizens to travel to the United States. In 1936, Foreign Minister Maxim Litvinov indicated that an increasing number of Soviets would be allowed to go abroad, but there was no noticeable increase in the traffic to the United States.[12] While thousands of Americans saw both the featured spots along the Intourist trail and the eyesores between, only a handful of Soviets saw the good and bad of America.

In the late twenties, the State Department expressed the opinion that Moscow encouraged tourism to promote recognition.[13] If so, that motive was gone after 1933. After recognition, the desire for western currency was probably a major motive, for American tourists brought valuable dollars with them. If creating a favorable image of Soviet material progress was a primary aim, Moscow was taking a large chance, for although Intourist featured model factories and farms, it could not hide the rest of the country, and apparently made little effort to do so. Whatever its reasons, Moscow deserves credit for encouraging the tourist travel, for without it the personal contact between American and Soviet citizens would have been far less than it was. Though Soviet controls restricting foreign travel by its own citizens obviated the possibility, it is difficult to believe that Washington would have welcomed up to ten thousand Soviet visitors pouring into the United States each summer.

In addition to those who traveled as tourists, a number of Americans went to the Soviet Union during the postrecognition thirties to exchange ideas and information relevant to their particular interests. In 1935, a large delegation of American scientists and medical men attended the fifteenth International Physiological Congress in Moscow, at which Harvard professor Walter B. Cannon delivered the first major address.[14] When not attending formal sessions the Americans exchanged notes and made acquaintances with Soviet colleagues in their laboratories. "Every conceivable kindness was shown and honor done us," wrote one delegate, "and we had the best possible opportunity ... of making ourselves acquainted with Russian physiologists and physiology. We came away with affection for our Russian colleagues and deeply touched by their welcome." If the contacts made during the congress were pursued, added another, "it might well mark an important milestone in the development of physiology."[15] During the same summer, Frank Lloyd Wright and a fellow American architect attended the first All-Union Congress of Soviet Architects in Moscow, likewise finding themselves well received and duly impressed with the ideas of their Soviet counterparts.[16]

A few actors and singers also made the journey. In 1934, black baritone Paul Robeson, graduate of Rutgers and Columbia Law School, Walter Camp All-American football player and Phi Beta Kappa scholar, made the first of many trips to the USSR, traveling at the invitation of

Sergei Eisenstein, who proposed casting him in the role of Toussaint L'Ouverture in a planned film.[17] Two years later a number of Soviet cities gave Marian Anderson a tumultuous welcome, though the acclaimed performer was not quite sure whether the adulation stemmed from her singing or from the opportunity it presented to exploit her race for propaganda purposes.[18] A number of representatives from the theatrical world studied the techniques of Soviet actors at the Moscow Theatre festivals, and in 1935 the composer Nicholas Slonimsky visited a number of Soviet musicians, including Dmitri Shostakovich, whom he invited to the United States.[19]

Shostakovich never made it to the United States during the thirties, but a handful of Soviets, in addition to those who came as students or members of technical delegations, did make the journey. The head of Soviet cinema production came in 1938, finding much to like in technique and much to dislike in content in American films, and Serge Prokofiev, making his first visit since returning to live in the Soviet Union, came in 1938.[20] The most visible Soviet presence was at the World's Fair in New York City in 1939. But even at the fair, Americans and Soviets could not refrain from competing. The discovery that the red star atop the Soviet building towered over the American flag proved occasion for careful strategy to preserve the national honor, culminating in a maneuver directed by fair president William H. Standley, naval admiral and future ambassador to the USSR, that placed the stars and stripes firmly in command atop the parachute jump.[21]

The pattern of contacts begun in the twenties continued into the post-recognition thirties in a number of incidental ways as well. American literature remained highly popular with Soviet readers, Soviet writers such as Mikhail Sholokhov began attracting an American audience, and a number of Soviet films appeared in the United States.[22] After 1932, Soviet jazz musicians were again permitted to play for Soviet audiences as well as foreigners, an American jazz band called the Syncopators performed for Soviet enthusiasts, and Soviet officialdom stamped its approval by creating the USSR State Jazz Band.[23] Alexander Tsfasman, disciple of Sidney Bechet and worshipper of America and its jazz, became overnight, in the words of one member of the Soviet state jazz band, the "uncrowned king of Russia," drawing the kind of fame and fortune accorded popular performers in the United States.[24]

For many Americans the closest proximity to Soviet culture came through the activities and exhibits which the American-Russian Institute promoted during the years immediately after recognition. In 1934 the Institute arranged for a Soviet section at the International Exhibition of Theatre Arts at New York City's Museum of Modern Art and sponsored a Soviet display at the International Exhibition of Children's Paintings at

Rockefeller Center.[25] In conjunction with the Philadelphia Museum of Modern Art and the College Art Association, it sponsored a large exhibition of Soviet art which, after opening in Philadelphia in 1934, toured the country from coast to coast, appearing in the nation's largest cities as well as in places such as Denton, Texas, and Kalamazoo, Michigan, before closing to the praise of critics in New York in 1936.[26] In 1935 the Institute collaborated with VOKS to arrange an elaborate Soviet educational touring exhibit which opened at the Museum of Natural History, and in the same year sponsored a display of modern Soviet printing at the International Typographical Exhibit in New York City.[27] In late 1937, a Soviet exhibit tracing the history of architecture in the USSR appeared under Institute auspices at Columbia, Harvard and other universities in the United States.[28]

In addition to sponsoring exhibits the Institute arranged dinner, previewed Soviet films, staged concerts and musical programs, sponsored lectures and shipped material of a cultural nature, such as the photographs and drawings that it sent to Moscow's Museum of World Architecture, to the USSR.[29] It was particularly active in honoring the fetes of Soviet aviators and explorers and their American counterparts. In 1929 the Institute honored two Soviet aviators who flew across Siberia to the United States, in 1934 gave a dinner for members of the Cheliuskin Arctic expedition, and in 1937 paid tribute to three Soviet flyers who flew across the North Pole to America.[30] The latter occasion drew a particularly luminous crowd from the American aviation and exploration world, as well as a number of noted persons from abroad. The explorer Vilhajalmur Stafansson presided, Lowell Thomas gave the principal address and Ambassador Troyanovsky represented Soviet officialdom. Charles Lindbergh, Admiral Byrd and Jimmy Doolittle, among many others, sent messages of congratulation and goodwill, all stressing the international significance of the flight and its potential for increasing American-Soviet contacts.[31] The Soviet flyers replied in kind, emphasizing the cooperation between the two nations in planning and executing the flight. Not only was it a unique achievement in science and aviation, one remarked in the spirit of the occasion, it also represented a further step toward "the cultural and economic rapprochement of the Soviet Union and the United States."[32]

During the early thirties a new American-Russian Institute, entirely separate from the New York organization, developed in San Francisco. Librarian Harriet Eddy, two physicians who had worked with Soviet colleagues in the USSR during the twenties and a number of faculty members from Stanford and the University of California founded the Institute; businessmen interested in trade relations with the giant nation lying directly across the Pacific joined and supported it.[33] Valdivostok, one pointed out, was closer to San Francisco than to Moscow. Alexander

Kaun, chairman of the Department of Slavic Languages at the University of California was an early member, as was Stanford University professor Holland Roberts, who became the organization's president in 1943 and remained in that capacity for over 30 years.[34] Like the New York Institute, the one in San Francisco maintained contacts with voks, hosted visiting Soviet dignitaries, exchanged material with various Soviet agencies and featured exhibits portraying Soviet life, many of which it staged in the city's leading galleries and museums.[35]

Though sharing the same name and performing many of the same functions, the two institutes differed in philosophy. While the New York Institute maintained its customary neutrality and impartiality toward noncultural relations and emphasized objective knowledge as the proper path toward mutual understanding, the San Francisco organization expressed a more overt approval of and sympathy toward the Soviet state. Whereas those in New York proceeded from the belief that friendly relations between the two countries would result from mutual understanding, those in San Francisco operated on the a priori assumption that its function was at least in part to promote that friendliness.[36]

In the immediate postrecognition period the American Embassy in Moscow also tried to promote more intimate contacts. At his own initiative and expense, Ambassador Bullitt imported enough baseball equipment to equip four teams in an effort to transplant the popular game to the communist camp, and at least a few Soviets learned the rudiments of the American pastime, though it never became theirs.[37] The ambassador likewise taught polo to the Red Army cavalry, though evidently for purposes political as well as pleasurable, hoping thereby to gain increased influence with military leaders, especially Kliment Voroshilov.[38] Though not particularly successful as a means toward establishing contacts, Bullitt's efforts at least indicated a willingness and an optimism in that direction before Embassy officials became disillusioned and discouraged in their dealings with the Soviets, both of which were developments not long in coming.

If in some ways the pattern of cultural contacts continued the same as before through the mid-thirties, disappointment marked the pattern in others. Efforts to increase the level of interaction in the area of education failed, as did those aimed at increasing the exchange of performing groups. As the flourishing tourist trade ground to a halt, as the American engineers left the USSR and as the Soviet delegations departed the United States upon the expiration of the technical assistance contracts, the personal interaction that had characterized the previous years ceased to exist.

Conditions on neither side were conducive to contacts in the late thirties. The Depression left little room for such matters in the minds of even the most interested Americans, and recognition was not sufficient to overcome the fears and suspicions of the Soviet state that lingered in the minds of many. When the Cleveland Symphony Orchestra first staged Shostakovich's "Lady MacBeth of Mtensk" in New York City in 1935, for example, it was asked to neither use the term "soviet" in the production nor to invite the Soviet ambassador or the consul to the performance.[39] But conditions on the Soviet side were even less propitious. New York only objected to the use of the term: Moscow informally but effectively banned the entire opera.[40]

Beginning with the assassination of Sergei Kirov in late 1934 and continuing through the purges at the end of the decade, the Kremlin tightened its grip on all phases of Soviet life, including the cultural. The relative freedom of artistic expression prevalent during the twenties became dangerous and useless formalism, to be eradicated at all costs. The new task for artists became that of portraying the virtues of socialism in such a way as to contribute to the collective effort. In an epoch of class struggle, wrote Andrei Zhdanov in 1934, still some twelve years before the heights of his notoreity, "a supposedly unpolitical portrait of historical reality which does not picture the Soviet system as the best of all systems is not fit for Soviet literature and art."[41] A year later A.M. Gerasimov, president of the Academy of Arts, stated even more explicitly the case for socialist realism in art, literature and music. "Ideology," he wrote, "is the decisive factor in art, in the science of aesthetics and in criticism. The militant struggle to create an ideological-artistic life can be the only accepted position for our artists."[42] Writers, artists, dancers and composers disappeared along with generals and Party members. The famed theatrical figure Vsevolod Meyerhold, hero to the Soviets during the twenties because of his revolutionary theatre, vanished, and his wife was brutally murdered. Boris Pilnyak was sentenced to death even though he publicly repented and asked his readers to remove his books from their shelves; Boris Pasternak was forcibly silenced and permitted to publish only translations.[43] Music for domestic consumption was likewise harnessed to the needs of the state, though the great composers were left relatively free because their music drew international praise and thus provided proof, at least to the Soviet leaders, that socialism advanced the arts. Thus Shostakovich's censure for his "Lady MacBeth of Mtensk" was not long lasting; by the end of the decade he had worked himself back into good standing.[44] But the USSR State Jazz Band, ridiculed by the public because its music was not real jazz, perished because Stalin considered its jazz altogether too real.[45]

While tightening its inward grip, Moscow undertook an intense anti-foreign campaign which, by 1937, portrayed foreigners in the USSR as spies and saboteurs, causing many to disappear along with vanishing legions of Soviet citizens.[46] Though Americans fared well in comparison, rarely suffering arrest or imprisonment, the climate thus created did little to advance cultural contacts, and on occasion even Americans were arrested and held by the Soviets.[47]

The antiforeign campaign was only one item in a long list of grievances that turned America's official relations with the Soviets into a steady stream of bickering and indignation. Restrictions on contacts between diplomatic personnel and Soviet citizens, obstacles blocking the construction of a new Embassy building, difficulties in securing official visas and the vexations of Soviet customs practices, though mundane problems in individual instances, created in the aggregate a tension and an irritation that carried over into other matters. Failure to reach agreement on the larger matter of debts and claims stemming from the revolutionary period further strained the relationship, and the Moscow meeting of the Comintern in 1935, considered by Washington a violation of the Soviet promise in the recognition agreement not to interfere in America's internal affairs, stretched it even more.[48] Both Washington's formal protest against the Comintern meeting and its less formal complaints concerning the other matters elicited Soviet denials on each of the points, prompting some Embassy officials to suggest that the ambassador leave the Soviet Union, that the Embassy staff be drastically reduced or that some other form of action be taken as a form of protest.[49] None of the suggestions were followed and the official relationship formally remained as before, but the words of a State Department official seemed to have proven prophetic. The experience of other countries, the Chief of the Division of Eastern European Affairs wrote in July, 1933, had shown that increased official intercourse following recognition of the Soviet regime seemed to create division and rancor; tended to be "the source of friction and ill will rather than the mainspring of cooperation and goodwill."[50]

It was within this atmosphere of official tensions and Soviet internal repression that Americans desiring closer cultural contacts with their Soviet counterparts had to operate in the late thirties. But unlike a decade later, Moscow's excursion into the artistic world evidenced itself not so much in dramatic ideological attacks on American cultural life as in day to day disappointments and frustrations. Particularly was this true regarding efforts toward increased interaction in the field of education.

In the fall of 1933 a man named I.V. Sollins, representing himself as New York University professor, approached Institute of International Education president Stephen P. Duggan in the name of the Soviet government, asking for advice as to the best means of establishing closer cultural relations with the United States. Specifically, as Duggan informed Secretary of State Cordell Hull, Moscow wanted to talk about exchanging students and professors, arranging joint conferences on educational matters, and establishing a summer school for American students in Moscow similar to those which the Institute had arranged at the University of Berlin and at the Sorbonne.[51] With Hull's approval and expressed hopes that the trip would contribute to "the mutually beneficial relations between the peoples of the two countries," Duggan traveled to the Soviet capital in the spring of 1934 to pursue the matter.[52]

In Moscow, Duggan discussed various proposals with Soviet officials and made definite arrangements for a summer school to open at Moscow University in 1934. The arrangement gave VOKS, Intourist, Open Road and Moscow University ultimate responsibility for the school, placed one American and one Soviet in charge of educational matters, and stipulated that all instruction was to be given in the English language. No more than 50 students were to be enrolled, Duggan understood, and these were to be carefully selected and recruited by Sollins, who was to act as liaison between the students and Soviet officials.[53]

During the negotiations Duggan began to suspect the motives and aims of some of the Soviets involved, and upon his discovery back in New York that Sollins had misrepresented himself, that he was an expelled student rather than a professor, his suspicions became even greater. Consequently, Duggan asked L. Henry Schapiro, an acquaintance living in Paris, to go to Moscow to make sure that the Soviets properly fulfilled the terms of the agreement.[54]

Schapiro found Duggan's fears well founded. Upon Duggan's departure, each of the Soviet agencies pursued its own aims and interests with little concern about the consequences for the summer school. Intourist and Open Road treated the entire matter as a money-making enterprise; VOKS as a way to create a favorable image of Soviet accomplishments. Only Moscow University viewed the school from the angle of education. Instead of the 50 well chosen students that Duggan envisioned, Intourist enrolled approximately two hundred people with widely varying backgrounds, abilities, interests and levels of education. The youngest enrolled was seventeen; the oldest, 70. Of these, 64 were undergraduates, 57 held bachelor's degrees, 40 were masters graduates, thirteen possessed doctorates and seven were medical doctors. Some considered the venture a cheap vacation, some were ideologues and a few were serious students.[55] The uneven assemblage portended problems; the situation in Moscow assured them.

Classes began toward the end of July in a welter of anger and confusion. Those who had not preregistered encountered scheduling problems; once enrolled, most found the classes either too difficult or too easy. Transportation, laundry and other incidental services provided by Intourist were inadequate, even at prices the students considered fraudulent.[56] Almost no contact with Soviet students was permitted, which caused some of the most bitter complaints. Schapiro tried to correct some

of the problems, only to be scorned and ridiculed by Sollins, who was the
source of many of the difficulties. Having got off to a good start under the
aegis of a respected organization, Sollins told Schapiro, the school no
longer needed the services of either Duggan or the Institute.[57] Duggan
considered withdrawing from the agreement, but believing his organization had committed itself too deeply to withdraw without adverse publicity, settled for complaining to the Soviet Embassy in Washington.[58]

If Sollins felt the services and the name of the Institute of International Education were no longer necessary, the Soviet Foreign Ministry
evidently felt otherwise. After Duggan complained in Washington, conditions at the school improved dramatically. Officials from both VOKS and
the Foreign Ministry began placating Duggan and other Institute officials,
and even Intourist's services took a turn for the better.[59]

If the students had complaints about other aspects of the school, they
had only praise for the quality of instruction and their personal relations
with the university instructors. Once the registration problems were overcome and the students placed in classes appropriate to their interests and
background the school progressed smoothly. In one area the instructors
were particularly circumspect. When presenting the Marxist point of view,
Schapiro reported, the lecturers made an obvious attempt to be detached,
quickly squelching the ideologues who tried to engage others in debate.[60]
By the end of the school term the students had largely forgotten the early
difficulties. "The special efforts made on behalf of the students, the large
number of excursions, the generosity of the lecturers with their time and
the social activities arranged for them, combined with the novelty of life
in the Soviet Union," wrote Schapiro, "combined to create a very favorable impression on the majority of the students."[61] When the school was
over the students selected one of three extensive tours of the USSR as a cul-
mination of their summer studies, and most departed the country satisfied
with the outcome of their efforts.[62]

Given the happy note on which the 1934 summer school ended, prospects for the following summer looked bright. Intourist again insisted on
selling tickets to anyone wanting to attend the school, but a satisfactory
compromise was reached by designating as auditors those not properly
qualified for academic credit. Columbia University professor George S.
Counts, eminently qualified for the position by virtue of his acquaintance
with Soviet educators and his knowledge of Soviet educational practices,
accepted the position of American director of the school, but upon being
unable to fill the role turned it over to fellow Columbia professor Heber
Harper, likewise well qualified for the position.[63] As time for the school
approached, Harper went to Moscow to assume his duties, confident that
the lessons of the previous summer would prevent similar difficulties
during the coming session.

The school never opened. Simultaneously with the arrival of some two hundred and twenty-five American students, the president of Intourist called Harper to his office and announced that the school had been cancelled.[64] Intourist offered to refund the unused fees for food and lodging that the students had been required to pay in advance, and to allow them to travel anywhere in the Soviet Union, but would do no more.[65] Some accepted the offer, but few were satisfied and many outraged. At least one tried to retrieve his money through appeals to his congressman and the State Department, but to no avail.[66]

The Soviets never gave a satisfactory explanation for the cancellation. The president of Intourist told Harper that the newly announced program of industrial and agricultural expansion required the services of so many faculty members that the school was forced to close, but according to rumor, Ambassador Bullitt told Washington, the reason stemmed from conflict among the various Soviet agencies as to the proper aims and goals of the school. Moreover, the ambassador added, some Soviet officials were blaming the cancellation on interference in the school by the American Embassy, an allegation that Bullitt vigorously denied and denounced as a ploy to direct the anger of the students away from those responsible.[67]

The closing of the summer school typified the changing Soviet attitude toward contacts, and provided a portent of future difficulties. Whatever the specific reason for the cancellation, the students returned angry, the Institute of International Education withdrew from any further efforts for the remainder of the decade, and hopes for a significant degree of cooperation in the field of education vanished.

Similar difficulties prevented American entertainers appearing in the Soviet Union in significant numbers during the years immediately following recognition. In this instance, however, the problem stemmed at least in part from the dubious dealings of a New York booking agent and the entertainers' own failure to make adequate inquiries about the nature of the contracts under which they agreed to appear in the Soviet Union.

In early 1935 an individual named Alexander Basy, head of Amsov, a New York agency with connections to Gomez, the Soviet state trust in charge of entertainment, traveled to Moscow to arrange reciprocal performances by American and Soviet entertainers. Basy particularly wanted to bring a Soviet ballet to the United States, but Moscow, arguing uncertainty as to how the dancers would be received, refused permission. Basy did, however, arrange for some thirty American groups, including vaudeville troupes, opera singers, a black jazz band, a girls' jazz band, acrobats and an assortment of other acts, to appear in the USSR.[68]

The contracts arranged by Basy were explicit and detailed, but written in straightforward and easily understood terms. The Soviets agreed to pay transportation both ways, to provide free transportation and lodging while in the Soviet Union, and to pay a stipulated monthly salary to be negotiated with each group. The contracts specifically stated, in large letters so as not to be overlooked, that the performers were to be paid in Soviet money exclusively, that they could not demand payment or compensation in any other form, that the money could not be taken out of the Soviet Union, and that all disputes arising under the contracts were to be settled in Soviet courts.[69] What the contracts did not explain was that Soviet money was divided into gold or "foreign" rubles worth approximately eighty-eight cents, and paper or "native" rubles worth about three cents, and that the performers were to be paid in the latter currency. Nor did Basy explain these facts to the performers even though the Embassy in Moscow specifically pointed them out, cautioning him particularly about the requirement that all disputes be settled in Soviet courts.[70]

The first group, billing itself the Mangean Four, arrived in Moscow in April, immediately encountered the realities of the contracts, and appealed to the Embassy for help. The stipulated salary of 4,500 "native" rubles per month, the leader of the group complained, was insufficient to buy food, much less to purchase the furs and jewels that the group had anticipated buying at the Torgsin stores.[71] And even if the salary were sufficient, they discovered, the Torgsin stores would not accept the paper rubles.[72] In order to warn other groups preparing to depart for Moscow the Embassy informed Washington of the situation and, at its specific request, provided the Mangean group with an interpreter to act in an unofficial capacity to solve its dilemma.[73]

Considering the fact that the Mangean singers had signed an explicit and binding contract, the Soviets were by no means unreasonable about the matter. Though refusing the Mangean demand for a new contract raising its salary to 25,000 paper rubles per month while retaining the other benefits such as free lodging and transportation, Gomez did agree to provide food as well as lodging, and to provide transportation back to the United States at the end of 30 days, even though the contract stipulated that the group must perform for at least 60 days in order to qualify for free return transportation.[74] When the Commissariat of Finance refused to provide the necessary funds to pay for the return trip at the end of 30 days, Gomez, largely at the diplomatic persuasion of Embassy official Loy Henderson, wrote a completely new contract raising the salary by 12,000 rubles, changing the date on the new agreement to make the sum appear a part of the original salary.[75] The Mangean Four left the USSR without further incident, though at Leningrad they were accosted by Basy, just arrived to straighten out his problems, who threatened both bodily harm and intervention by the Soviet secret police if the group insisted on leaving.[76]

Had the incident ended at that point it would scarcely have deserved notice, but its repercussions continued. Upon persistent inquiries from reporters about the American singers "stranded" in the Soviet Union, Under Secretary of State William Phillips explained their problems during a Washington news conference on April 19, and the following day newspapers across the country carried accounts of the performers' plight as reported by Phillips and as described by an American correspondent in Moscow.[77] On the 21st, *Billboard* gave the story even wider circulation.[78] The news created a furor in the entertainment world, particularly among those directly involved. Some one hundred performers stormed Basy's office demanding to know the truth about their contracts, and a number of them contacted the State Department.[79] Basy in turn, after bitterly condemning the Department for interfering in private matters, issued a press statement designed to placate his clients. Gomez had informed him, Basy stated, that the American Embassy had specifically approved the contracts and determined that the Mangean singers were well treated and well satisfied.[80] Embassy officials had done neither, as Basy later admitted, but the assertion served to momentarily satisfy those with contracts.

Moscow was less satisfied. On May 13, three groups holding Gomez contracts contacted the Embassy from New York, saying that they wanted to perform in the Soviet Union despite the ruble situation, and asking Embassy personnel to persuade Gomez to provide free transportation as promised.[81] Because of the problems and difficulties associated with the Mangean tour, Gomez replied to the subsequent Embassy inquiry, only one additional group would be permitted to enter the country. Only after that group had given assurances that it was fully satisfied with its salary and working conditions would others be admitted. But even that arrangement failed when the Commissariat of Finance refused money for transportation, though at least one of Basy's clients made the trip.[82]

In the meantime, Basy traveled to the Soviet Union to salvage matters, arriving just in time to try to prevent the Mangean singers boarding their boat. Failing in that, the booking agent verbally attacked Embassy officials in Moscow, accusing them of meddling in private matters and ruining his plans.[83] Within a few days, however, a contrite Basy appealed to the Embassy for support for his failing scheme, admitting while doing so that he had lied about a number of matters connected with the venture.[84] But despite his efforts, Gomez would neither fulfill the terms of the remaining contracts nor allow Basy, who represented an American organization willing to pay $12,000 a week to the dancers, to make arrangements for a Soviet ballet company to tour the United States.[85]

Whether the Soviets would have fulfilled the terms of the contracts had not the first group complained, or whether they used the occasion to cancel the remaining groups under contract for the same reasons that they cancelled the 1935 summer school are questions impossible to answer. There was seemingly no valid reason to cancel the appearances of the groups that wanted to perform in the Soviet Union even with the explicit understanding that they were to be paid in three-cent rubles, and restricted as to where they could spend those rubles; as far as the Soviets knew, those groups and individuals understood the currency situation from the first and were satisfied with the terms of the original contracts. The reason for refusing to fulfill the agreements, it would appear, had as much to do with Moscow's retreat from foreign contacts as with problems concerning the contracts themselves. But whatever the Soviet reasoning, the cancellation of the Basy contracts effectively eliminated large scale contacts in the entertainment field just as the cancellation of the 1935 summer school eliminated organized contacts in the area of education.

By the mid-thirties, problems had replaced promises for those who hoped for a heightened level of cultural interaction in the postrecognition period. The difficulties defeating the efforts in the fields of education and entertainment seemed, for the moment at least, to have rendered organized exchanges in those areas impossible, and additional problems were soon to follow.

Nineteen thirty-seven was to have been a banner year for tourism in the USSR. Anniversary events celebrating 20 years of socialist progress were planned throughout the country, and advertised widely. Intourist and the travel agencies booking passengers to the Soviet Union highlighted the special events, featuring particularly a series of North Cape cruises with short trips to Leningrad and Moscow.[86] Over three thousand Americans, Intourist anticipated, would book passage on six ships for these cruises alone.[87] American travel to the USSR, Intourist reported in May, was up 40 per cent over the same date the previous year.[88]

But in July the friendly attitude toward tourists began to cool. Several dozen passengers on four different ships, most of whom were Americans, were refused permission to enter Soviet territory with their fellow passengers, even though all possessed either visas or Intourist entry permits.[89] In late July, Soviet authorities refused entry to fifteen Americans from the Hamburg-America liner *Reliance*, and ten from Holland-America's *Rotterdam*.[90] A month later fifteen were barred from the Swedish liner *Gripsholm*, and 40 "undesirables" aboard the Italian liner *Roma*, cruising in the Black Sea, were refused entry at Yalta.[91] The five hundred passengers who were allowed ashore were forced to stand in line for hours while Soviet agents searched each thoroughly, and once ashore were permitted to visit only the czar's palace and one restaurant. Westerners not accustomed to nude bathing, the Soviets stated in an explanation that many refused to believe, might be offended if allowed to visit the beaches. Even more infuriating was the fact that the passengers were encouraged to exchange their dollars for rubles, and, having no opportunity to spend the money, were refused the opportunity to convert the rubles back into dollars.[92] Two Americans were arrested for taking pictures of innocent objects, though such a practice had previously been allowed.[93] The antiforeign rhetoric and the fear of spies and saboteurs was manifesting itself fully in the Soviet tourist trade.

American tourist traffic to the USSR fell off sharply thereafter. Though Intourist early in 1938 denied a report that it was no longer interested in the American tourist trade, and indicated that it planned to place advertisements in a dozen magazines and 31 newspapers in nineteen cities, a search of the publications in which the advertisements usually appeared revealed none, and in magazines such as *Travel* which over the previous years had carried feature articles and short items about the USSR, such features became conspicuous by their absence.[94] According to the *New York Times*, Moscow began reducing the number of visas issued to Americans in the spring of 1938, limiting them primarily to professional men, newspaper reporters and travelers on cruise ships, all of whom were restricted to beaten paths.[95] The Embassy increasingly complained about delays in the issuance of visas, and by the fall of 1938 was suggesting that Americans with no real need to be in the USSR leave the country.[96] The flourishing American tourist traffic to the USSR lasting from the late twenties to the late thirties was over, to lie dormant for two decades.

Nor did the approximately one hundred American delegates planning to attend the seventh International Congress of Genetics get to make their planned trips to Moscow in 1936. More than forty were preparing papers to read at that conference, which was of special interest due to the fact that Herman J. Muller, serving as head of the Department of Mutations of the Soviet Institute of Genetics while on leave from the University of Texas, was to be the chairman of the program committee.[97] But the same internal developments that contributed to the regimentation in artistic life and to the purges in the political realm, surfacing in scientific circles in the form of T.D. Lysenko's attacks on classical genetics and geneticists, caused the Soviets to cancel the program.[98]

Minor problems further discouraged contacts. In the mid-thirties, Moscow refused to allow its young scientists to accept further Rockefeller grants and fellowships, stating that it could afford to pay for such matters itself, though it was willing to accept the assistance provided it was tendered through an international agency such as the League of Nations rather than directly through the Rockefeller Foundation.[99] And when the Bibliofilm Services, a nonprofit agency operated by several United States government offices, asked the Soviets to copy some Voltaire manuscripts, they refused, explaining that they were preparing a catalogue for publication and unable to make microfilm copies at the time. Since they had announced the same catalogue years before, since microfilm copying was a rapid process, and since Bibliofilm had performed the same service for the Soviets on a number of occasions, Bibliofilm officials pointed out, the Soviets were obviously unwilling to undertake the task.[100] Minor in itself, the incident provided a foretaste of future difficulties.

Washington did little to encourage the cultural relations that Moscow's actions discouraged. Despite the changed official relationship, the State Department's attitude toward cultural matters remained the same: willing to acquiesce, unwilling to promote. Though not opposed in principle, the active encouragement of cultural intercourse still lay beyond its authorized or accustomed function.

When, for example, the American Council of Learned Societies asked the Department to assign an "intellectual attache" to the Moscow Embassy to serve the same function in cultural matters as that performed by military and commercial attaches in their fields, the Department demurred. Rather, it suggested, the Council should support a private representative in the USSR for that purpose, though at the insistence of Council President Mortimer Graves it did agree to instruct an Embassy officer to handle such matters as long as it did not interfere with his regular duties, and Graves found some Embassy officials, particularly Loy Henderson, helpful and cooperative.[101]

If Washington did little to promote cultural contacts, the nation's schools did little to educate the country about the USSR. Despite the increasing importance of the Soviet Union in international affairs, American academic study of its institutions remained almost nonexistent. A handful of universities offered courses in Russian language, literature and history, and in the summers of 1934 through 1937 the Institute of Pacific Relations taught intensive language courses at, respectively, Harvard, Columbia and the University of California, but the minuscule nature of the effort only illustrated the enormity of the need.[102] In that respect the Soviet Union was well ahead, for their schools widely taught the English language as well as American political, social and economic history.[103] Even though the courses were taught from the Marxist point of view, the Soviet Union did not at least, as Ernest J. Simmons noted, "make a virtue of ignorance of the United States, however much it may have cheerfully anticipated the collapse of our way of life."[104]

The Nazi-Soviet Pact, the outbreak of World War II and the subsequent Soviet moves into Poland and Finland destroyed whatever hopes remained for cultural contacts during the thirties. The relatively free and easy relations of the prerecognition period had proved to be not a prelude to more intimate interaction in the postrecognition years, but rather to an increasing discord and divisiveness. Only a drastic change in the relationship between the two nations could alter that reality.

V
War and Increased Contacts, 1941–1946

The Nazi invasion of the Soviet Union instantly created a new American-Soviet relationship, replacing much of the animosity aroused by the Nazi-Soviet Pact with a sense of shared purpose and common danger. Washington immediately promised aid; within months started a new flow of equipment and technique to the USSR. After Pearl Harbor the relationship became even closer as the two countries became partners in war. In the United States that partnership translated itself into both a new interest in cultural friendship and a new emphasis on understanding the culture of its ally. Organizations formally devoted to cultural relations, individuals and groups desiring simply to share their cultural achievements, and, for the first time, official Washington, all worked together to heighten the level of cultural cooperation while the nation's universities and libraries expanded their efforts to provide the means of cultural understanding.

The New York American-Russian Institute played a leading role in the endeavor, both in maintaining contacts with the Soviets and in supplying reliable, accurate information to the American people. In the latter regard it served a particularly valuable function, for despite the earlier traffic in tourists, technicians and performers, the United States had little systematic, detailed information with which to assess its new ally. Considering the Institute's wartime importance and popularity — and considering its postwar fate — its activities during the war years are worth examining in some detail.

The sudden and urgent demand for information about the Soviet Union made painfully apparent the pre-World War II academic neglect of the USSR. In 1938 only four universities maintained departments of Slavic languages and literature. In the six years prior to the war, American universities awarded only four doctoral degrees in all areas of Russian and East European studies; in 40 years prior to the war the University of California at Berkeley produced only five Ph.D.'s in Russian area studies, four of whom were native Russians and one a Yugoslav. Immediately before the war there were only twelve specialists in Russian history in the

United States, and of the dozen "specialists" employed by military intelligence only two knew the language and had professional training in the field. The Department of State employed six specialists in Soviet affairs; the Departments of Agriculture and Commerce, one each.[1]

Individuals, organizations and institutions therefore turned to the American-Russian Institute for information and assistance; as one Institute researcher commented during the war, "the phone began ringing the day Hitler invaded the USSR and has not stopped."[2] The Associated Press, the United Press and the *New York Times* paid retaining fees for its consulting services, as did *Time, Life, Newsweek* and other publications.[3] Columbia, Yale, the University of California, West Point, the Naval Academy and the Army Air Force Instructor's School sought its assistance, along with General Electric, Westinghouse, the Veteran's Bureau, the Department of Agriculture and similar organizations.[4]

Having maintained the professionalism it exhibited before 1936 as the Society for Cultural Relations with Russia, the Institute was well qualified to serve the new demands placed upon it. As before, the quality of its leadership shaped the quality of its efforts. In 1945 its board of directors included Mortimer Graves of the American Council of Learned Societies, Columbia sociologist Robert S. Lynd, Arthur Upham Pope of the Asia Institute and Columbia professor Ernest J. Simmons, one of the nation's leading scholars on Russian history and literature.[5] Ernest C. Ropes, head of the Russian section of the Department of Commerce for more than twenty years, became the board chairman upon his retirement from government service in 1947.[6] During the war the Institute's staff acted as advisers, translaters and language teachers in military programs. Bernard Koten, head of the Institute's language school, for example, earned the Legion of Merit for using his language skills to help capture a German division, organized the Russian section of the U.S. Army School at Biarritz, France, and acted as adviser to such projects as the March 29, 1943 issue of *Life* devoted exclusively to the Soviet Union.[7]

As earlier the library, which by 1948 contained over thirteen thousand volumes and listed over four hundred titles of Russian language newspapers and periodicals, constituted the core of the Institute. The clipping file, having accumulated some 350,000 indexed items since the late twenties, continued to be a heavily used asset, yielding answers to thousands of inquiries.[8] The combination of books, periodicals, clipping file and professional staff, along with numerous exchange arrangements with various Soviet institutions, made it perhaps the public's best source of information on contemporary Soviet affairs during the war.

Drawing on its resources, the Institute issued its own publications and carried on a number of organized cultural activities. In the late thirties it began publishing the *Russian Review of the Soviet Union*; in 1946 began issuing the *Russian Research Technical News*, listing Dow Chemical, Du Pont, Monsanto and the Bethlehem Steel Company among its subscribers.[9] Bell Telephone, *Life, Time* and the Wilson Library used its translation services, as did individuals such as John Hersey who commissioned the Institute to prepare a complete translation of a Moscow symposium on his novel, *A Bell for Adano*.[10] The Institute's language school, noted for its quality and professionalism, enrolled as many as one hundred and eighty students per session during the war years, in courses ranging from elementary to highly specialized.[11] Along with the National Council of American-Soviet Friendship, the ARI sponsored in-service courses covering various aspects of Soviet life for New York City school teachers.[12] Similar classes acquainted Soviets living in the United States, most of whom were serving in some war related capacity, with the complexities of American life. In both instances the instructors for the courses were highly competent, and in some instances the ranking authorities in their fields. Margaret Mead and Sir Bernard Pares, to mention only two, indicate the quality of professionalism to which the Institute aspired in conducting the courses.[13]

Prominent speakers, both American and Soviet, both in government and out, addressed the Institute's regular gatherings. In 1944, Ralph B. Turner, Assistant Chief of the State Department's recently created Division of Cultural Cooperation, outlined the emerging government role in American-Soviet cultural relations at an ARI dinner, stressing in his presentation the past and future importance of the Institute and similar private agencies.[14] At the same function, Ambassador Andrei Gromyko emphasized his country's desire for closer cultural relations, likewise pointing out the importance of private cultural agencies and the ARI in particular.[15] The following year Ernest C. Ropes, still in charge of the Commerce Department's Russian Division, spoke to an Institute audience in the same vein. The American people were largely ignorant of the Soviet Union, Ropes stated, and government agencies were at a disadvantage in trying to overcome that ignorance for such efforts were instantly denounced as "communistic." Therefore, he urged, the ARI must continue to perform that vital task; must continue to "gather and distribute information about the Soviet Union ... in trade, culture, science and many other fields."[16]

In late 1943 a new organization devoted to promoting American-Soviet cultural friendship developed in New York City and grew rapidly, attracting support from a wide segment of the American public. Through its exhibits, cultural exchanges and speakers' bureau the National Council of American-Soviet Friendship performed many of the same functions as did the New York American-Russian Institute, but its public orientation, mass rallies, and, most importantly, its views on official Washington-Moscow relations, set it apart. Whereas the New York ARI stressed the importance of increasing knowledge on the assumption that this would naturally lead to better relations, the Council, following a philosophy similar to that of the San Francisco ARI, was much more vocal in its opinion that the official relationship between the two nations should — indeed must — be one of friendship and cooperation. And like the New York ARI, the Council deserves extended notice because of both its war-time activities and its postwar problems.

Its membership, like that of the ARI, was impressive. Albert Einstein, Judge Learned Hand, Helen Keller, Mary McLeod Bethune, Raymond Robbins, Lillian Hellman, Leverett Saltonstall, George Vernadsky, Howard Mumford Jones, E.W. Burgess, Charlie Chaplin and W. Rose Benet, to mention only a very few members, indicate the diverse nature of the people it attracted.[17] Equally impressive were the members of the Council's numerous committees. Aaron Copland, Roy Harris, Benny Goodman, Andre Kostelanetz, Fritz Reiner and Serge Koussevitsky belonged to the Music Committee, as did Arthur Feidler and Bruno Walter.[18] Rockwell Kent, Paul Manship and Max Weber were members of the Art Committee.[19] The Book Publishers Committee, headed by M. Lincoln Schuster of Simon and Schuster, included the presidents of Dodd, Mead and Company, the W.W. Norton Company, and Little, Brown and Company, with others representing Brentano's and Doubleday.[20] Walter B. Cannon and Irving Langmuir served with other prominent scientists on the Science Committee, and individuals equally well known in their professions belonged to the Education and Architecture committees.[21]

The various committees actively promoted cultural relations during the war. Through art sales, donations from art houses and individual contributions, the Art Committee shipped art supplies to its Soviet colleagues, thereby establishing contacts that lasted throughout the war years.[22] At the request of VOKS the committee sent books, reprints and magazines portraying the historical development of art in the United States, and in September, 1945, some one hundred and fifty American artists sent eight hundred reproductions of their works to the Soviet Union in an effort, as one contributor stated it, to further "the mutual knowledge and friendship between the artists of the two countries."[23] The Music Committee shipped works of contemporary classical, jazz and folk music to the Music Section of VOKS, and the Womens Committee exchanged books, photographs and child care exhibits with Soviet womens' organizations.[24] The Book Publishers Committee sent books to replace those destroyed by the Nazis and on one occasion restored, largely through the efforts of Mrs. Frank N. Doubleday, the American sections of two libraries destroyed by German armies.[25] The Science Committee both sent and received scientific publications, translating the material received and giving it wide circulation through scientific journals in the United States.[26]

The Architecture Committee was especially active in promoting contacts during the war, hoping thereby to "create a basis for constructive cooperation after the war ... leading eventually to exchange visits by architects, engineers, technical personnel and students."[27] In collaboration with the Office of War Information the committee sent an extensive exhibit to the Soviet Union in the fall of 1944. Designed to provide both architects and laymen with a coherent picture of American architectural development, the exhibit traced the history of American building from indigeneous designs through contemporary community planning and development. Organized in part by the Dean of the Harvard School of Design and professionals from the Columbia School of Architecture, the display drew warm praise from the Soviets.[28] In the spring of 1945 the committee sponsored an American-Soviet building conference, featuring films, speakers and exhibits from both nations. The conference, a Soviet official wrote, was "a tremendous contribution to the exchange of experiences between the builders and architects of your country ... and our men who were visiting in the United States."[29] In the fall of the same year some two hundred Americans attended a reception at which still another architectural exhibit was presented to the Soviet consulate-general, to be shipped to Moscow and thence to other Soviet cities.[30]

In November, 1945, the various committees of the Council cooperated in a widely publicized exhibit featuring Soviet art, music, science, and education. Noted authorities in each of the fields conducted panel discussions to familiarize those attending with Soviet activities and accomplishments, and the State Department, demonstrating its support, sent an official from its cultural relations division to explain Washington's developing role in cultural contacts between the two countries.[31]

A series of mass rallies designed to publicize the cause of postwar friendship made the Council highly visible. Held in Madison Square Garden, the rallies featured nationally known speakers, drew large crowds and received messages of support and encouragement from the nation's most powerful leaders, including the president of the United States.

The first rally, based on the theme that victory was near and planning for postwar partnership imperative, was held in November, 1944.[32] A large and festive second rally staged in May, 1945, celebrated the victory in Europe and gave special honor to the efforts of the Red Army. Tributes, praises and expressions of goodwill looking forward to future close relations flowed freely. The U.S. Army Combat Infantry Band played Soviet marching songs, and gave a special performance of Prokofiev's "March to Victory." Paul Robeson, a controversial figure in some quarters because of his expressed admiration of the Soviet Union, sang Red Army songs.[33] General Joseph Stilwell was scheduled to be the featured speaker but military duties kept him away, forcing the audience to settle for a message read by his wife.[34] Secretary of State Stettinius, Henry A. Wallace, Harold Ickes, Eleanor Roosevelt and Soviet Ambassador Andrei Gromyko likewise sent messages, as did President Truman. "We must now," the President's message read, "bend every effort to work together to assure that these sacrifices shall not have been in vain."[35]

A third rally was held in November, 1945, again in Madison Square Garden, and again President Truman sent a message expressing his "continued interest in all efforts to continue the good relations between this country and the Soviet Union."[36] General Eisenhower wired his congratulations along with his conviction that American-Soviet friendship was "one of the cornerstones on which the edifice of peace must be built." Nothing was more important, the general's message read, than "mutual understanding on the part of each of the institutions and customs of the other."[37] Albert Einstein stressed the necessity of "permanent close collaboration" with the Soviets and a number of others, including Under Secretary of State Dean Acheson, the principal speaker, expressed similar sentiments.[38] The Dean of Canterbury flew to the United States to speak at the rally, afterward touring the country promoting American-Soviet understanding and visiting with President Truman at the White House.[39]

On the west coast the San Francisco American-Russian Institute played a similar role in promoting wartime cultural contacts. Architects, musicians, theatre workers and movie cameramen contributed materials and supplies to their Soviet counterparts, which the Institute, through the use of a Lend-Lease plane, flew to Moscow.[40] Over six thousand books, along with microfilm recording and reading equipment, were shipped to Soviet libraries, and more than seventy exhibits on various phases of Soviet life were provided to American museums, schools, universities, art galleries and army orientation centers.[41] Its publication, Soviet Culture in Wartime, was requested by public and university libraries throughout the nation.[42] A film on wartime Soviet medicine attracted eight hundred medical people, including many from the Stanford and University of California medical schools, both of which dismissed classes to allow faculty and students to attend the event.[43] After the war the demand for its materials remained strong. In 1946 and 1947 the Institute received more than five hundred requests for materials from schools located in every state in the union; on one morning alone, in September, 1946, requests arrived for such materials from 26 cities in seventeen states.[44]

A highlight of the San Francisco Institute's activities was its Shostakovich Music Festival, during which radio stations played the composer's music, lecturers discussed his life and musical contributions and the San Francisco Public Library featured exhibits based on his works. A 45 minute shortwave broadcast beamed to Moscow at the height of the Nazi push on Stalingrad, featuring both Shostakovich's music and greetings from such eminent musicians as Leopold Stokowski, Serge Koussevitsky and Yehudi Menuhin, culminated the festival.[45]

The Institute also welcomed a number of Soviet officials during the war and postwar years. During the United Nations Conference at San Francisco the Institute held a reception for Foreign Minister V.M. Molotov, after which the entire Soviet delegation was honored at a banquet attended by Governor Earl Warren.[46] In turn, a number of Soviet scientists in the United Nations delegation hosted a reception for 85 of their American colleagues in the Bay area.[47] In 1946, Dr. V.V. Parin, Secretary General of the Soviet Academy of Medical Sciences, was honored at an Institute dinner, as were a number of others, including the poet and newspaper correspondent Konstantin Simonov, who voiced warm appreciation for America's contribution to the Soviet war effort and expressed hope for continuing cultural cooperation even as the postwar divisiveness lessened the chances of those hopes being realized.[48]

While the organizations dedicated to American-Soviet cultural relations took the lead in widening contacts during the war, other Americans not formally committed to such a cause contributed to the same end. Wartime conditions rendered direct human contact difficult, but music, films and printed material provided a link between the people of the two countries. And once the conflict was over, scores of individuals and organizations approached the State Department with schemes for maintaining friendly relations between the former allies through the strengthening of cultural interaction.

Music served as a particularly important medium of cultural interchange. Orchestras throughout the United States performed concerts of all-Russian and all-Soviet music, prompting at least one critic to complain that the outpouring of Russian music represented less a tribute to another nation and its composers than an attempt by certain schools of music to promote their preferences.[49] Programs dedicated to Prokofiev and Shostakovich were particularly prevalent, but others received attention as well. In some cities such concerts had been presented before the war, but in others they were something new. The Houston Symphony Orchestra presented an all-Soviet concert in 1943 which one trade magazine deemed, for instance, an historical event in the musical history of the Southwest.[50]

If Americans became familiar with Soviet songs during the war, the same was true of the Soviet people regarding American music. In the fall of 1942, American composers and publishers donated the complete orchestration for 21 symphonies plus the music and lyrics to more than sixty popular songs which, after being reduced to microfilm, the Office of War Information sent to Moscow. Years later, Americans in the USSR were still surprised to hear such numbers as "Alexander's Ragtime Band," "There's A Tavern in the Town," "By the Light of the Silvery Moon," "Over There,"

"Tea for Two," "Stardust," "White Christmas," "Deep in the Heart of Texas," or any number of old favorites, all part of the wartime shipment.[51] "Alexander's Ragtime Band" became a particular favorite in Moscow's nightclubs, and Moscow jazz orchestras clamored for even more jazz tunes.[52] In addition to hearing American music the Soviets — at least a favored few — were afforded the opportunity to see the latest movies via an ambitious project begun by Ambassador William H. Standley in 1942.[53]

Libraries also joined the effort to acquaint Americans with the culture of their wartime ally. Throughout the war years local libraries displayed material on Soviet life, with the effort reaching its peak in May, 1944, when the American Library Association, in conjunction with a "Russia Book Week" sponsored by the National Council of American-Soviet Friendship, urged its members to feature books, exhibits and posters on the Soviet Union.[54] The Library of Congress used the occasion to announce the opening of its new Slavic Center, made possible by a Rockefeller grant and intended, stated library director Archibald MacLeish, to play a particularly important role in meeting the postwar demands for more extensive materials on the Soviet Union.[55] To honor the occasion, the Soviets presented the Library of Congress with a portfolio of pictures from an exhibit on American life shown in Moscow while that city was under seige.[56] The following month the Library of Congress featured another exhibit on the Soviet Union, emphasizing the development of the USSR Academy of Sciences and its role in Soviet society.[57]

On a more academic level, both universities and libraries expanded their efforts in order to accomodate the increased demand for knowledge of the Soviet Union. Army and Navy subsidies and private foundation grants allowed scores of schools to either expand existing programs or create new ones: by late 1947, the dozen or so colleges and universities teaching Russian language and literature at the beginning of the war had grown to more than one hundred and forty, and that number was climbing rapidly.[58]

The increased academic interest forced both private and university libraries to devise better methods of acquiring and distributing scholarly materials relevant to the USSR. As early as 1943 the Rockefeller Foundation, concerned over the lack of knowledge, sponsored a conference to discuss the dilemma. A resulting grant accelerated the cataloging of the Slavic Collection of the Library of Congress, and, more significantly, a second grant financed the compiling of a checklist of materials considered necessary for the scholarly study of the USSR.[59] Upon completion the checklist showed that many of the necessary items were not available; that the United States was little prepared to undertake a serious study of the Soviet Union.[60]

In June, 1945, eighteen of the nation's leading university libraries sent representatives to Washington to further deal with the problem. In order to assure a reasonably complete collection of materials, the librarians agreed, it was necessary to establish a more systematic means of cooperation among themselves. Individual institutions, they decided, must take responsibility for building complete collections in specific areas to avoid duplication and delay. Moreover, they agreed, Washington's help was essential in securing the desired materials from Soviet institutions.[61] Consequently, a three man delegation approached the State Department concerning the matter, finding there both concern and promises of assistance; promises which, Department officials were shortly to find, were easier made than fulfilled.[62]

In November of the same year approximately fifty delegates representing 42 of the nation's leading private libraries met in New York City to discuss their particular problems relevant to the acquisition and distribution of Soviet material. Sponsored by the American-Russian Institute, the meeting attracted delegates from such organizations as the Hoover Institution on War, Revolution and Peace, the Council on Foreign Relations, the Foreign Policy Association, the OWI and the Department of Agriculture. Leading newspaper and book publishing firms sent representatives, as did universities such as Brown, which was in the process of building a collection covering Soviet mathematics. Acting Librarian of Congress Werner Clapp attended to answer questions for his institution, the secretary of the Soviet consulate replied to inquiries concerning exchange possibilities, and the Lenin Library wired its willingness to cooperate with the libraries represented at the meeting. Those attending traded information, established channels of communication and cooperation and generally informed themselves of the resources and activities of the others.[63] Prior to adjournment the delegates drafted a message to be sent to Moscow through the State Department, requesting the Soviets, now that the war was over, to resume the normal flow of publications between the two countries.[64]

While the librarians sought to improve the availability of materials, others concerned themselves with translating selected Russian titles into the English language. In 1944 the American Council of Learned Societies, operating under a Rockefeller grant, began translating distinguished Russian and Soviet works in the humanities and social sciences in order, as a spokesman stated, "to promote a better understanding of Russian culture and the Russian mind."[65] By 1948 the undertaking, known as the Russian Translation Project, had already published a number of articles, had some thirty full length works in various stages of completion, and had agreed, at the request of the State Department, to begin translating newspapers and periodicals.[66] The following year the Joint Committee on Slavic Studies,

established by the American Council of Learned Societies and the Social
Science Research Council, began publishing the *Current Digest of the
Soviet Press*. With Philip E. Moseley as chairman and Ernest J. Simmons
as secretary, the Committee undertook the translation of most of the
articles in *Pravda* and *Izvestia* as well as selections from 40 other magazines, thus making important sources of Soviet thought available to
Americans within three weeks of their publication in Moscow.[67]

During the war years numerous magazines and periodicals likewise tried to increase America's knowledge of the Soviets. Publications
ranging from popular to scholarly featured articles and information about
the USSR, and some, such as *Life* and the *American Sociological Review*,
devoted entire issues to the Soviets.[68]

American scientists and medical specialists also maintained contacts
with Soviet colleagues during the war, exchanging information, publications and delegations and stressing the need for continuing such contacts
in the postwar period. The American-Soviet Medical Society, founded by
Walter B. Cannon and housed in the same building as the New York
American-Russian Institute, played an especially important role in maintaining relations between nongovernment agencies. Drawing on the Institute's facilities and connections, the Medical Society published the results
of Soviet research in its *American Review of Soviet Medicine*, hosted
visitors from the Soviet medical community and sponsored similar visits
to the USSR.[69] Dr. Stuart Mudd of the University of Pennsylvania Medical
School, president of the Society, visited a number of Soviet institutions
during the autumn of 1946, and in turn Soviet physicians attended the
Society's annual meetings during the war and early postwar years.[70]

The United States Public Health Service also maintained friendly contacts with Soviet agencies. In January, 1944, Dr. Michael B. Shimkin,
chief of the Health Service's Office of International Relations, traveled to
Moscow to study advances in a number of fields. Accompanied by Harvard professor A. Baird Hastings, Shimkin found the Soviets friendly and
frank. "The Soviet medical authorities," the two wrote upon their return,
"made every effort to provide us with unsupervised contacts with their
medical scientists ... to accede to our requests for specific information on
matters pertaining to medical research."[71]

For a time it appeared as though American and Soviet researchers
might collaborate on a cancer research project. During the early thirties
the husband and wife team of Nina Klyueva and Georgi Roskin developed
a promising serum for cancer treatment, attracting thereby the attention
of a number of American scientists. In September, 1945, Dr. Theodore
Hauschka of Philadelphia's Laukenau Hospital Research Institute applied
for a visa to travel to Moscow to observe the Soviet experiments; in mid-
October the National Cancer Institute, increasingly intrigued by the

researchers' results, decided to send doctors Michael B. Shimkin and Murray J. Shear to accompany Hauschka.[72] Ambassador Walter Bedell Smith also took a personal interest in the matter, contacting a number of high Soviet officials about the possibility of American cooperation and personally visiting the Soviet scientists in their laboratory.[73] The Americans left no doubt that they were interested in the Soviet serum and desired to collaborate in its further development, but the desire was ultimately to prove more frustrating than fruitful.[74]

Scientists in nonmedical fields cooperated with Soviet colleagues in their respective fields during the war and early postwar years. In addition to the exchanges carried on by the Science Committee of the National Council of American-Soviet Friendship, the National Academy of Sciences mailed its *Proceedings* to over forty Soviet institutions, receiving in turn the publications of a variety of Soviet agencies.[75] In 1942 the American Philosophical Society elected the Soviet scientist I.M. Vinogradov to its membership, and four years later elected Pavel Alexandrov, both of whom Princeton University invited to visit its campus during the early postwar months.[76] Individual scientists such as Harvard astronomer Harlow Shapley carried on personal correspondence with their Soviet counterparts, exchanging in the process both scientific information and nonscientific expressions of goodwill.[77]

James B. Conant, Harvard president, scientific adviser and atomic bomb researcher, formally stated the informal sentiments of many of his fellow scientists. Washington should place scientific interchange on a systematic and rational basis, he suggested to Secretary of State Byrnes in December, 1945; should sponsor alternating annual conferences in the fields of agriculture, medicine, physics and other branches of science, between which a minimum of two distinguished scientists, representing the National Academy of Sciences and the Soviet Academy of Sciences should work in the country of the other. Scientists from each nation should periodically tour the other's basic research laboratories and scientific attaches should be assigned to the Embassies in each country to facilitate the flow of information from these laboratories. "Personally," Conant concluded, "I believe that everything that can be done to increase the flow of basic scientific information between Russia and the United States and the interchange of scientists will work for the benefit of both countries ... indeed it seems to me that it is through the medium of science, education and the arts that we can build bridges of communication between the two countries."[78]

The kind of scientific interchange that Conant envisioned seemed well within the realm of reality in the early postwar period. In 1946 the Soviets invited 30 American scientists to help celebrate the 220th Anniversary of the Soviet Academy of Sciences, to begin in the latter part of June. Sixteen of the scientists accepted the invitation, along with approximately two hundred from other countries, with Moscow paying — or offering to pay — all expenses.[79]

From the viewpoint of international cultural contacts the anniversary celebration was a huge success. Each scientist conferred with colleagues in his own field; attended meetings and visited laboratories during formal sessions; enjoyed banquets, receptions and a variety of social pleasures during informal gatherings. The Soviet government honored the Americans as special guests at the great victory celebration held in Moscow on June 24, and afterward entertained them at a special Kremlin banquet hosted by Stalin and attended by top members of the Soviet heirarchy.[80]

More importantly the Soviets, according to delegation spokesman Harlow Shapley, appeared eager to open a new era of cooperation with western scientists. The Soviet Minister of Education, the Harvard scientist reported, expressed a deep interest in exchanging scientists and science students, and the Soviet Embassy had confirmed that interest.[81] Shapley therefore devised a plan to reciprocate the Soviet invitations to the anniversary celebration. The American Philosophical Society and National Academy of Sciences, he suggested to State Department officials, should invite approximately fifty Soviet scientists to the United States, paying all expenses except transportation, which was to be the responsibility of the Army Transport Command. Both Frank B. Jewett and Thomas Gates, the respective presidents of the sponsoring scientific bodies, Shapley assured Department officials, favored the proposal.[82]

President Truman and Secretary of State Byrnes, both of whom listened to Shapley's suggestions, endorsed the idea, agreeing with the State Department's Elbridge Durbrow that the plan represented a serious step toward improved cultural relations.[83] Moreover, as Durbrow pointed out, it was a plan the Soviets would most likely accept, since it represented a return invitation to their earlier overture.[84]

But Shapley had acted prematurely in promoting his bilateral program. Though such invitations had been discussed, Frank B. Jewett informed the State Department, no steps had been taken to implement them because many scientists believed they represented the wrong approach. Detlev Bronk, foreign secretary of the National Academy of Sciences, best expressed the reasoning of the opponents. The Soviets themselves, Bronk argued, had set a better example by the multilateral nature of their earlier invitations; a bilateral approach might thus be considered little more than high level propaganda. Moreover, Bronk continued, a number of Soviet scholars had expressed hopes of achieving the same easy give and take relationship with Americans as those enjoyed by other nations, and those hopes might well be harmed rather than helped by inviting Soviet scientists to the exclusion of others.[85]

The State Department remained neutral concerning the form and scope of the invitations, but adopted a significant attitude toward the larger issue. It was the general policy of the government to encourage as much scientific interchange with the Soviets as possible, a Department official wrote, but the invitations should be worked out insofar as possible on a nonpolitical basis; should be handled from the viewpoint of scientific relations rather than from that of international politics.[86] Ultimately the Bronk view prevailed. Only four Soviet scientists were invited, along with representatives from other nations, to attend the 1946 meetings of the National Academy of Sciences and the American Philosophical Society.[87] But despite the small number of Soviet scientists invited as compared to the earlier invitations from the USSR, there were no political motives or anti-Soviet sentiments involved. Hopes for postwar cooperation remained high among influential segments of the nation's scientists during the early postwar period.

Educators, actors, producers, musicians, sports promoters, universities and students also devised projects for furthering cultural contacts during the early postwar years. In October, 1945, Ella Winter, former wife of the deceased writer Lincoln Steffens, sought the assistance of both the State Department and the Soviet Embassy in trying to bring the Red Army Chorus to the United States.[88] The following spring the Boston Symphony Orchestra invited Eugene Mravinsky of the Leningrad Symphony Orchestra to visit Boston as its guest conductor, and shortly thereafter volunteered to give a series of concerts in the USSR, hoping thereby "to repay in some small part the magnificent cooperation of the Soviet Union during the war."[89] In both instances it offered to pay all expenses; in the latter offered to donate all proceeds to a Soviet-designated agency.[90] The Sol Hurok agency invited a Soviet ballet company to participate in the International Dance Spring Festival at the Metropolitan Opera House, to tour the United States, or do both.[91] The president of the Metropolitan Opera Association contacted Department officials concerning means of establishing closer relations with Soviet opera and ballet circles, and the mayor of New York City invited the Soviets to send either the Moscow or Leningrad ballet companies or the Moiseyev Dance Ensemble to help celebrate the city's golden jubilee.[92]

Movie producer Mike Todd devised one of the more ambitious postwar projects, proposing to sponsor an American tour by the composers Shostakovich and Prokofiev, the Red Army Chorus, a Soviet symphony orchestra and a number of other groups. In arranging the tour, Todd assured the State Department, he would spare no expense; would present the Soviet artists with a dignity "commensurate with their position, their art and the nation they represent." Millions of Americans, he envisioned, would attend the Soviet performances in large outdoor stadiums and indoor auditoriums, thereby promoting warm human relationships on all sides and "goodwill and understanding between the two nations."[93]

The nation's universities joined the effort. The Association of American Colleges, representing some six hundred colleges and universities, sought permission through Secretary of State Byrnes to send a film crew into the USSR to make documentary films and to gather materials for educational purposes, assuring the Soviets while making the request of the objective and scholarly nature of the proposed endeavor.[94] Cornell University invited four graduate students and a ranking professor of Soviet literature to lecture on its campus during the 1946–1947 school year.[95] Princeton invited two eminent Soviet scientists to spend a year lecturing to its students, and asked two other Soviet representatives to attend its bicentennial celebration.[96] Yale geology professor Richard Flint sought Moscow's permission to work with Soviet colleagues on a research project in Siberia, the National Colloid Symposium, meeting at Stanford, invited a noted Soviet scientist to be its principal speaker, and the American Society for Russian Relief, acting through Dr. Edward L. Young, offered to build a plant to produce penicillin on Soviet soil.[97] The Rockefeller Foundation offered to pay all expenses for a trip to the United States by two Soviet mathematicians, and on behalf of a number of universities the United States Commissioner of Education asked VOKS to suggest a professor who would be willing to spend a year in America, lecturing for varying periods of time on a number of campuses.[98] Several other universities, responding to an officially sponsored State Department proposal, indicated a willingness, indeed an eagerness, to engage in academic exchanges with Soviet institutions.[99] Dr. William G. Carr of the National Education Association made a plea on behalf of his organization for increased contacts between the two powers, arguing that catastrophic consequences were likely if either practiced "educational and cultural isolation."[100] An eleven member CIO delegation echoed the plea, urging an exchange of workers as well as students, while the YWCA drafted a resolution at its 1946 annual meeting both commending the State Department for its efforts toward cultural relations and urging it to broaden and strengthen its initiatives.[101]

Large numbers of students also approached the State Department in the early postwar period, requesting information about the possibility of studying in the USSR. Some wanted to study under specific professors or in specific fields, but most desired to study in the Soviet Union because wartime contacts had increased their interest in Soviet affairs and heightened their awareness of the Soviet role in the postwar world. Regardless of the motive, almost all expressed an appreciation of the role of cultural contacts between the two powers of the postwar period.[102]

The sports-minded sought to strengthen cultural cooperation through athletic events. The Chicago YMCA suggested volleyball contests between the two nations; Alabama coach Champ Pickens, undaunted by earlier failures, proposed to take college athletes to the USSR to perform exhibition matches in football, baseball, track and swimming events.[103] The Army and Navy Association suggested that one thousand Soviet teams be equipped and taught the game of baseball, doubtless convinced that the virtues Americans assigned to their national sport would accompany the balls and bats to Moscow, and in 1947 the New York American-Russian Institute negotiated an agreement to stage a number of athletic contests between representatives of the two countries.[104]

Chess enthusiasts met a particularly favorable reception from their Soviet counterparts. As early as 1942, *Chess Review* resumed prewar negotiations aimed at arranging a series of matches, but wartime travel conditions rendered the project impractical.[105] In late 1943 the American Chess Federation tried to defeat the travel problem by arranging a long distance radio match, but nothing came of the initiative at the time.[106] Two years later, however, the radio match was held, and even though the American team was badly beaten it stressed the larger benefits of the competition. The match, a spokesman stated, was of great importance "not only in the chess world, but even more so as one of the steps to promote relations between the two nations in a field other than war."[107]

In 1946 an American team accepted a Soviet invitation to compete in Moscow upon condition that the Soviets return the visit the following year. To coordinate the matches a U.S.-USSR chess committee was organized, with the president of the Manhattan Chess Club serving as chairman. After working out plans to alternate annual matches between the two countries, the American team traveled to the Soviet Union in the fall of 1946, finding itself well received but badly beaten.[108] As earlier, however, both teams emphasized the noncompetitive benefits of the game. "Such exchanges will help promote better understanding between the American and Russian people," the American chairman of the joint chess committee stated, and he hoped, would "lead to other exchanges in the whole sports and cultural field."[109] The Soviet Embassy in Washington was even more optimistic in its opinion regarding the possibilities of such matches, seeing them as "another means of further strengthening the ties of friendship between the two great peoples," and hoping that this "latest in a growing series of exchange visits from representatives of various fields of culture and national life of the two countries," would add to the "growing understanding and goodwill between the American and Soviet peoples."[110]

By the end of World War II, it was apparent that many people in the United States desired to strengthen the cultural relationship between the American and Soviet people, both for the intrinsic values and benefits inherent in friendly foreign contacts and for the possible beneficial effects that such contacts might have on the official relationship between Washington and Moscow. There was sufficient reason to believe that the Soviet people, and even the Soviet government, reciprocated the desire. And Washington, abandoning its earlier neutrality in such matters, had begun to view the possibilities of international cultural contacts from the same perspective.

VI

Washington Assumes a Role:
Official Contacts, 1942–1946

That the American public took an increased interest in the Soviet Union during the war years is not surprising. The Soviets were, after all, comrades in a common cause; fellow fighters against a deadly foe. But significantly, the public was not alone. Official Washington shared its interest and, in many instances, took the initiative in turning that interest into action. In some instances congressional legislation and Justice Department rulings hindered the free flow of people and ideas, but regardless what other aims and interests Washington may have had vis-à-vis Moscow, the State Department made a serious, sustained effort to establish friendly cultural contacts with the Soviet Union during the war and early postwar years.

Prior to 1938, Washington concerned itself little with international cultural relations, largely limiting its role to that of expediting or restricting private initiatives through its control over visas and passports. But in that year two small steps stemming from the Pan American Conferences of the thirties marked the beginning of an effort destined to assume significant proportions. In May, an Interdepartmental Committee of Cooperation with the American Republics linked a number of federal agencies for the purpose of promoting cultural amity within the western hemisphere, and in July the Division of Cultural Cooperation was created within the State Department for the same purpose.[1] In 1942 the program was extended to China; in 1943 to the Near East and Africa.[2] And as Ralph B. Turner, one of the principal architects of the cultural relations program pointed out in a speech at the American-Russian Institute in 1944, throughout the war years Washington sought the means to extend its activities to the European countries.[3]

From the beginning there was a split regarding the proper role of an officially sponsored cultural relations program. Some considered it primarily a means to serve America's national interests abroad; a tool to

79

implement the nation's foreign policy. Others strenuously opposed linking cultural activities to foreign policy, arguing that such efforts should serve no ulterior purpose; should do no more than promote mutual knowledge and understanding among nations. Whatever benefits such a program produced, they contended, should be long term gains derived from the atmosphere of goodwill and understanding created in the process of cultural interaction.[4]

The General Advisory Committee on Cultural Relations attempted to reconcile these opposing views. To the extent that American foreign policy sought to achieve mutual understanding by promoting the exchange of ideas and information, the committee recommended, cultural relations should serve to implement that policy. But on the other hand, it asserted, no program should try to achieve noncultural objectives, nor be "an instrument by means of which one people attempt to impose its ideas and conceptions on another."[5]

Moreover, policymakers agreed, government efforts should facilitate private initiatives rather than supplant them. From the beginning the State Department stressed that its role was not to replace or diminish the work being done by private individuals and institutions, but "to assist them in producing more effective results toward nation-wide cooperation."[6] As Under Secretary of State Sumner Welles noted, the concept of an "official" culture was alien to American thinking; therefore the proper function of the Cultural Relations Division was to serve as a clearinghouse, as a coordinating agency for the private groups and individuals interested in promoting cultural contacts.[7]

During the war and early postwar years Washington largely adhered to these concepts in its cultural relations efforts vis-à-vis the Soviet Union. There were exceptions to be sure, but the preponderant aim during the period was to promote mutual knowledge and understanding, not to propagandize American cultural achievements in the interests of political partisanship. The explicit statements of State Department officials, the readiness with which Department officials facilitated private efforts and the Department's own initiatives in sponsoring cultural relations programs all bear witness to the fact.

Throughout the war years various government officials made references to the importance of postwar American-Soviet relations, but none stated the case more explicitly than did Ralph B. Turner, Assistant Chief of the Cultural Relations Division of the State Department and Dean Acheson, Under Secretary of State.

The same circumstances that had stimulated cultural relations between America and other countries, Turner told an American-Russian Institute audience in New York in 1944, had stimulated closer cultural relations between the American and Soviet people as well.

"The normal relations of these people," Turner remarked, "is cultural."

> Each has achieved results in ways that can help the other. They are in the forefront of medical and other scientific advances. The agriculture of each has much it can teach the other; their industrial technologies support each other. Both can take pride in their war effort, and in this shared leadership is the guarantee of mutual understanding and mutual services between the American and Russian peoples that can be developed in a broad program of cultural exchange. The way to do this is to develop cultural exchanges between the two countries on an agreed basis.

"Indeed," Turner concluded, "the time is now opportune for the negotiation of a bilateral agreement under which all kinds of exchanges may be carried out between the American and Russian peoples."[8]

Several months later, Dean Acheson, speaking at a rally sponsored by the National Council of American-Soviet Friendship, echoed Turner's sentiments. One of the most important elements in friendship among nations, Acheson remarked, was understanding: enduring friendship could be built only on understanding and trust, not only between governments, but peoples as well. The problem was that of how the American and Soviet people could come to know and understand each other. Both wanted to know the other better, yet both were proud and strong, and both committed to their own way of life, thus creating barriers between themselves. "I confess," he continued, "I see no other way to draw people into closer understanding except by persistent efforts, on both sides, to free the lines of communication through the press and radio, through books and magazines, through the exchange of knowledge and culture, through travel and personal acquaintance." What the American and Soviet people need from each other, and are entitled to ask, the State Department official went on, had been summed up by Marshal Stalin in a conversation with Florida's Senator Pepper. "Just judge us objectively," Acheson quoted Stalin as having remarked to the senator, "do not either praise us or scold us. Just know us as we are and base your estimate of us upon fact and not rumor." We have so much to learn about each other, Acheson concluded, that only in an atmosphere of candor, knowledge and understanding could the task be accomplished.[9]

Ernest C. Ropes of the Justice Department, long an advocate of closer ties with and greater understanding of the Soviet Union, stressed the same theme. The potential existed for a greatly expanded trade with the Soviets, Ropes remarked at the American-Russian Institute, but the potential could be realized only if Americans knew more about the Soviet people. We often alluded to them as mysterious, Ropes told his listeners, but they were not. We were simply ignorant of the Soviets and their culture, and it was mandatory that we correct that shortcoming.[10]

It was easy of course for official spokesmen to express such a co-operative attitude toward cultural contacts during the war, but such expressions meant little if not implemented by action. But the State Department proved more than willing to turn rhetoric into reality. Private individuals and organizations bringing projects and proposals to the Department met a favorable reception as the Cultural Relations Division encouraged and assisted in myriad ways the initiatives stemming from rising public interest in broadened cultural relations with the Soviets.

Perhaps the most valuable form of assistance came simply in the readiness with which the State Department transmitted and supported privately proposed projects. Messages in this vein traveled between Washington and Moscow in large numbers, with correspondence concerning individual projects frequently reaching impressive proportions. Mike Todd's proposal to bring Soviet artists to the United States, for example, touched off an extensive round of messages between Todd, Washington and Moscow, and other projects followed a similar pattern. In transmitting Ella Winter's proposal to bring Soviet performers to America, Washington instructed the Embassy to inform VOKS that even though the Department was not directly involved in the invitation, it encouraged and supported that particular project as well as all others aimed at furthering cultural contacts between the two nations.[11] Embassy officials equalled those in Washington in their support and encouragement, at times going to great lengths to implement the proposals streaming from the United States. The American Council of Learned Societies' project for securing and translating Soviet materials received full and enthusiastic Embassy assistance, as did the efforts of Ernest J. Simmons, whom the Council sent to Moscow in 1947.[12] Embassy officers assisted the Yale University Library in its efforts to secure academic materials from Soviet institutions and made extensive efforts to establish the library exchange program as envisioned by the three man committee that had earlier approached the Department.[13]

Embassy officials encouraged efforts in other directions as well. Charge d'Affaires George F. Kennan urged the Department to invite Soviet youth delegates to America to reciprocate Soviet invitations to American youths, and particularly supported the Chicago YMCA proposal to arrange American-Soviet volleyball matches.[14] Ambassador Harriman likewise encouraged sporting events. "I wish to endorse the idea that intercountry sports contests, particularly with the Soviet Union," he wired in late 1945, "are a valuable contribution to better understanding between peoples." The United States should do everything possible to encourage such contests, he continued, "so that by mutual acquaintance and travel in our respective countries, individuals may come to have a broader knowledge of the customs and life in each country."[15]

In matters concerning visas and passports the State Department proved similarly cooperative, frequently instructing the Embassy to do whatever possible to facilitate the granting of passports to Soviets traveling to the United States and the issuance of visas allowing Americans to enter the Soviet Union. During the war years the registration requirement pertaining to individuals acting as agents of their governments was suspended in the case of allied countries, thus obviating the necessity of Soviet registration, and, insofar as possible, State Department officials sought during the war to make it easier for Moscow to comply with the publications provisions of the Foreign Agents Registration Act.[16]

At home too the State Department was helpful and cooperative. Department spokesmen attended the dinners and functions of the privately sponsored cultural agencies, participated in panel discussions arranged by those organizations and frequently referred inquiries to them. And when answering the numerous questions and inquiries received from private citizens — many of which were of a nebulous nature — Department officials invariably provided thoughtful answers that provided factual information, expressed gratitude for the inquirer's concern, and encouraged continued interest in the same.[17] To accommodate the numerous students who wished to study in the USSR, Washington placed a number of Soviet institutions on the list approved for study under the G.I. Bill, and the Department took up details of the matter with Moscow.[18]

An episode stemming from the Soviet invitation to the American scientists to attend the anniversary celebration of the Soviet Academy of Sciences well illustrates the lengths to which Washington was willing to go toward cooperation in cultural matters. To encourage American participation in the celebration the Soviets provided a plane to transport the delegates to Moscow and back, but after a quick inspection the scientists refused to board the craft. Although 20 people were scheduled to make the flight, the plane seated only twelve, contained no accommodations for food services, no sanitary facilities, and, although scheduled to fly the Alaska–Siberia route, contained no insulation against the cold.[19] Since the proposed trip was already public knowledge the refusal of the scientists created a potentially embarassing situation for both Washington and Moscow, which both wanted to avoid. Consequently, following a series of meetings involving Joseph Grew, Elbridge Durbrow, President Truman and a number of others, the President ordered the Army Transport Command to provide the necessary transportation.[20] The resulting trip, largely made possible by the President's decision, turned into one of the more rewarding instances of postwar cultural contact.

The Department made a particularly extensive effort to satisfy the requests of the committee of librarians seeking its assistance following the Washington conference held in June, 1945.[21] Pointing out the problems and the potentialities as determined at that conference, the committee specifically asked Department officials to arrange for an exchange of at least one copy of every piece of printed matter published in each of the two countries, to assign an official to the Embassy in Moscow to facilitate the flow of publications, and to place the entire matter on the Potsdam agenda.[22] If the Department would assist in getting Soviet material to the United States, the librarians explained, the Library of Congress would assume responsibility for its proper distribution, thus assuring the reasonably complete collection called for at the Washington meeting.

The committee's request touched off a series of conferences in July within the State Department. A meeting on the thirteenth approved the idea of coordinating the flow of materials through the Embassy in the manner suggested, with Ambassador Harriman cabling his consent from Moscow, but cancelled the idea of placing the matter on the Potsdam agenda due to difficulties in time and scheduling.[23] A subsequent meeting, citing the scope of the task and the difficulty of procuring certain Soviet publications, likewise rejected the suggestion of exchanging at least one copy of all printed matter.[24] But the difficulties of the task made it all the more necessary that the Department play a role: only through an official government connection, the participants concluded, could a well co-ordinated program of publications exchanges be devised and implemented.[25] To carry that decision into effect the Department assigned J. Wentworth Ruggles to the Embassy as cultural attache in 1946 with the principal duty of coordinating the flow of publications between the recent wartime partners.[26]

While collaboration with private individuals and organizations was an integral part of the effort, the State Department also devised its own programs to advance its aims. Ambassador William H. Standley took an early interest in promoting friendly cultural relations, and Ambassadors Harriman and Smith followed his lead. And State Department officials in Washington, both in and out of the Cultural Relations Division, made a genuine effort to follow policies and devise programs to broaden contacts between the two countries.

As early as mid-1942, Ambassador Standley devised one of the most ambitious projects undertaken by Washington. Designed to exchange information and promote understanding through the use of motion pictures, printed material and radio broadcasts, Standley's program admittedly emphasized giving more than it stressed receiving; offered more information about America than it elicited about the Soviet Union.[27] But it contained elements of reciprocity as well, particularly in the area of newsreels and feature films. And it was with these that the Ambassador was primarily concerned; that comprised his "pet project," as he termed it, to "educate the Russian people about us through the selected use of motion pictures."[28] The other parts of his program were soon largely forgotten, but the film project became a major feature in the official effort to promote cultural contacts.

In selling his program to the Soviets, Standley talked to the heads of VOKS, Tass, the Soviet radio bureaucracy and the Soviet Film Committee, arguing that such an exchange of information would promote better understanding on both sides, and offering printed, recorded and filmed material for that purpose.[29] The Soviets expressed willingness, even eagerness to participate in the project. The head of VOKS was particularly enthusiastic, observing, for example, that the program would solve his problem of constantly having to refuse requests for materials on American life because he had none available.[30] And as for the Soviet public, Standley wrote at the time, "my own observations confirm the interest of the Soviet people in all things American."[31]

Having convinced the Soviets of the virtues of the project, Standley turned to Washington, presenting his arguments both through cables from Moscow and a personal visit to the United States. In his selling campaign the ambassador talked to Department officials and interested persons such as the Chief of Naval Operations, the Army Chief of Staff and Robert Sherwood of the Office of War Information, stressing to all the prime importance of such a program of information exchange.[32] In order to be successful, Standley insisted, it was necessary to develop the program gradually and carefully, to take into account the structure and peculiarities of the Soviet government, and, above all, to conduct it through the Embassy and to consider it an integral part of its work, for only in that way could the project be controlled and regulated in accordance with the degree of Soviet cooperation.[33]

Standley's arguments convinced the State Department. Considering the importance the ambassador attached to the project, the insistence with which he promoted it and its possible positive impact on future relations, Department officials recommended, the program should be implemented, and, in keeping with Standley's suggestion, should be kept under strict Embassy supervision and control in order to properly adjust it to the level of Soviet reciprocity.[34]

Standley quickly put the project into motion, making arrangements while in Washington for the Office of War Information to supply documentaries and newsreeel to the State Department for overseas shipment, for the Ferry Command to provide transportation, and for the viewing of commercial films by Soviet representatives looking toward possible purchase.[35] By mid-September, 1942, a number of newsreels were on their way to Moscow, followed shortly by documentaries and somewhat later by feature films.[36] To direct the program in Moscow, Standley sought the assistance of Douglas Fairbanks, Jr., but failing in that direction chose

Lt. Commander John Young, a public relations specialist with whom he had worked as director of the New York World Fair.[37]

Standley left Washington confident of the value of his film project and optimistic about Soviet cooperation in fulfilling it. A temporary stop at Kuibyshev, where part of the Embassy staff was working during the wartime emergency, heightened his optimism. At the conclusion of a feature film screened for a number of American and Soviet officials, Standley made a short speech explaining his program, then turned to the Soviet officials Solomon Lozovsky and Georgi Zarubin.[38] "Here's why I brought Commander Young with me....," he remarked, "your people like our American films. They could teach you a lot about America and Americans. We could learn much about Russia from your films. I hope to see good American films, both feature and educational pictures, screened every week in the Soviet Union."[39] In reply Lozovsky, according to Standley's account, waved his hands excitedly and stated, "that would be wonderful, Mr. Ambassador. I wish you all success in your plans. In fact, I publicly challenge you to the fullest cooperation in carrying them out."[40]

The film program progressed smoothly during the spring of 1943. In late May, Young and the Soviet film agency Soyuzintorgkino signed a formal agreement governing the exchange of scientific, technical and educational films, under the terms of which American companies agreed to deliver films to the Embassy for transmittal to Soviet authorities, who in turn agreed to supply films to the Embassy, with the latter having the option of rejecting those it considered unsuitable.[41] By June, 1943, the Soviets had screened eighteen feature films and were negotiating for the purchase of eight, were regularly forwarding newsreels to be incorporated into American news films, and were using excerpts from American newsreels in their features; were in fact asking for even more newsreels, particularly for more footage depicting the North African campaign and featuring everyday industrial life in the United States.[42]

By early summer the film program was functioning so smoothly that Standley sent Young back to the United States where, repeating the ambassador's arguments regarding the merits of the program, he persuaded both Washington and the film industry to cooperate even further.[43] Hollywood loaned 40 of its latest and best commercial features, the OWI supplied documentaries, the Army Transport Command provided a plane, and Young, his four motored craft armed with over five thousand pounds of celluloid cargo, left Washington in early July bound for Moscow via Cairo and Teheran.[44]

In September, Standley urged the Department to allot the necessary money and manpower to broaden the scope of his program and to reach an agreement with Moscow permitting regular air transportation of the required material and personnel. Specifically, he suggested, the Department should continue the film and newsreel program, should supply magazines, war posters, novels and scholarly works for distribution by the Embassy, and should consider publishing a serious Russian language magazine devoted to cultural, scientific, historical, social and industrial topics. As an alternative, or possibly a supplement, the ambassador recommended an illustrated popular magazine. But any American cultural or informational program, he concluded in a caution worthy of consideration, should be based squarely on the actualities of American life, for otherwise the result would be "distinctly harmful to the cause of good relations between the two countries." Moreover, the dictates of any particular school of thought concerning the Soviet Union should be avoided, for a narrow approach would "provoke internal controversy in the United States and impair the unity of desire on the part of the American people to go forward with a program of collaboration with the Soviet Union."[45]

Before Washington could respond to Standley's suggestions, Averell Harriman replaced him as ambassador to the Soviet Union. Like Standley, Harriman took a personal interest in cultural relations, particularly in promoting knowledge of the United States among the Soviet people. Shortly after his arrival the new ambassador, following Standley's lead, wired Washington that he wanted to distribute a monthly magazine in Russian text, containing "state papers and speeches, authoritative articles on war, science, agriculture, industry, music, theatre, painting and motion pictures," to be aimed primarily at Soviet leaders and secondarily at the Soviet public through libraries and clubs.[46] Citing transportation problems and other difficulties, Washington suggested instead a deliberately unpretentious illustrated weekly or biweekly publication using cable and radiotelephone material.[47] Ultimately a magazine following the popular format of *Life* and *Look* was agreed upon, after which Harriman, in early 1944, sought Foreign Minister Vyacheslav Molotov's permission to distribute the publication, titled *Amerika*.[48] After several weeks the Soviets consented, receiving in turn the right to circulate an English language publication in the United States.[49]

Amerika first appeared in October, 1944, and, judging from numerous observations and remarks, was an immediate and huge success. The allotted 10,000 copies per issue sold instantly upon appearance, worn copies became black market items, and even single pages passed from person to person.[50] "When Amerika appears it is a great day in Moscow," a *New York Times* reporter wrote in October, 1945, and early the following year a *Time* correspondent elaborated as to why. "Amerika," he wrote, "was hot stuff. Russians liked its eye-filling pictures of Arizona deserts, TVA dams, the white steeples of Connecticut towns, Radio City, the Bluegrass district."[51] It quickly became apparent that the circulation figure of 10,000 was far too limited, prompting the Embassy to press for higher numbers. In June, 1947, after a number of requests by Ambassador Walter Bedell Smith, the Soviets agreed, allowing the circulation to increase to 50,000 copies per issue.[52]

At the end of the war Harriman, asserting that the tremendous interest of the Soviet people in the United States represented a powerful asset in dealing with Moscow, and observing that the Kremlin was for the first time allowing Americans to present information directly to the Soviet people, strongly urged Washington to continue publishing *Amerika* and supporting the other cultural relations efforts being carried out under Embassy direction. "I feel it important," he cabled, "that there be no break in carrying out the present program," for though it was difficult to get high level Soviet approval of such projects, "once approved we find those involved on the operational level are much interested to cooperate in the work."[53]

Harriman's message met a favorable response, for Washington's thinking ran in the same direction. Shortly after receiving the ambassador's cable, William Benton of the Cultural Relations Division, explaining that the State Department wanted to make a public statement concerning American-Soviet cultural relations and therefore needed more precise views and information from the Soviets, instructed George F. Kennan to pose a number of questions to Soviet authorities. When, Benton wanted to know, could Moscow send ballet, theatre and orchestra groups, including the Red Army Chorus, when could it send exhibits of art, architecture and handicrafts, and when could it participate in a series of conferences to arrange cultural interchanges between the two countries?[54]

A month later Secretary of State Byrnes, noting that Molotov had welcomed increased contacts at a function of the San Francisco American-Russian Institute, again instructed the Embassy to sound out the Soviets on the matter.[55] Accordingly, Harriman informed Deputy Foreign Minister Andrei Vyshinsky in mid-November that the United States would welcome a "frank discussion" of the possibilities of cultural exchanges, particularly exchanges involving students and teachers. Did the Soviet government, Harriman inquired, have any "objections in principle" to a student-teacher exchange program during the 1946–1947 academic year, and if not, with whom should he discuss details?[56] The inquiry was no afterthought, for the State Department was already shaping an educational exchange proposal to present to Moscow.

The details of the proposed academic program were worked out during a February, 1946 State Department meeting attended by various government officials, academic figures and representatives of the Institute of International Education.[57] As a first step, the conference concluded, the Institute of International Education should conduct a survey among several major universities to determine their willingness and ability to provide grants to Soviet students and teaching positions for Soviet professors. Should the replies be favorable, the participants decided, the State Department would transmit the offers to Moscow, indicating in the process its role as sponsor and coordinator and asking for reciprocity in the form of exchange scholarships from the Soviets.[58] "All persons who attended," a Department communication noted, recognized that "a program of cultural exchange with the USSR was of the greatest importance in view of the necessity for better understanding between this country and the Soviets."[59]

The universities contacted by the IIE responded enthusiastically. Some offered teaching posts, some offered grants, and some offered both, prompting Lawrence Duggan, head of the Institute, to see something significant in the response. Though the universities contacted did not represent a fair sampling of America's institutions of higher education, since they had over the years expressed a special concern for all aspects of international relations, he wrote, their favorable response did furnish a clue to the thinking of administrators and faculty regarding cultural interchange with the Soviet Union; did give an approximate indication of the readiness of higher educational institutions "to do their bit in attempting to get to know the Soviet Union better through exchanges of students and professors."[60] They wanted such exchanges, and wanted them badly enough to take the necessary steps to secure them. "Were the Institute to circularize all the institutions on the accredited list," Duggan concluded, "I am confident that the display of countrywide interest would be truly astounding."[61]

Having compiled the university offers the IIE sent them to the State Department for transmittal to Moscow, optimistic that the rancor beginning to pervade American-Soviet relations in other areas posed no insuperable obstacle in the realm of academic exchange. The joint effort between private individuals and institutions on the one hand and the State Department on the other seemed to be working well indeed.

VII
A Cooling Relationship, 1946–1947

The optimism that postwar Moscow would respond favorably to proposals for formal exchanges was not unwarranted. Throughout the war years the Soviets expressed both in word and deed a willingness to engage in cultural contacts; in many instances initiated those contacts. Those in the United States who hoped and planned for more intimate postwar connections had justifiable reason for doing so; had sufficient cause to believe that both Moscow and the Soviet people shared their hopes and plans.

But even during the war, Americans in the USSR encountered a number of frustrations and difficulties in implementing cultural projects, particularly if those projects were in any way connected with the Embassy, and the cumulative effect of those frustrations produced pessimism over postwar prospects among Americans resident in the Soviet Union. By the war's end, Embassy officials were urging Washington to proceed cautiously; to plan its programs in accordance with Soviet actions rather than announcements; to refrain from encouraging expectations likely to result in illusion.

That the majority of the Soviet people wanted intimate cultural connections with Americans seems beyond doubt. Embassy officials, journalists and visitors commented on the fact, and Stalin himself seemed to confirm it. The Soviet people, Stalin remarked to War Production Board Chairman Donald Nelson in October, 1943, "liked Americans better than the people of other nations...."[1] A year later he gave similar assurances to Eric Johnston, President of the United States Chamber of Commerce. "The Russian people," the red ruler remarked to Johnston, "have the highest regard for Americans." And since Hitler had brought the American and Soviet people together, he further commented during the same conversation, "we must never allow anything to come between us again. We must work together after the war."[2] Ambassadors Standley and Harriman both alluded to the Soviet interest in and friendliness toward Americans, and lower ranking officials such as Frederic Barghoorn found scholars, artists, librarians and educators surprisingly friendly and cooperative. Within the limits possible, Barghoorn wrote, Soviet professional people "did everything possible to cooperate and expand the area of contact with their foreign counterparts." Friendliest of all were the "ordinary nonintellectual Soviet citizens," who seemed to believe there was an affinity between Russians and Americans based on common characteristics. Once one got to know them, Barghoorn concluded, they were almost "pathetically eager" to reciprocate friendliness.[3] All groups from workers and peasants to intellectuals, a Soviet history professor assured Embassy officials in 1944, wanted to know more about America.[4]

French correspondent Alexander Werth recorded similar sentiments. There were unmistakable signs of liberalization during the war, he wrote, and the Soviet people held deeply cherished feelings that the regime would be softer when the conflict ended. "When the war is over," Werth quoted a Party official as saying at a voks function in 1944, "there will be much coming and going and a lot of contacts with the West ... there will be exchanges of students and foreign travel for Soviet citizens will be made easy."[5]

Top Soviet officials expressed the same attitude. During a speech at the San Francisco American-Russian Institute, Foreign Minister Molotov expressed surprise at the American lack of knowledge of his country and a desire to enter into a closer cultural relationship, particularly in the area of educational exchange, to overcome that lack.[6] Stalin remarked to Harold Stassen on one occasion and to Elliot Roosevelt on another that the Soviet Union welcomed more intimate cultural ties, and lesser officials routinely made such statements in their speeches both in the ussr and in the United States.[7]

What these said in short, Ambassador Andrei Gromyko said in full. Sharing the American-Russian Institute platform from which Ralph B. Turner in 1944 outlined America's cultural relations program vis-à-vis the Soviet Union, Gromyko traced in great detail the various ways in which the collaboration between the two nations expressed itself not only in military, political and economic cooperation, "but in the strengthening of the cultural relations between our peoples and countries" as well. Capsulizing the entire range of cultural contacts, the ambassador dwelt on the reciprocal popularity of Russian and American literature, on the Soviet enthusiasm for popular American music and the American taste for Russian classical composers, on the growing trend toward scientific cooperation and on the festivals and exhibits being staged in each country to honor the accomplishments of the other. There was no doubt, he concluded, that the tendency to "study each other's cultural and scientific achievements would grow stronger and stronger."[8]

In a variety of ways the Soviet expressed in action what they proclaimed in words. Wartime festivals and exhibits featured American art,

architecture and music, Soviet agencies sent and received cultural delegates and Soviet spokesmen made special efforts to honor American
accomplishments. American literature remained as popular as ever, as did
adaptations of American plays, particularly those of Lillian Hellman.[9]
American movies, though rarely made available to the general public,
were in great demand.[10] Soviet musicians performed music provided in the
OWI shipment, making particular hits out of numbers such as "Alexander's
Ragtime Band" and "Tavern in the Town," while orchestral arrangements
popularized the creations of Roy Harris, whom Moscow invited for a
visit in 1944.[11] American scientists received special attention at the Soviet
celebration honoring its Academy of Sciences, and Soviet acknowledg-
ments of Lend-Lease contributions, though somewhat slow in coming,
raised even higher the reputation of American technique.[12]

Festivals and exhibits were particularly common. On July 4, 1943,
VOKS sponsored nationwide concerts featuring American jazz, popular,
and classical compositions. Obviously the Russians, wrote Ambassador
Standley, who accompanied New York Times publisher Arthur Sulz-
burger to the celebration staged in Moscow, "spared no effort to make the
concert a success; it was a beautiful tribute to Americans resident in Moscow."[13] Later in the same year VOKS arranged a series of lectures and discussions honoring the 450th anniversary of the discovery of America,
afterward shipping some of the exhibits marking the occasion to be featured at the Library of Congress.[14] Even Standley's film project grew out
of such a celebration, receiving its impetus from a Soviet request for recent
Hollywood films to feature in a festival dedicated to the American motion
picture industry.[15] Displays of art and architecture shipped from the
United States appeared in various Soviet cities, while on a local level,
schools, clubs and libraries arranged their own tributes to American
culture.[16]

As in the prewar period, the Soviets demonstrated an omnivorous
appetite for American writers. In late 1945 Jack London still led the list
in sales and popularity, followed by Mark Twain and Upton Sinclair.
Theodore Dreiser and Sinclair Lewis remained highly popular; Ernest
Hemingway, John Steinbeck and Erskine Caldwell were becoming increasingly so.[17] The Union of Soviet writers, wrote Frederic Barghoorn,
clamored for modern short stories, while less sophisticated readers demanded detective novels—a demand that Barghoorn met on occasion by
trading thrillers for war posters.[18]

The treatment accorded American visitors during the war and early
postwar years gave further evidence of a cooperative and friendly attitude. Medical and scientific representatives praised their reception in
fulsome terms, as did violinist Yehudi Menuhin, who performed before
enthusiastic audiences at Moscow's invitation in late 1945.[19] A delegation

of religious leaders, including among its numbers the president of the Southern Baptist Convention, gave a similarly favorable report on all aspects of is trip, even managing kind words for the state of religion under the Soviets.[20] Representatives of the business and production world were particularly well received. The ten day visit of War Production Board Chairman Donald Nelson, the Embassy informed Washington, "was marked by extreme cordiality and exceptional cooperation on the part of all Soviet officials with whom he came in contact."[21] Eric Johnston met the same treatment, traveling where he pleased, inspecting what he wished and asking what he desired. "I could talk with anybody and everybody," Johnston wrote, "and I did—from Stalin down through his commissars to Ivan himself, typical citizen, USSR."[22] Public Works Administrator Philip B. Fleming found a surprising degree of interest in and friendliness toward Americans, and Vice-President Wallace publicly expressed his gratitude for the treatment accorded him in a letter prominently published in the Soviet press.[23] The remarks of a congressional delegation typified the comments of all these visitors. "Our movements were unhampered," the members of a House Foreign Affairs subcommittee stated upon returning in late 1946, "and on every hand we were treated with great friendliness."[24]

The traffic was not all in one direction. Soviet organizations sent books, music and exhibits to the United States, largely for distribution through the cultural agencies dedicated to that purpose.[25] Representatives of Soviet culture came as well, among them such well known figures as Sergei Eisenstein, Ilya Ehrenberg and Konstantin Simonov. Vasily Parin, Secretary General of the Soviet Academy of Medical Sciences, spent three months in the country during late 1946 and early 1947, turning over to American colleagues while here, in a generous gesture that was to produce repercussions, an unpublished 250 page manuscript describing the cancer research of Roskin and Klyueva.[26] Many of the visitors appeared at functions across the country, some contributed to articles in American publications, and all stressed the need for cultural friendship. Simonov, for instance, made a particularly stirring appeal at the San Francisco ARI, and professor Parin, upon his departure, strongly encouraged the exchange of cancer research specialists that he suggested was soon to take place between the two nations.[27]

Such public appeals and statements by both Americans and Soviets, along with the overt manifestations of cultural cooperation in both countries, gave cause for optimism over future prospects; provided reason to believe that the difficulties straining political and diplomatic relations in the postwar period would not necessarily lead to cultural estrangement as well.

But even at the height of Soviet cooperation, Americans in Moscow experienced a number of difficulties in implementing cultural projects.

Though the Soviets worked closely with the private American cultural organizations, in instances involving the Embassy the expressed desire to cooperate was not necessarily followed by action, or, even more frustratingly, an explanation of the lack of action. Many of the difficulties and irritations were minor and would perhaps have been forgotten had the Soviets taken time to explain themselves, but their cumulative impact discouraged Embassy officials, causing them to cable their reservations to Washington.

Embassy Charge d'Affaires George F. Kennan stated those reservations most fully. Noting that Molotov's San Francisco call for increased cultural cooperation had drawn a great deal of attention, Kennan advised Washington to be wary; to view the comments in proper perspective and not to interpret them as any basic shift in attitude. Such remarks, he wired in July, 1945, were by no means unusual; were in fact similar to those made to distinguished guests at VOKS functions. But State Department officials should know from sad experience, Kennan asserted, that while it might appear that the Soviets were promoting a new era of cultural friendliness, in reality they were placing insuperable obstacles in the way of even the most rudimentary contacts; were holding exchanges to a minimum carefully censoring correspondence, importing only those foreign plays containing no threatening ideological germs and exporting only approved views of Soviet life. Concerning student exchanges, few foreigners not ideologically acceptable would be permitted to enter the country; only those approved and carefully prepared allowed to go abroad, and then only under a system of controls representing the antithesis of genuine intellectual and cultural exchanges. Especially would it be dangerous to allow the impression to grow in intellectual circles that the two nations were on the verge of a new era of closer cultural relations, for to do so would saddle the government with an obligation it could not fulfill and place an even greater burden on America's relations with the Soviet Union. It behooved the State Department, Kennan concluded, to find a way to make clear exactly what Molotov's remarks entailed without, at the same time, offending the Soviets.[28]

Several months later, Ambassador Smith echoed Kennan's sentiments. Prior to arriving in Moscow, he informed his superiors, he held many of the same optimistic ideas that prevailed in Washington regarding the possibilities of cultural exchanges, but those ideas had undergone drastic changes. Smith was particularly pessimistic about student-teacher exchanges. The availability of tuition scholarships — a prime consideration at the February 27 State Department meeting — was of little importance, he cabled, for if Moscow considered it politically advantageous to engage in academic exchanges it would gladly pay the expenses involved; if not, it would refuse under any conditions. Though living conditions and housing shortages posed a real obstacle, the ambassador concluded, the fundamental problem was the Soviet desire for security. Moscow simply would not allow unsupervised mingling of American and Soviet students, and that fact effectively eliminated any real chance for an exchange program.[29]

The warnings and advice from Moscow, unfortunately for the cause of cultural contacts, proved altogether too prophetic and increasingly so as the war wound down and the two nations began adjusting to their new roles as former partners.

Ambassador Standley's film project began experiencing difficulties as early as mid-1943, providing a foretaste of some of the problems to follow. Having convinced Washington and the film industry of the value of an expanded program, Lt. Commander Young prepared to leave Washington with his load of films at the end of July, anticipating a quick and uneventful flight to Moscow. Early in the month, Standley applied for Young's visa, but contrary to expectations received no quick response.[30] On the twelfth he applied again, asking permission for Young to enter the USSR via Cairo and Teheran rather than through Alaska and Siberia. On the same day he took up the issue with Zarubin, but still no response came.[31] On the 26th an angry Standley talked to Lozovsky, accusing the Soviets of failing to live up to their agreements, but still no answer was forthcoming.[32] On September eighth, Standley instructed Young to proceed as far as Teheran and discharge his cargo there. "We will get the films to Moscow," he wired Young, "if need be can by can."[33] As instructed, Young started for Teheran but at Cairo was detailed to duty elsewhere. The films finally arrived in December, but by that time Averell Harriman had replaced Standley as ambassador. Not until years later did Standley learn the fate of the cargo he valued so much.[34]

Whatever the reason for the delay—and Moscow never bothered to explain it—the films served their purpose well for a number of months. The Soviet Film Committee kept each film for approximately three months, showing it to various organizations and individuals including, the Embassy understood, Stalin himself.[35] The feature films were particuarly favorites, prompting considerable maneuvering to obtain them, including offers of bribes to Soviet employees at the Embassy.[36] The Artists Club, Film Club, Actors Club, Red Army Club, Red Navy Club, and the Bolshoi Theater Club were all on the Film Committee's approved list and therefore able to see the movies, as were the personnel of VOKS, the Soviet Information Bureau, the Soviet Foreign Office and others who, as Kennan cabled, were considered capable of withstanding the bourgeois wiles of Betty Grable and Errol Flynn.[37] That the Film Committee purchased only sixteen films between 1943 and 1945 was not viewed with great concern. More importantly, as Harriman pointed out, the films served a valuable purpose by reaching the opinion making audience in the USSR.[38] Kennan expressed even more satisfaction with the program. "The amount of goodwill gained in this connection," he wired, "cannot be overestimated."[39]

The cooperative attitude began to change in the fall of 1944. According to information received at the Embassy, Harriman informed Washington, the Film Committee was under orders from political authorities to purchase far fewer films than originally intended, and those purchased were to portray American life and society in a bad light.[40] Other reports indicated that dubbing and editing were to be done in such a way as to give the impression that an inferior product was being shown, and indeed, Harriman confirmed, recent examples indicated either gross incompetence or deliberate bungling on the part of Soviet film technicians.[41] A similar shift was detected in the newsreel exchange program. At the time of the Normandy invasion the Film Committee urgently requested newsreels of the landings, but once arrived the newsreels were never used. Furthermore, Harriman cabled, he had information to the effect that no material indicating the scope and magnitude of the Allied operations in the West would be publicly shown.[42]

A month later Harriman confirmed his earlier reports and fears. High Soviet officials, he wired, indicated that only one film, "Song of Russia," was to be purchased despite earlier plans to buy as many as fifteen, explaining only that "conditions did not warrant" further purchases. The invasion newsreels were not being used, and only negligible footage from other news films was being shown.[43] By the end of the year the Soviets were no longer supplying their newsreels for American use, despite continued American shipments to the USSR under the terms of the agreement signed between Young and Zarubin; were in fact avoiding the Embassy in all matters pertaining to the film program.[44]

A changing attitude was expressed in another way as well. In response to an earlier joint Anglo-American request for a theater in which to show exclusively British and American films, the Film Committee had compromised by giving permission to show the films in five leading Moscow artistic and intellectual clubs. In September, stating that the clubs had already arranged their winter schedules and were in no position to undertake the project, it withdrew the permission.[45] Viewing the cancellation as representing something more significant than simply the denial of the use of the clubs, Harriman took the occasion to express his thoughts concerning the changing Soviet attitude. "It is obvious," he cabled, "that the explanation given is flimsy,

> and is being used to cover up the real situation and for some reason which is as yet not clear the political authorities have decided against the project. The official who gave it to me showed considerable embarrassment

and indicated that all these decisions had been made on a higher and more political level and could be dealt with only by the British, myself and Molotov.... [T]hese developments in the motion picture field are parallel to a greater or lesser extent in other fields of Soviet-American relations and reflect a development which is far greater in its implications than the mere dissemination of American motion pictures. I can see it only as a reflection of a trend toward increasing restrictions on foreign influences and contacts within the Soviet Union and at least partially as a return to earlier attitudes and policies. I have no way of knowing whether this trend is temporary or one that may expand and develop in the coming months. It is, however, something that should be born in our mind in our relations with the Soviet Union and will be watched with the utmost care.[46]

One reason for the changing Soviet attitude became apparent in late 1944. While ignoring the Embassy film program, the Soviets and RKO Studios signed a contract that supplied American films to the Soviet Union, provided direct access to American markets for their own motion pictures, and, most importantly, gave Moscow almost total control over the acquisition and distribution of films, allowing it to select both the films imported from and exported to the United States. For its part, RKO received the financial benefits of being allowed to participate in what amounted to a worldwide monopoly over the selling and purchasing of films for the USSR.[47]

The agreement, to go into effect on the first of December, created a great deal of consternation in Washington. Following a series of internal Department meetings and conferences with RKO executives, State Department officials decided to ask the Justice Department to begin antitrust action against RKO to prevent the contract being finalized but the film studio, disenchanted over financial and business arrangements as finally determined in the agreement, dropped out of the scheme of its own accord.[48]

The attempt to bypass the Embassy in favor of a program totally controlled by Moscow did little to forward the cause of cultural friendship. It could be argued of course that the Soviets were only trying to do the same thing that the Americans were doing through their program; that they were simply trying to control the Soviet image as portrayed abroad through films in the same way that the United States controlled the image it projected through the Embassy operation. But the fundamental aim of the Embassy program — as it operated in 1944 — was not to peddle propaganda: while there were elements of propaganda in the program, its principal purpose was to promote goodwill and cooperation between the war partners. Had its primary purpose been propagandistic, it would have largely been ineffective because of the restrictions under which it operated. According to the terms worked out by Standley, each country selected the films and newsreels it presented to the other, from which representatives of each nation chose the films and footage they desired, assuring thereby that each maintained control over both that which it offered and that which it accepted.[49] But under the terms of the new contract only RKO Studios had any influence on the American side as to the quality and content of the motion pictures sent and received by the Soviets, and RKO officials readily admitted that in reality Moscow would make the final decision regarding such matters.[50] The potential of the arrangement as a propaganda tool was infinitely greater than any such possible use of the Embassy program, and the fact that the Soviets negotiated it created a wariness and restraint among American officials that was not present before.

Failing in the effort to obtain films through the RKO connection the Soviets again turned to the Embassy, repeatedly requesting films during the next several months. The requests, made personally on occasion by such highly placed officials as the heads of VOKS and the Soviet Information Bureau, culminated in a rather peremptory note from the head of SovExportFilm in June, 1946, pointedly reminding Embassy officers of the length of time that had passed since the last films had been made available.[51] Still valuing the opportunity to reach the Soviet opinion-making audience, the Embassy was willing to meet the renewed requests, but Hollywood, disturbed over the difficulties encountered in retrieving the movies already sent, was reluctant.[52] At Embassy insistence, however, the films started flowing to the USSR again, though under stricter controls governing usage and return.[53] Upon resumption of the flow the demand for feature films was as great as ever. Even "the Minister" wanted to see the movies, requiring special and complicated arrangements by the Embassy staff to accommodate his desire to see the films at his own convenience and in his own quarters.[54] Sunday night movies at Spaso House, the official residence of the American ambassador in Moscow, became regular and highly popular events, attracting a select crowd of Soviet intellectuals along with guests from the embassies of a number of countries.[55]

Minor irritations continued to plague the program. In February, 1946, for instance, representatives of the Film Committee stopped the screening of "Casablanca" at the Actors Club, confiscating Bogart and Bergman and carrying them off to some unknown place.[56] After repeated inquiries and requests failed to secure the film's return an irate Kennan wrote Assistant Foreign Minister Vladimir Dekanazov concerning the matter. "I am obliged to tell you the Embassy sees in these developments not only an unjustified sequestration of Embassy property," Kennan wrote, "but an act of discourtesy as well...."[57] A month after being seized the film was returned to the Embassy by two messenger boys, unaccompanied by either explanation or apology.[58] It was a minor incident to be sure, but nonetheless one which, along with similar episodes, heightened the pessimism over the possibilities of reciprocal relations.

Similar difficulties befell the publications program so optimistically envisioned by the librarians who gathered at the nation's capital in June, 1945.[59] Responding to the librarians' request the State Department agreed to coordinate the flow of publications between the two countries, assigning J. Wentworth Ruggles to Moscow for that purpose, but the project that seemed so simple and expedient from the American side quickly ran into obstacles from the side of the Soviets.

During the war, Soviet officials worked closely with Embassy personnel in the exchange of library materials, but once the fighting was over the same desire to avoid the Embassy that plagued the film program surfaced in the matter of publications as well. In July, 1945, for example, Lenin Library officials indicated that if they had the proper microfilm equipment they could supply more printed material to American libraries, but when the Library of Congress offered to furnish the needed machines the Soviets declined. Not only was he not interested in receiving such equipment, the assistant director of the library told Kennan in early 1946, he did not wish to even discuss the matter with the Embassy.[60]

Shortly thereafter the library confirmed in writing that which had become evident in practice. The use of diplomatic channels for book exchanges had served a useful purpose during the disruptions of the war years, the assistant director informed the Embassy, but now that the conflict was over the Lenin Library intended to re-establish "normal" channels linking it directly to American institutions. The services of the Embassy were therefore no longer needed.[61]

The system of exchanges desired by Moscow promised to work greatly to its advantage, for by centralizing its operations in the Lenin Library on the one hand while dealing with separate American libraries on the other, the Soviets could exchange a limited number of titles for, in the aggregate, a wide selection of American publications. Embassy officials therefore insisted on the right to centralize and coordinate the flow on the American side as well, resulting in a voluminous and increasingly acrimonious correspondence between the Embassy, the Lenin Library and the Soviet Foreign Office. A rather imperious note from Kennan to the head of the American Section of voks typified the exchange. "I wish to make it clear," Kennan wrote in March, 1946, "that if there is any tendency to inhibit this Embassy or any other organ of the United States government in the exercise of their normal part in the promotion of cultural exchanges or any other form of cultural collaboration, I would not be able to view this as consistent with a desire to improve cultural relations between the two countries."[62]

Confronted with such a situation upon his arrival in early 1946,

Ruggles shortly suggested that he be recalled and that the Embassy abandon its efforts in the area of library exchanges. The Lenin Library, he wired in July, did not intend to exceed the strict controls under which it was operating, and obviously resented the presence of an American official whose function it was to encourage it to do so.[63] Other Embassy officials felt much the same way, considering their repeated overtures and the subsequent Soviet refusals in the field of publications exchanges to be demeaning as well as nonavailing.[64]

Despite Ruggles' suggestion the Embassy effort continued. In October the Lenin Library again confirmed its refusal to deal with the Embassy, prompting Ruggles to try a new approach in early 1947. Reasoning that American institutions should be allowed the same approach to individual Soviet institutions as that permitted the Lenin Library in the United States, the publications officer informed VOKS that the Library of Congress wished to arrange an exchange of atlases and maps on physical geography with the Geography Department of Moscow University.[65]

The Soviets refused the request, pointedly remarking that the Lenin Library was properly responsible for such exchanges, that the request had been forwarded to that institution, and that it would directly contact the Library of Congress concerning the matter. "I think," the Soviet official handling the matter wrote, "that you share my opinion of the impracticability of setting up intermediate stages for affecting exchanges of geographical publications, considering the fact that it will be much simpler and faster to decide these questions directly between the Lenin Library and the Library of Congress."[66] Certainly, Ruggles replied, he shared that opinion, and that was why the Library of Congress wanted to engage in direct exchanges with the Moscow University faculty. "That the Lenin Library should act as an intermediary as you propose," he wrote, "is not in accord with the principle of direct relations upon which we agree ... just as your great institutions enjoy direct relations with numerous American organizations, so would the Library of Congress like to exchange publications directly with large numbers of their Soviet counterparts."[67]

To no avail. The Soviets maintained their insistence on centralizing their end of publications exchanges while carrying on open-ended arrangements on the other. As the irritations stemming from political disagreements mounted and the frustrations attendant to the cultural program accumulated, the strained relations between Embassy officials and the Lenin Library grew accordingly. Though exchanges between the library and individual American institutions never completely ceased, a phone call in late November, 1947, put an end to any hopes for an inclusive coordinated program operating under Embassy auspices. All future business between the Embassy and the library, a Soviet official informed Ruggles, must be handled through the Ministry of Foreign Affairs. To

Ruggles's protestations that the Embassy had always dealt directly with the library, the official, stating that new instructions had been received, replied that he could not discuss the matter further.[68] "It is the opinion of this Embassy," Ruggles cabled concerning the conversation,

> that the developments in the case of the Lenin Library are indicative of what can be expected from Soviet institutions in general. If the Lenin Library has new instructions which forbid direct contact with the Embassy, it must be assumed that the other institutions with which the Embassy has attempted to foster exchange relationships also have such instructions.[69]

The assumption, developments were to prove, was well founded.

Even more frustrating was Moscow's attitude toward proposals involving individuals and groups. In the projects relating to books and movies the Soviets cooperated at least to a degree, but in instances involving individual exchanges they overwhelmingly refused all invitations tendered through the Embassy, regardless whether those invitations were privately sponsored or officially proposed. Some of the overtures they rejected outright, some they talked to death, and others they ignored altogether.

Cornell University's invitation to a Soviet professor and several graduate students to lecture on its campus during the 1946-1947 school year well illustrates the pattern and the problem of dealing with the Soviets on such issues in the early postwar period. Cornell's simple and straightforward proposal, containing provisions for salaries, living accommodations and required dates of arrival, was one that could have been either readily accepted or easily refused with a simple explanation and an expression of appreciation for its being offered.[70] Embassy officials certainly anticipated no problems in receiving some sort of an answer to such a simple communication.

On August 31, Embassy officer Elbridge Durbrow made his first attempt to deliver the proposal to Deputy Minister of Education Samarin, but on that day the Soviet official was unable to either see Durbrow or, despite a specific request, return his call. Advised by Washington on September 4 that Cornell must soon receive some definite answer or cancel its invitation, Durbrow tried again.[71] On the second effort he succeeded in talking to Samarin, who promised to contact the Embassy concerning the matter on the 7th.[72] But on the 7th no call came, so the Embassy tried, unsuccessfully, to contact the deputy minister.[73] On the 13th Samarin again failed to contact the Embassy as promised, making it necessary for Embassy officials to call him. He could not say anything on that day, Samarin said, but if Durbrow would call the following day he would have some information.[74] On the following day Samarin delivered as promised. Four students, he stated, had been selected and passports were being prepared: all would be ready within a few days.[75] Having received no further word by the 18th, however, the Embassy again tried to contact Samarin, to no avail.[76] A call on the 19th produced the same results.[77] On the 20th, Samarin's office promised information on the 21st, but no call came on that day.[78] On the 23rd, Embassy officials informed the Soviet Ministry that Cornell must cancel the project if there were further delays, requesting that the Ministry at least confirm that the professor and the students had been selected and that preparations were being made for departure.[79] Receiving no response, the Embassy called again on the 24th and on the 25th, but was unable to talk to any responsible official in Samarin's office.[80]

Despite the delays, Dean Acheson advised Durbrow on October 4th, Cornell still wanted to go through with the project, even though it would have to be postponed until the following semester.[81] A week later an irritated and disgusted Durbrow suggested cancelling the invitation altogether, pointing out that despite his calls, letters and personal conversations no progress had been made over a two month period.[82] Finally, in February, 1947, Samarin contacted the Embassy concerning the matter. The Minister of Education, he said, favorably regarded the Cornell invitations — but it would be difficult to accept them that year.[83] The professor and the graduate students never made it to Cornell.

Much the same pattern of inquiries and delays marked the attempts of the medical researchers Hauschka, Shimkin and Shear to travel to the USSR to observe the cancer research being conducted by Roskin and Kluyeva.[84] Hauschka applied for a visa in mid-September, 1946; Shimkin and Shear, representing the National Cancer Institute, shortly thereafter.[85] Despite repeated Embassy efforts to facilitate the applications the Soviets took no action. On November 16th, following a number of communications between Washington, the Embassy and the Soviet Foreign Office, the latter was still unable to make a decision on the visa requests, but promised to do so within a few days.[86] Four phone calls from the Embassy to the Foreign Office failed to elicit a response by the 18th, however, nor was any answer forthcoming during the following week.[87] On the 26th, Washington again urged Embassy officials to take up the matter, but their compliance still produced no visas.[88]

Other overtures met a similar fate. The Rockefeller invitation to the Soviet mathematicians Pontrijagin and Vinogradov went unanswered even though it was tendered twice, nor was any answer received to the proposal that a Soviet scientist make the principal speech at the National Colloid Symposium at Stanford University.[89] The same was true in the case of Alexandroff and Kolmogoroff, invited by Princeton to spend a year at its Institute for Advanced Study. Despite the fact that the two scientists had earlier received permission to spend a year in the United States, the director of the Princeton program wrote the State Department, they had neither arrived nor contacted the school.[90] At Princeton's request Washington checked into the matter, discovering that the two had never applied for visas, nor had they done so two months later when the Department checked again.[91] Like the others, the two never made the trip.

Likewise the proposals of Mike Todd and Ella Winter, insofar as State Department records indicate, went unanswered, as did New York City's request that a Soviet ballet company appear at its Golden Jubilee celebration and Sol Hurok's offer to arrange for an American tour by a Soviet ballet.[92] Some of the others eventually received answers, but all were unfavorable.[93]

VIII
Final Efforts, 1947

Nineteen forty-seven produced further American efforts toward cultural relations with the Soviets. As earlier, the efforts represented at least in part a response to encouraging Soviet remarks, but the new overtures met the same fate as the old. Some of Washington's own policies, however, did little to forward the success of the American efforts; indeed, provided Moscow with a patented reason for doing that which in all probability it would have done anyway.

Stalin himself provided the impetus for a new Embassy effort. The Soviet Union, he told Elliot Roosevelt in December, 1946, was willing, even eager, to participate in a cultural exchange program with the United States.[1] Responding to Stalin's published remarks, Ambassador Walter Bedell Smith sent a letter to Foreign Minister Molotov in early February, 1947, submitting again the various proposals made earlier. Although the time limit had expired on the offers and overtures already extended, the ambassador wrote, they would undoubtedly be renewed should Soviet authorities show any inclination to accept them. "I should be very glad," Smith told Molotov, "to have your views with regard to the foregoing proposals and particularly if anything can be done to further the important matter of scientific and cultural exchange."[2]

The aroused hopes were premature. Three months passed before the Soviets mentioned the proposals in Smith's letter, and then only in an incidental and incomplete way. The "proper authorities," Deputy Foreign Minister Andrei Vyshinsky informed Smith, were examining the offers made by Mrs. Dickensen, by the Boston Symphony and by the scientists Hauschka, Shimkin and Shear, but as for Yale geologist Richard Flint's request to work with Soviet colleagues in Siberia and the trans-Baikal region, there were no field investigations planned for that area.[3] The offer of Dr. Young and Russian War Relief to build a penicillin producing laboratory met a similar reception, degenerating into a series of accusations of bad faith on both sides.[4] Neither Dr. Young's project or any of the others were carried out. Nor did an April, 1947 Embassy proposal to exchange some fifty American and Soviet scholars meet a favorable response, although in all fairness to the Soviets there were extraneous considerations that complicated the issue.

The suggestion that American and Soviet scholars reciprocate visits stemmed from the February, 1946, State Department conference and the subsequent survey conducted by the Institute of International Education.[5] Despite the favorable response from American universities the project had long been delayed, largely at the urging of Ambassador Smith, who pointed out that both security concerns and postwar living conditions in the USSR assured a Soviet rejection of any offer of academic exchanges.[6]

Toward the end of 1946 the project was renewed, but this time it involved professors only, and depended on the governments of each country, not the generosity of individual institutions, to pay the costs involved.[7] After lengthy correspondence concerning details, Washington instructed Smith to present the proposal in early January, 1947.[8] But again Smith delayed, pointing to an obvious problem that, he argued, had to be resolved before the Soviets would even consider the project.[9] And indeed, from the Soviet point of view, there was reason for pause.

The problem developed from the Justice Department's application of the Foreign Agents Registration Act. During the war that part of the act calling for registration of individuals had been suspended in the case of the allies, but in early October 1946, Attorney General Tom Clark, acting on orders from President Truman, removed the suspending clause and ordered a number of Soviet citizens to either register as agents of their government or face fines and imprisonment.[10] "Your position as a member of a delegation from a foreign organization and the activities in which you have engaged since your entry into the United States," the Justice Department informed the members of two separate delegations on the same day that the Attorney General announced the removal of the suspending clause, "makes you subject to the regulatory provisions of the act as the agent of a foreign principal." Therefore unless an "immediate response" were forthcoming, the Justice Department would be "forced to conclude that your deliberate refusal to comply with the act constitutes a violation of the criminal provisions thereof."[11]

The Justice Department requirement was aimed largely at a delegation of five Ukranians, in the United States at the invitation of the Music Committee of the National Council of American-Soviet Friendship, and a six member delegation to an All-Slav Congress being held in America. Among the Ukranians were two internationally known singers, a member of the Supreme Soviet, a professor of Jurisprudence at Lwow University and a war correspondent; among the second delegation similar representatives, including the writer Alexander Korneichuk.[12] The Ukranian singers had already appeared in concerts in New York City and were scheduled for further appearances across the country when the announcement came.[13]

The registration requirement touched off a flurry of protests. Aaron Copland, Serge Koussevitsky and the heads of the Eastman School of Music and the Columbia University Music School sent letters of protest to President Truman and Attorney General Clark, and *New York Times* music critic Olin Downes complained even more vociferously, as did the American Civil Liberties Union.[14] The Soviet Embassy naturally opposed the action, condemning it as "compatible neither with the personal dignity of these outstanding people or with the self-respect of the country which they represent," and stating that it would make even "more difficult the establishment of cultural ties between us and the people of the United States."[15] Despite the protests the registration requirement remained in effect.

When the State Department instructed Ambassador Smith to deliver the invitation to the 50 Soviet scholars it was unable to say definitely whether they would be required to register under the act. Its "preliminary view" was that the visitors would not be required to register as long as they restricted themselves to professional interests and refrained from political activities, but it was still discussing the matter with the Justice Department.[16] Because of the uncertainty, Smith recommended that the invitation be further delayed, and Washington agreed.[17]

On February 10th the Attorney General confirmed the opinion. As long as the Soviet scholars limited themselves to scientific, academic and scholarly pursuits, he ruled, they would not have to register, but the ultimate decision rested upon their activities while here, not upon their general status as academics; any scholar who engaged in political activities or participated in public meetings of a political nature would have to register as an agent of the Soviet government.[18]

Having received the desired confirmation, Smith delivered the invitation in early April, taking care in the process to explain the Justice Department ruling regarding registration. The United States, the message read, would welcome the arrival of approximately fifty scholars to confer with their American colleagues, and, in view of the great interest of American scholars in visiting the Soviet Union, would in turn welcome the early receipt of corresponding invitations to American scholars. Ideally, the Soviet visitors should arrive in groups of five or six and spend 45 to 60 days in the country. Each of the two nations should pay its own expenses. For its part, the Department note continued, it was willing to facilitate travel arrangements, to place Soviet scholars in touch with American counterparts and to help in various ways to assure the success of the endeavor.[19] Though the invitation mentioned specific fields of scholarly interest, it suggested, at Smith's insistence, no individual names. To invite particular scholars, the ambassador reasoned, would provide the Soviets with the opportunity to do the same, permitting them to select politically partisan Americans instead of representative scholars. Moreover, Smith argued, the Soviets would not allow any scholar to travel abroad unless politically secure, regardless how distinguished in his specialty.[20] The Department therefore suggested specific areas in which exchanges should occur, but mentioned no names.

Moscow replied two weeks later. The proper authorities, Vyshinsky informed Smith, were carefully studying the proposal, but, he continued in a vein that precluded optimism, "the practices of the organs of the Department of Justice with respect to Soviet citizens arriving in the United States creates difficulties in the development of cultural relations between our countries, irrespective of the opinion of the Attorney General."[21] The recent examples of the two delegations in the United States, the Soviet official concluded, "speak for themselves."[22]

The Soviets never agreed to the exchanges. Only they knew whether the registration requirement played a significant role in the refusal, but had the situation been reversed and had American scholars been subject to registration as agents of the United States government if they made remarks interpreted as political, it is readily apparent that such a requirement would have posed a major obstacle. The Justice Department would have acted more wisely had it waived the requirement in this instance, for there was little reason to anticipate that the Soviet scholars would use their positions as political platforms, and, even had they done so, it would have been easier and more diplomatic to quietly cancel the remaining exchanges rather than force a choice of either registration or prosecution. The country would hardly have folded had a Soviet scientist said a good word about communism, or a bad one about capitalism. But regardless of the Justice Department's attitude, it is highly unlikely that the registration requirement, given the existing pattern of Soviet refusals and the growing tensions between the two countries, was the determining factor in the rejection of the offer. In the final analysis it is difficult to disagree with Ambassador Smith's assessment. The State Department's inability to give Moscow absolute assurances that the visitors would not have to register as foreign agents might be used as a reason for not entering into an exchange agreement, the ambassador wired, but "such a consideration would not be a determining factor but rather a convenient out for that government if it wanted one."[23]

Some individuals and institutions, still convinced that the Soviets could be induced to cooperate if only the correct formula could be found, were unwilling to abandon the effort. Among these was the American Council of Learned Societies, which in the summer of 1947 sent Ernest J. Simmons to Moscow in a last-ditch effort to establish an exchange program. Hoping that the Soviets would respond more favorably to private overtures tendered through academic institutions than to official efforts under Embassy auspices, the entire venture, financed by the Rockefeller Foundation, was deliberately planned with minimum connections to Washington.

That the Council chose Ernest J. Simmons to represent it said a great deal about the program and its sponsors. Simmons was perhaps the ranking American scholar on Russian and Soviet affairs; certainly among the select few. Chairman of Columbia's Department of Slavic Languages, author of numerous articles and books and chairman of the Executive Board of the New York American-Russian Institute, Simmons had spent most of the previous fifteen years trying to improve cultural relations between the two countries.[24] Like the others connected with the New York ARI, Simmons viewed cultural relations not as a means to a political end, but as an end in itself; an end which, pursued in the proper way, could produce understanding and reduce fear. Interest in the culture and the aspirations of another country did not necessarily imply admiration or encourage imitation, Simmons and the like-minded believed, but it did represent a quantum leap over the ignorance that resulted from a lack of such interest and understanding. Simmons' reputation within academic circles, his fluency in the language, his acquaintances and contacts with Soviet intellectuals and his concept of cultural relations made him the perfect choice to present the proposals of the American Council of Learned Societies to the Soviets.

Simmons had reason to be optimistic about the outcome of his efforts. In the process of obtaining a visa he talked to a number of high-level Soviet officials in the United States, all of whom offered encouragement and support. Soviet Ambassador Novikov assured him of Moscow's desire for better cultural relations, observing that although postwar conditions made student exchanges difficult at the time, the situation would, hopefully, soon change.[25] And as Simmons himself remarked upon receiving his visa, "the very fact that I was granted one at all, which is usually not done without an acceptance on the part of the Ministry of Foreign Affairs of the applicant's reason for applying, gave me a slight feeling of hope that some of my requests might be favorably received by Soviet officials."[26]

An added feeling of hope came from the enthusiastic response of the academic institutions contacted by the American Council of Learned Societies as potential participants in the program. As on earlier occasion when the Institute of International Education contacted a number of schools regarding their willingness to engage in exchange activities, the replies were overwhelmingly positive, prompting Simmons to remark on the seriousness of the schools and the extent of their readiness to make commitments toward improving contacts with the Soviets.[27] From the various replies and offers received, Simmons selected five, deliberately choosing those that required no quid pro quo arrangements. In addition, the Library of Congress asked Simmons to present a number of proposals on its behalf, and Simmons readily agreed.[28]

Thus equipped with a visa, armed with a number of proposals and backed by a prestigious academic body, Simmons traveled to Moscow in mid-July, 1947. Given the credentials, the sincerity and the lack of ulterior motives on the part of both Simmons and his sponsors, the Soviets, had they been equally sincere in their statements favoring cultural relations, could hardly have ignored the new overture. But like the earlier attempts, the new proposals met delay, frustration and failure. Even a token degree of interest and a reasonable explanation of Soviet reluctance could have changed the outcome of Simmons' mission and produced a more favorable reaction among those supporting the effort in America, but that token was not forthcoming.

On the morning of the 16th, Simmons met with Smith and Ruggles at the Embassy, at which time they agreed that Simmons, in keeping with the private nature of his visit, should work as independently of American officials as possible. But if Simmons met with little success in talking to representatives of cultural agencies, the ambassador insisted, the Embassy would, in order to assure that his proposals received a fair hearing, arrange for him to meet with high level officials at the Ministry of Foreign Affairs.[29] While at the Embassy, Simmons also examined the records of the earlier attempts to improve cultural contacts, expressing both surprise and satisfaction at the extent of the effort.[30] Prior to that time, Smith wired Washington, Simmons and presumably others in the academic community were largely unaware of the efforts that Embassy officials had already undertaken in the cause, and therefore some means should be devised to keep them informed of such activities.[31] The record as written in the Embassy's files proved, however, a portent of Simmons' success.

On the second day of his visit, Simmons outlined a number of his proposals to voks Vice-President Karaganov. Karaganov received Simmons cordially, expressed interest in his ideas and asked for a written memorandum covering specific items.[32] Accordingly, Simmons prepared the requested document, explaining in detail the various measures that he desired to submit, and sent it to the voks official.[33]

In his memorandum, Simmons first presented the proposals submitted by Chief Librarian of Congress Luther B. Evans. The Library of Congress and the Lenin Library, he suggested, should jointly compile a comprehensive bibliography covering the cultural, historical and economic relations between the two countries during the revolutionary and prerevolutionary periods, and, for preliminary purposes, might link that project to one calling for the exchange of two librarians from each of the institutions as a means of familiarizing them with the problems and procedures of the other. And the Library of Congress, Simmons further noted, was both interested in receiving a number of Soviet publications not on its list and willing to restore to the Soviet Union the Yudin Collection, valued by many because it contained works once used by Lenin.[34]

In the remaining proposals Simmons extended invitations from a number of American universities. Columbia, Yale and the University of Chicago, among others, requested that Soviet scholars spend either a semester or a year lecturing to their students, and several other schools, among them Stanford, Northwestern, Bryn Mawr and the University of Kansas, asked that those scholars, once in the United States, spend at least a short time on their campuses.[35]

To facilitate his mission in Moscow, Simmons continued in his memorandum, he would appreciate Karaganov arranging for him to meet with the Soviet Minister of Education, the head of the Soviet Academy of Sciences, the director of the Lenin Library and the director of the Marx-Engels-Lenin Institute. Also, he specified, he would like to meet with certain scholars in the field of Russian literature and Slavic philology, and with the head of the Foreign Section of the Writers Union.[36]

Five days passed — very valuable days considering Simmons' limited time in Moscow — before he was invited back to Karaganov's office, and then only after considerable telephone prompting on his part.[37] Appropriate authorities were studying the memorandum, Karaganov told Simmons, but it appeared that he would not be able to meet with some of the officials whom he had specified. The Minister of Education was away for several days and thus not available, and it was highly doubtful that the head of the Academy of Sciences would agree to a meeting.[38]

Simmons and Karaganov next discussed the possibility of a broadened exchange of books and periodicals. The VOKS official expressed some interest in receiving such popular American periodicals as *Life*, *Time* and *Newsweek*, and in acquiring new books on literature, art, music and theatre, but when Simmons suggested that the entire process of publications exchanges be centralized, explaining past American difficulties with book exchanges as presently carried out, Karaganov demurred. Reverting to the same position as expressed to Ruggles and Embassy officials earlier, Karaganov argued that the Soviets would receive fewer publications under such an arrangement.[39] Upon Simmons' suggestion for an overall exchange between the Lenin Library and the Library of Congress, however, the VOKS officer displayed an active interest, prompting Simmons to immediately send a telegram to Washington asking for further instructions and information.[40] Despite the glimmer of hope on the last point, Simmons was discouraged by the meeting. "Obviously," he later wrote of his conversation with Karaganov, "something had happened between my first and second interviews to lower the temperature of his interest in my mission, probably a talk with the authorities in the Ministry of Foreign Affairs."[41]

Five more days passed before Simmons received the opportunity to proceed further with his mission, and then only in a minor way. On July 26 he met with the director of the Marx-Engels-Lenin Institute, but only for the purpose of being brought abreast of developments in that body since his last visit some ten years earlier. Upon Simmons' query, the director expressed a mild interest in the return of the Yudin Collection from the Library of Congress, but as for exchanging students and professors, he volunteered, the time was not yet ripe.[42]

Still another five days lapsed before Simmons, hearing nothing further concerning his proposals, was able to contact Karaganov. The Lenin Library was still considering the parts of the memorandum pertaining to it, the VOKS official informed Simmons, and, hopefully, an appointment could soon be arranged, but he had no information concerning the American's other suggestions. On the same day, Simmons discussed his problems with Ambassador Smith. If no results were forthcoming within a few days, the two agreed, the ambassador would try to arrange an interview for Simmons at the Ministry of Foreign Affairs.[43]

Yet another five days slipped away before Simmons was again afforded the opportunity to talk to Karaganov, and then all the answers he received were negative. It would not be possible, the VOKS official stated in confirming that which he had earlier implied, to talk to either the Minister of Education or the head of the Academy of Sciences: the former had just left on vacation, and the latter was too busy.[44] "The implication was clear," Simmons wrote, that "if Mr. Karaganov had informed Mr. Kaftanov and Mr. Vavilov about my proposals for Soviet professors to visit and teach in the United States, and these two gentlemen had found it impossible to see me, the obvious answer to the proposals from that quarter was no."[45]

During the following few days Simmons called on Karaganov's office at VOKS on a number of occasions to discuss the projected visit with the director of the Lenin Library, and, in the meanwhile, provided the Embassy with material for an *aide memoire* for the proposed interview at the Ministry of Foreign Affairs. On each occasion Karaganov tried to be helpful, expressing surprise—either real or conjured—that certain Soviet agencies, particularly the Lenin Library, were making so little effort to avail themselves of the opportunity presented by Simmons' presence.[46] On August 9 Karaganov finally informed Simmons that an interview had been arranged for that day at the Lenin Library. But he would have to talk to the acting director—the director of the Library had just left on vacation.[47]

During his interview with the acting director, Madame Kamenetskaya, the two covered point by point the relevant items as outlined in Simmons' memorandum.[48] Concerning the proposal for a joint bibliographical enterprise, Kamenetskaya stated, her institution was involved in revamping its bibliographical facilities in connection with the current five year plan, and therefore could not undertake any new projects at the time, though perhaps the scheme might be considered again once the revamping was completed. And since the proposal for a joint bibliographical enterprise was linked in Simmons' memorandum to the proposal for exchanging librarians, the latter idea would also have to be dismissed for the time. Upon Simmons' rejoinder that there was no absolute need to link the two, the acting director replied that the matter would have to be taken up with the director, but most probably the full assistance of all Soviet librarians would be needed for the five year plan. As for the local, provincial and bibliographic items that the Library of Congress indicated that it would like to receive from the USSR Kamenetskaya continued, the Lenin Library's means for exchange were limited, but it would do what it could to supply the desired items. As for the return of the Yudin Collection, she indicated, her superiors might be interested in receiving some of the materials, but were by no means anxious for the return of all.[49]

Having received a cable from Washington urging him to explore further the idea of an overall exchange program between the two libraries, Simmons next alluded to that possibility. Unfortunately, Kamenetskaya replied, the Lenin Library simply did not have the books to embark on a bigger or more inclusive exchange program, either on an overall basis or in specific categories. Therefore the exchange relationship would have to remain as it presently stood, though efforts could be made to improve the procedures within the framework already established.[50]

Simmons' long awaited visit with Lenin Library officials thus accomplished little of a positive nature. The outcome was indicated beforehand by the fact that it was necessary to talk to an assistant rather than to the director himself. It was clear, Simmons wrote, that the answers to each of the proposals had been decided upon earlier and that Kamenetskaya had no authority to do anything other than follow those decisions.[51]

On the same day that he talked to Kamenetskaya, Simmons and Ambassador Smith discussed the American proposals with Vice-Minister of Foreign Affairs Jacob Malik. The interview stemmed from a comment that Smith had made a few days earlier, during a discussion with Vyshinsky involving matters of a political nature. At the end of the meeting the Ambassador reminded the vice-minister that Simmons was in Moscow on a mission to promote cultural relations, that he represented the highest academic circles in the United States, and that he was acting in a completely private capacity. Since a cultural relations program between the two nations was of utmost importance, Smith observed, and since it was beneath the dignity of the United States government to further pursue the possibilities, having been rebuffed on so many earlier efforts, he would consider it a personal favor if Vyshinsky would agree to discuss with Simmons the concrete proposals brought from America. Vyshinsky replied that he would do what he could regarding the matter, though since Molotov was away he was very busy at the time.[52]

A few days later — and after more prompting on Smith's part — the Foreign Ministry invited Simmons and Smith to discuss the matter, though it would be necessary, the invitation pointed out, to talk to Vice-Minister Malik rather than to Vyshinsky.[53]

Smith began the interview with a statement of the importance which the United States attached to cordial cultural relations with the Soviet regime, a resumé of efforts made to that point in the interest of achieving those relations, and an explanation of Simmons' position and importance. Malik in turn assured his visitors of his government's interest in maintaining friendly cultural contacts, and then, the preliminaries out of the way, the two sides moved quickly to the issue at hand.[54]

Realizing that this was his last chance, Simmons used his most persuasive pitch. American academic interest in the Soviet Union, he began, had grown tremendously since the outbreak of the war. Prior to that time scarcely a half-dozen American universities were teaching nor more than a hundred students were studying the Russian language, but since the war began some thirty thousand students had enrolled in language courses taught by more than one hundred schools. A similar increase had taken place in the area of Soviet studies. But the students' learning would be incomplete at best, Simmons argued, unless they were allowed to spend some time in the Soviet Union. Moreover, Simmons continued, he was prepared to immediately extend invitations to Soviet professors of literature, history, economics, jurisprudence and international relations if the Soviets were willing to accept. The American representative then concluded his presentation with a recitation of his proposals, the negative responses they had elicited, and an implied plea to prompt the various agencies into action.[55]

To Simmons' statement concerning the growing interest in Soviet studies among American universities, Malik expressed both surprise and gratification, although, he observed, the number of Soviet students studying English was far larger. But as far as student exchanges were concerned, the possibilities seemed slight. Over one hundred students applied for every available spot in Soviet universities, the vice-minister remarked, and, moreover, the war had created terrible housing difficulties. And for the same reason that it could not accept American students, Malik continued, the Soviet Union could not send its professors abroad: the demand for them at home was simply too great. Upon Ambassador Smith's re-joinder that the crowded conditions were understood and appreciated, but that it was common knowledge that the Soviets were accepting foreign students from countries other than the United States, and that to accept as few as four or five Americans as a token of goodwill would do much to improve the state of cultural relations between the two countries, Malik simply remarked that he hoped this could be done in the future.[56]

The Soviet vice-minister then raised the issue of the registration re-quirement, observing that scholars from his country greatly feared what could happen to them under the provisions of the Foreign Agents Regis-tration Act. Smith's explanation that those engaged solely in cultural pur-suits were not required to register, and his reiteration of the lengths to which he had gone to obtain an authoritative ruling on that point left Malik unconvinced, at least outwardly. The act, Malik repeated, created a great "psychological fear" of visiting the United States.[57] Earlier a VOKS official had raised the same point with Simmons, protesting strongly against the treatment of the Ukranian visitors and the delegates to the All-Slav Congress. "We are proud," the official remarked to Simmons, "and though it is possible that the law might apply to visiting historians and economists, we do not see how it could apply to Soviet writers and artists in your country."[58]

At the conclusion of the conference Malik promised, at Simmons' request, to provide definite answers to the various proposals discussed during the interview. But no further word came from either VOKS or the Ministry of Foreign Affairs. On the 14th of August, Simmons left on schedule without further discussions with any Soviet official; a week later the Embassy received an *aide-memoire* acknowledging the interview and noting that the proposals had been sent to the appropriate Soviet author-ities.[59] Simmons was eventually to receive a reply to his overtures, but the form and substance was to be far different than that anticipated when he arrived in Moscow.[60]

Simmons' efforts marked the last major attempt to improve cultural relations during the 1940's, and the failure of those efforts had an impact both in Washington and within academic circles. The lack of response, the delaying tactics and the outright refusals based on flimsy excuses, Ambassador Smith cabled the State Department, followed almost exactly the pattern of Soviet reaction to earlier proposals made by Embassy officials. "The fact that Simmons was acting in the capacity of a repre-sentative of the highest organs of learning in the United States and that until the last stages of his visit he worked quite independently of the Em-bassy," the ambassador continued, "provides discouragingly conclusive evidence that the Soviet government does not intend within the forseeable future to accept any overtures from the U.S. regarding actual and concrete projects in the field of cultural and scholarly exchanges."[61] Moreover, Smith urged, Department officials should make sure that future Embassy efforts toward improved contacts were well publicized within scholarly and educational circles. Had those circles been aware of past efforts, he asserted, they would have better understood the reasons for the lack of success; would have been less critical in their attitude. Particularly in the field of publications exchanges, the ambassador recommended, there should be more communication between private and official bodies: had Simmons known of certain files and documents beforehand, he contended, the scholarly institutions that he represented would have been more tolerant of the Embassy's performance.[62]

Simmons drew his own conclusions from the experience. For the moment, he wrote, there could be no hope of negotiating cultural exchanges with Moscow. Since the Soviets still needed vast quantities of American information and printed material they would maintain a thin façade of relations, but there could be no free exchange of people and ideas. Only if at some future date the Soviets deemed it to their advantage would extensive contacts be possible. "If such a time ever comes," Simmons concluded, "they will make it abundantly clear, and then there will be no great difficulty in negotiating cultural exchanges with the Soviet Union."[63]

Simmons was both right and wrong. Such a time was to come and the Soviets were to make it abundantly clear, but the negotiations were not to be without difficulties. And those difficulties, reflecting both a changed mood and a changed concept of cultural relations in the United States, were to lie at least in part on the American side.

IX
Cold War and Cultural Contacts,
1947–1952

Simmons' failure coincided with the beginning of a rapid deterioration in the cultural relationship already grown tenuous. Within weeks of his departure the Kremlin erected additional barriers to contacts between foreign and Soviet citizens, intensified its campaign against western influences within, and turned its cultural organs into weapons to attack those influences without. Books, magazines, newspapers, films and plays praised the glories of Soviet culture; ridiculed American pretensions in the same direction. Only socialist realism, the message read, could aspire to true art; decadent capitalism, for all its riches, could neither purchase nor produce it. For the moment, Moscow's actions made clear, hostility and isolation better served its purpose than did contacts and cooperation.

The United States, perceiving a threat in Stalin's measures at home and in his ventures abroad, sought protection in its own version of cultural isolationism and internal purges. As American anger and apprehension rose over Soviet activities in eastern Europe and over reported machinations aimed at Iran, Greece and Turkey, the State Department increasingly abandoned the reciprocal and educational aspects of cultural relations in favor of a unilateral "campaign of truth" against communism, congressional legislation prevented Soviet citizens entering the country, and the House Un-American Activities Committee rooted out signs of communist contamination at the slightest sign of infection. Officers of the National Council of American-Soviet Friendship went to jail; the New York American-Russian Institute, even less fortunate, went to its grave. As the successive shocks of the Berlin Blockade, the communist victory in China and the outbreak of war in Korea increased American-Soviet tensions, cultural estrangement kept pace with political alienation; except for the slimmest of threads, cultural contacts between the former war partners ceased to exist. By 1950 the people of the two nations largely looked upon each other as alien and hostile beings, each deeply suspicious of the other. The cultural curtain had become as impenetrable as that of iron.

During the latter half of 1947, Moscow effectively eliminated all nonofficial contacts between its citizens and foreigners. A June decree went far toward that end; a November one completed it. And to assure that it plugged all loopholes, Moscow renewed and extended its wartime travel controls during the following year. Communication became difficult at best on the official level; next to impossible on the cultural.

The State Secrets Act announced in June categorized, in effect, all material not already in print as a secret of the state, particularly material pertaining to technical, military and industrial matters. Statistics and figures routinely published in the United States became classified data, as did information relating to foreign policy and foreign trade.[1]

Since the act contained harsh penalties for anyone violating its provisions, most Soviet citizens, Ambassador Smith informed the State Department, viewed it as a warning to avoid foreigners. Embassy personnel suddenly found old contacts distant and evasive; old sources of information silent.[2] The artists, intellectuals and entertainers who frequented the ambassador's weekly movies at Spaso House stopped coming; even stopped speaking at social functions.[3] On at least one occasion Smith refrained from speaking to an old acquaintance in the lobby of the Bolshoi Theater to avoid embarassing him — or perhaps doing something worse, for some of those who formerly attended Embassy functions were being arrested.[4] Newsmen reported the same pattern, noting that at times they nodded to former friends, but did not speak.[5]

If the June decree was insufficient to eliminate all connections between Soviets and foreigners, a December law requiring that all ordinary contacts be arranged through the Ministry of Foreign Affairs went far toward correcting that deficiency. Foreigners could no longer directly approach Soviet individuals or institutions, nor could Soviet citizens reply should such overtures be made in violation of the law. All oral approaches, the law stipulated, were to be rejected and reported to the proper authorities. A number of institutions whose ordinary functions required foreign contacts were exempted, but cultural, scientific and educational institutions were not among those specified. Only in instances involving fire, police and hospital cases were foreigners permitted direct contact with Soviet citizens without prior approval.[6] Foreign correspondents, required to arrange all contacts through the Foreign Ministry's press department, were limited by the same restrictions.[7]

In the fall of 1948, Moscow added more provisions, placing certain areas of the USSR off limits to foreigners, limiting travel in the vicinity of Moscow to a radius of 50 kilometers, and requiring prior notification of travel beyond those limits.[8] In practice the limitations were even more severe than on paper. Though legally applying only to diplomatic and consular officials, administrative procedures largely extended the limitations to nonofficial foreigners as well, since the necessity of traveling through forbidden zones closed many of the areas theoretically open, and police barricades routinely reduced the 50 kilometer limit around Moscow to fifteen.[9] In 1952 and again in 1953, Moscow redrew the restricted zones, opening some areas formerly closed while simultaneously closing zones previously open, and in 1954 precisely stipulated the objects and areas that foreigners could photograph within the open zones.[10]

At the same time that it isolated the Soviet people from foreigners, Moscow waged a campaign to eradicate the alien cultural influences which had infiltrated the country. A succession of decrees from the Central Committee of the Communist Party affected every facet of cultural life. Attacking the bourgeois sympathies of "homeless cosmopolitans" who "toadied to the West" and providing guidelines for the creation of proper Soviet art, the decrees educated and exhorted those willing to conform; pressured and punished those who proved reluctant. Government and Party publications joined the crusade, providing further guideposts to direct Soviet artists along the path to socialist realism and marking pitfalls along the way.

The Kremlin began cautioning against cultural subservience to the West as early as 1944, warning that the nation must return to "Leninist purity" in all matters and consequently creating rumors of an imminent cultural purge.[11] In August, 1946, the rumors attacked a number of Leningrad writers and literary magazines, pointing to their "servility before contemporary bourgeois culture" and urging them to correct their errors.[12] Resuming the role he had played briefly in the thirties, Stalin's handpicked cultural cleanser Andrei Zhdanov stepped up the attack, charging that the Leningrad writers encouraged defeatism, pessimism and anti-Sovietism; imitated the art and literature of the bourgeois West; had nothing in common with the Soviet people and the Soviet state.[13] Subsequently the Writers Union expelled two of the writers, reorganized one magazine and liquidated another.[14] The message was clear: Soviet writers existed to serve the state, not to explore individual themes dictated by personal preferences and emotions. "Art for art's sake," proclaimed the "Resolution on the Journals *Leningrad* and *Zvezda*," was "alien to literature and harmful to the interests of the Soviet state."[15]

A host of similar decrees and articles followed the dictum aimed at the Leningrad writers. The first issue of *Culture and Life*, inaugurated during the purge by the Agitation Department of the Central Committee, explicitly stated the task of Soviet cultural organs. "All the forms and means of ideological and cultural activities of the Party and the State, whether the press, propaganda and agitation, science, literature and art, the cinema, radio, museums or any cultural and educational establishment," the magazine asserted, "must be placed in the serving of the masses."[16] Other decrees and resolutions warned against "false films" and films without ideological content, urged theatre groups to sharpen their social message, and cautioned architects against slavishly imitating the West.[17] Accusing dance pavilions and summer parks of succumbing to the pernicious influences of ballroom dancing and the evils of American jazz, of being "hotbeds of all kinds of tangos, blues, one-steps and fox-trots," *Evening Moscow* warned them to place more emphasis on traditional dances and Russian folk songs.[18] Even vaudeville actors drew criticism and advice. They must, an official proclaimed, give timely reaction to international events, expose corrupt western culture and, above all, promote the virtues of Soviet reality.[19]

Soviet scientists received similar advice and instruction. Their function, Minister of Higher Education Kaftanov informed them in a 1947 issue of *Culture and Life*, was to serve the Soviet state, not to pursue scientific knowledge for the advancement of mankind in general. Unfortunately, the minister noted, there were still some who liked to cast glances abroad; for whom an article in a foreign journal carried more weight than did the praise of fellow Soviet scientists. To such scientists who could not "erase the psychology of servility and obsequiousness" toward the West, Kaftanov quoted Zhdanov's admonition of the Leningrad writers. "Does this slavish attitude," Zhdanov had asked, "befit us who have built the Soviet regime a hundred times higher than any bourgeois regime?"[20]

For two years music escaped the regimentation imposed in other areas, but in early 1948 Zhdanov turned his attention in that direction, shortly reducing the proud and famous Soviet composers to functionaries of the state; forcing them to admit their musical mistakes and to conform to the Party concept of proper Soviet music. Shostakovich, Miaskovsky, Prokofiev and Khachaturian — the "big four" of Soviet composers, pride of Soviet cultural achievement and winners of numerous Stalin prizes — came in for especially harsh criticism. Their works, stated a Party decree, vividly demonstrated the unsound, antipublic, formalistic trend in music composition; led to antidemocratic tendencies that separated Soviet music from the Soviet people; strongly reeked of modern bourgeois compositions which reflected the "marasmus of bourgeois culture, the full denial of art, its impasse."[21] The solution was obvious. Those composers retaining "vestiges of bourgeois ideology, nourished on influences from the decadent West," must "permeate themselves with the high demands of the musical creation of the Soviet people" in order to write worthwhile compositions.[22] Whatever their private thoughts might have been, the composers, with varying degrees of humility, admitted the error of their ways and promised to do better in the cause of socialist realism.[23]

Sufficiently purged, Moscow used its cultural organs as weapons against the United States, portraying America as an aesthetically barren wasteland dominated by greedy capitalists and populated by culturally deprived people. An article in *Soviet Music*, though specifically aimed at American music, typified the Soviet portrayal of American culture as a whole. Music businessmen interested only in profit and reviewers who could be bought and sold, the article asserted, set standards and tastes; like everything else in America, artistic acclaim was gained by the dollar. *Musical America*, *Musical Quarterly* and similar publications contained "all the vices of reactionary ideological thought ... shameless propaganda for idealess formalism and cosmopolitanism—all those features which are characteristic of contemporary American culture as a whole."[24] And *Soviet Music* found a deeper meaning in all this. "Thus one may comprehend," it concluded, "the rapacious tendencies of militant imperialism ... revolting in its shameless nudity. All attempts to engulf the world with the scanty products of the venal American muse are nothing but frontier ideological expansion of American imperialism, propaganda for reactionary-obscurantist misanthropic ideas."[25]

American literary and scholarly figures drew similar epithets; in Soviet literary magazines, they were corrupt agents of the bourgeois; petty capitalists who sold their soul for the dollar. "Upton Sinclair," as Fueloep-Miller wrote, "was denounced as a man without honor, Dos Passos as a renegade, T.S. Eliot as a hyena with a fountain pen, O'Neill as a degenerate, Thornton Wilder as a fascist and Steinbeck as a Wall Street lackey."[26] Clifford Odets was "beyond the pale of civilized humanity."[27] But the most scathing remarks were saved for Ernest J. Simmons.

It was difficult to tell, *Izvestia* asserted in an October, 1947, review alluding to Gorki's characterization of the almighty dollar as the Yellow Devil, whether the works of this "learned servant of the Yellow Devil" contained more "ignorant jauntiness or deliberate lies."[28] In mid-November the same reviewer returned to the attack in *Literary Gazette*, labeling Simmons' newly published study of Tolstoy "an insult to the great writer," and charging that the author went beyond all bounds of sensationalism to insure the sale of his book.[29] In February, 1948, a second reviewer took up the charges in the same magazine, this time attacking both Simmons and Sir Bernard Pares, who had defended Simmons' works against the earlier Soviet denunciations. The critic emphatically rejected what he interpreted as an offer from Pares to "extend to us his senile hand from across the ocean ... were we willing to accept, falling to our knees," everything American. "Such a handclasp," he wrote, "will never take place. Such 'mutual understanding' will not occur between us."[30]

The attacks constituted the reply to his proposals that Simmons had earlier sought but never received. "Even should there have existed a slight possibility that any of the proposals Dr. Simmons brought to the Soviet authorities would be accepted," Elbridge Durbrow wired from the Moscow Embassy after the first attack on Simmons, "it is now practically inconceivable that a Soviet official would react favorably to a program of cultural cooperation presented by a person now belonging to the Soviet ideological rogue's gallery."[31] A firm lock, Embassy officials concluded from the denunciations, had been placed "on a door long ago slammed shut."[32]

Following a 1946 resolution making the writing of anti-American plays a patriotic duty, Soviet motion pictures and stage productions joined the chorus.[33] Konstantin Simonov's bitter condemnation of the American press in "The Russian Question" led the way. Before being transformed into a motion picture, Simonov's production, playing in over five hundred theaters throughout the Soviet Union, attracted one of the largest audiences ever to see a stage play.[34] Subsequent stage productions ridiculed President Truman, American racism, Hollywood, the Marshall Plan, the House Un-American Activities Committee, the Voice of America and numerous other aspects of American life.[35] On occasion as many as twelve anti-American plays ran simultaneously in Moscow theaters.[36]

Two stage productions, remarkably similar in theme, well illustrate the use to which the Soviets put the theatre. Both eloquently spoke the Soviet attitude toward the exchange of scientists and scientific information, and both served as a warning to Soviet scientists inclined toward cooperating with foreigners, particularly Americans. Neither mentioned by name the American doctors Hauschka, Shimkin and Shear, the Soviet researchers Roskin and Klyueva, or the head of the Soviet Academy of Medical Sciences, Dr. Vasily Parin, who gave to American colleagues an unpublished manuscript detailing the cancer research of Roskin and Klyueva, but the parallels were obvious.[37]

In "Court of Honor," first as a stage play and later as a motion picture, two Soviet scientists, both believers in humanism and international scientific cooperation, permitted an American magazine to first disclose a new medicine they had developed. A Red Army colonel, learning of the foul deed while leafing through a copy of *Amerika*, rushed to the Soviet laboratory to reprimand the two scientists. Upon arrival the colonel found two American visitors, from whom he demanded, in exchange for the Soviet knowledge they were seeking, the secret of a medical process that they had already patented. Sorry, the Americans replied, but they had already sold their patent to a large company, and could not reveal its secret. To the colonel the contrast and the inequity were obvious. Soviet scientists worked for the benefit of the Soviet people, even shared their knowledge with foreigners, but American researchers, in collaboration with grasping capitalists, worked only for themselves. So much for the international responsibilities of science!

Moreover, one of the Americans proved to be a spy, as was to be expected of those masquerading under the guise of cultural cooperation, and that fact necessitated a trial of the Soviet scientists. One recanted and was forgiven by a benevolent Stalin; the other refused and was barred from the laboratory. As the curtain closed the repentant one was exclaiming his determination to publish his findings only in the Soviet Union and to use his knowledge only to heal the Soviet people, not to enrich corrupt Americans interested only in their own welfare.[38]

Konstantin Simonov's "Alien Shadow" followed the same theme. Trubnikov, director of a Soviet bacteriological institute, made a discovery that could greatly advance medical science, but before he could publish his results an old friend from Moscow appeared and, with cunning talk of "universal science" and "humanism," persuaded him to turn over the results of his research to a visiting American delegation. Only then did Trubnikov discover that his friend was an American spy, and only then did his true friends inform him of the real nature of the international struggle and of the role of science in that struggle. The Americans, Trubnikov's real friends told him, wanted his secret because it could be used to destroy as well as to heal. As one colleague told him, "you see how good and evil clashed, two worlds, theirs and ours, over this discovery. You thought that humanism means to stand aside and love everyone. No. Humanism for the scientist means fight. Be a soldier in the struggle for the future of all people, all science, all cultures, against the darkness that is moving down upon us from that half of the world."[39]

Only a very courageous or a very foolhardy scholar would have exchanged information with an American colleague after a message such as that.

Only the Soviet leaders — and perhaps only The Leader — knew precisely why Moscow rejected the American overtures, isolated the Soviet people and attacked American culture. But undoubtedly the massive exposure of Soviet citizens to western culture during the war and early postwar years created an enormous anxiety in the Kremlin and greatly intensified the isolationist urge that had been building in the thirties, and which the war had only temporarily interrupted. For selected Soviet representatives to travel to the West or for foreign engineers and workers to expose the Soviet population to western technology during the prewar period was one matter; for massive numbers of wartime Soviets to observe western lifestyles beyond the control of the Kremlin was quite another. The unfortunate end of the Soviet prisoners of war and of the forced laborers whom the fates took to the West before delivering to Stalin provides only one measure of the lengths to which Moscow was willing to go to protect the nation against foreign contamination, and it is unlikely that any amount of persuasion or concession by the West could have altered that willingness. Moreover, the effort to rebuild the shattered Soviet economy would benefit from the portrayal of a foreign villain necessitating sacrifices; isolation made that villain easier to depict. A people convinced, as were Trubnikov's friends, that they must struggle "against the darkness that is moving down on us from that half of the world," were undoubtedly more pliable than a people still influenced by the praise of all things American.[40] But whatever their reasoning, the Soviets repeatedly refused American initiatives during the immediate postwar years.

Cultural relations exist, of course, within the framework of the total relations between nations, and the growing political tensions of the postwar period obviously exerted a strong influence in the cultural sphere. Only the Soviets knew the exact extent to which their actions reflected domestic as opposed to international concerns and aims, to which they represented reactions to American policies as opposed to their own initiatives, but as late as August 1947—after the Truman Doctrine and the Marshall Plan had delienated the depths of the diplomatic division— American officialdom was still supporting Simmons and the others who had tried to initiate contacts with the Soviet people. Perhaps Soviet acceptance of the proposals would have had little impact in the noncultural realm, but as Ambassador Smith pointed out to Vice-Minister Malik while Simmons was in Moscow, even a token effort on the Soviet side would have indicated a willingness to cooperate in at least one area of their relations.[41] And it was precisely at that point of increasing diplomatic discord that cultural cooperation was most needed, for while neither side had much to lose on the official level by continuing to cooperate on the cultural, they might possibly have found some means to prevent the almost total alienation between the two peoples that was soon to follow. It was easy enough for both governments to encourage contacts during the war, but the real test of their sincerity in promoting the merits of mutual understanding came not during those years of official accord, but during the following years when their relations strained toward the danger point. While it was perhaps only natural that the two powers clashed over fundamental differences in ideology and national interests in the postwar period, and while neither could reasonably have been expected to relinquish the policies that they deemed best served their vital interests and purposes, the leaders on both sides, if they were in fact sincere in their professions of peace, could reasonably have been expected to favor all means of cooperation and accommodation in areas not essential to the preservation of their security and ideology. If Washington was willing to continue supporting individual cultural initiatives even as the diplomatic disputes of the late

forties deepened, the Kremlin, had it possessed an equal desire to find
some common area of cooperation, could have responded in at least some
symbolically positive manner; at the bare minimum could have refrained
from crucifying Simmons as the bearer of the message. Moscow's rejection
of the American initiatives, its withdrawal into isolationism, and its attack
upon the culture of the West, particularly that of the United States, sug-
gests that the Kremlin, during Stalin's declining years, was not interested
in accommodation of any sort. If neither side was altogether blameless in
the burgeoning political, military and economic problems dividing the two
countries, the Soviets, even after considering their wartime devastation
and attendant postwar difficulties, must bear the burden of the blame for
the cultural impasse of the late forties and early fifties.

But not all the blame. While many in Washington and in the American public desired and worked for more intimate cultural intercourse with
the Soviets, the actions and rhetoric of others did little to establish conditions conducive to such collaboration. For like the Soviets, the United
States began staging its own version of cultural isolationism and national
purification during the postwar period, and intensified the effort after
the international argument turned to action in Korea. That both Stalin's
course in the late forties and the outbreak of war in 1950 rendered contacts
virtually impossible does not obviate the fact that certain American
actions and measures of the same period contributed to the same end.

As the political tensions of the Cold War grew, the division within the
State Department over the proper aims of a cultural relations program
grew accordingly.[42] For several months after the war those viewing cultural relations as a long term effort toward reciprocal education and mutual understanding held the upper hand — or at least held their own.[43] But
the diplomatic difficulties of the day proved too much for long range,
nebulous goals. Congressmen and diplomats clamored for a weapon with
which to engage the Soviets in the struggle for men's minds, and that
clamoring produced the United States Information and Educational Act of
1948, commonly known as the Smith-Mundt Act.[44] After 1948, Washington thus had a comprehensive cultural program to deploy, but from the
first it was expected to produce results in one direction. The fundamental
premise of its existence, as Thompson and Laves wrote, was the conviction that "if other people understood us, they would like us, and if they
liked us, they would do what we wanted them to do."[45] Reciprocity in
cultural relations thus gave way to dispensing "information" about America and Americans. Teaching became more important than learning; the
conviction of possessing the truth so strong as to largely obliterate the
urge to understand what it meant to others. And only within the newly
emerging view of international cultural relations is it possible to understand America's subsequent cultural relationship with the Soviet Union.

Those who favored the educational, reciprocal view of cultural relations urged from the beginning that two assistant secretaries be appointed within the State Department to administer the two functions, which they considered separate and distinct, implied in the title of the information and educational exchange act. But instead of two separate agencies, two advisory commissions — the Advisory Commission on Educational Exchange and the Advisory Commission on Informational Activites — were created to provide guidance to the secretary of state.[46] Subsequently the informational aspect, drawing the major share of the budget and the bulk of attention, overshadowed the educational function. Both in Washington and in the field, public relations experts and advertising specialists held the top positions, controlling those trained in education and related fields who carried on cultural activities.[47]

In 1950, the cultural relations program shifted even further in the direction of information and propaganda. In January, shortly after the Soviets exploded their atomic bomb, the National Security Council called for an enlarged and more powerful propaganda program to help strengthen the nation's defenses.[48] Three months later President Truman proposed a worldwide "campaign of truth" to fight the forces of communism.[49]

The phrase, like similar catch-phrases, caught on quickly. By the middle of the year, America's cultural relations effort had become, in essence, the "Campaign of Truth."[50] Under Assistant Secretary of State William Barrett, who originally penned the phrase, the program became well organized and sharply focused. By October, 1951 both its educational and informational aspects had become integrated into the military and economic programs of national defense as outlined by the National Security Council and approved by President Truman.[51] To fit its new function the Advisory Committee on Educational Exchange even restated its aims. Originally emphasizing the promotion of mutual understanding through educational exchange, the new purpose became that of promoting cooperation among "free" nations and strengthening resistance to communism in areas already dominated by the USSR.[52] Overseas libraries became "information centers," carefully designed to impart particular knowledge pertaining to selected subjects to certain citizens.[53] Student exchange programs increasingly focused on foreigners who made decisions and influenced opinion rather than on boda-fide students. As Secretary of State Acheson explained, the primary task was to bring to the United States such people as editors, commentators, labor leaders and others "who will yield results right away."[54] Many in charge of funding and directing America's cultural relations program would have agreed with the report of two officials who wrote that "culture for culture's sake has no place in the United States informational and educational exchange program. The value of international exchange is to win respect for the cultural achievements of our free society, where that respect is necessary to inspire cooperation in world affairs. In such a situation, cultural activities are an indispensable tool of propaganda."[55] Cultural relations had become for Washington, as for Moscow, a cold war weapon.

Washington likewise erected its own barriers to contacts with Soviet citizens, first through administrative procedures, later through legislation.

In early 1949 the National Council of Arts, Sciences and Professions, an organization of prominent Americans chaired by Harvard astronomer Harlow Shapley, invited a number of Soviets to attend, along with hundreds of others from the United States and abroad, a New York conference on world peace.[56] Seven, including composer Dmitri Shostakovich, novelist Alexander A. Fadeev, film director Sergei Geriasimov and biologist Alexander Oparin, head of the Biological Sciences section of the Soviet Academy of Sciences, accepted the offer and applied for visas to enter the United States.[57]

The applications touched off a flurry of conferences in the State Department, a spate of warnings in the newspapers and a round of denunciations in Congress. Walter Winchell, demanding that the Soviets be barred on the grounds that they would spread communist lies, urged his listeners to write their congressmen and demand action.[58] The United Press urged Department officials to not only bar entry, but to "crack down" on the sponsoring organizations as well.[59] Attorney General Tom Clark feared that the Soviet delegates might "act as transmission points for espionage agents in this country."[60] But none stated the case as colorfully and succinctly—if not altogether meaningfully—as California Congressman Donald L. Jackson. Shostakovich and his fellow "prostitutes of Soviet art," the congressman proclaimed to his colleagues, several of whom had already risen to express their indignation over the possibility of Soviet citizens defiling American soil, "have the same right in this land of freedom as rattlesnakes in a Baptist church."[61]

Since by 1949 Washington was strictly applying the immigration laws governing admission to the United States, the Soviet delegates could enter the country only if the Justice Department permitted it under the terms of Proviso Nine of the Immigration and Nationality Act of 1917.[62] Despite his reservations, Attorney General Clark agreed to apply Proviso Nine action if the State Department requested it in the national interest.[63] A State Department staff meeting, following the advice of the Advisory Committee on Educational Exchange, concluded that visas should be granted on the premise that the visit posed no threat to national security, and, more importantly, provided the opportunity to prove that no iron curtain existed in America.[64] Having made that decision, the Department decided that the matter should be exploited to the fullest to contrast the American and Soviet positions regarding such matters. Consequently, on the eve of the conference the Department issued a lengthy statement describing both the American efforts to establish cultural contacts and the Soviet rebuffs to those efforts.[65] By allowing "notable communist propagandists" to attend the peace conference "in accordance with the American view of freedom and intellectual interchange," the statement concluded, the nation had demonstrated the vast difference between the policies of the two governments.[66]

The Soviet delegates arrived in New York City on March 23, immediately ran into a barrage of reporters, and quickly fled to the residence of the Soviet delegation to the United Nations.[67] When the conference opened two days later a crowd of noisy, sign-carrying pickets surrounded the Waldorf-Astoria Hotel, protesting the presence of the Soviets.[68] When the meeting moved to Madison Square Garden to accommodate a gathering of eighteen thousand people, some two thousand "jeering, shouting, and booing" marchers, as the *New York Times* described them, followed.[69] Inside the Garden shoving matches erupted between delegates and photographers, but the massive number of policemen assigned to the conference kept the meeting orderly.[70] To the dismay of many of those present, particularly the sponsors, some of the Soviet delegates, including Shostakovich, could not refrain from either overtly or implicitly attacking the policies and institutions of the United States.[71]

At the conclusion of the conference the Soviet visitors prepared to participate in similar conferences scheduled for Newark, Detroit, St. Louis, Los Angeles and Philadelphia. The planned appearances stirred even more debate and controversy. Yale would not allow Shostakovich to perform a concert on its campus, Philadelphia denied the use of its town hall, and its Blackwood Hotel cancelled a dinner to be given in the composer's honor.[72] On March 29 the State Department, asserting that the purpose for which the Soviets had been allowed to enter the country had been fulfilled, cancelled their visas.[73] Shortly thereafter the delegation left the United States.

Had the World Peace Conference been held a year later, Shostakovich and his companions could not have attended, for beginning in 1950, Congress added new restrictions that prevented all but the most desirable foreigners entering the country. In addition to establishing the Subversive Activities Control Board to control internal dissent and authorizing the State Department to deny passports to American citizens on the basis of political beliefs, the Subversive Activities Control Act of 1950—popularly known as the McCarran Act—denied admission, in effect, to all nonofficial Soviet Bloc citizens, including those fleeing from totalitarian control.[74] Two years later the Immigration and Nationality Act of 1952—also known as the McCarran Act, and consequently the source of a lot of confusion relating to the measures—repeated the 1950 restrictions and added even more.[75] Significantly, the 1952 act removed the nonquota provisions of the 1917 act which allowed relatively easy entry for scholars, and, even more significantly, required that all persons applying for visas to enter the United States be fingerprinted.[76] President Truman condemned the measure both verbally and officially, but Congress over-rode his veto of the bill.

Washington next established regulations restricting the travel of Soviet officials in the United States. In March, 1952, the State Department required that all Soviet diplomats and employees of agencies such as Tass and Amtorg henceforth provide 48 hours notice before traveling more than 25 miles from the centers of Washington and New York.[77] In January, 1955, it extended the regulations to include all Soviet citizens, nonofficial as well as official, and placed large areas of the United States off limits to anyone from the USSR. Four states were completely closed, as were specific regions, counties and cities in 34 more.[78] And, like Moscow, Washington placed detailed restrictions on areas and objects that could be photographed or sketched. Buildings of cultural and architectural interest such as schools and theaters could be photographed, as could urban and rural scenes. With prior permission, foreigners could photograph industrial enterprises engaged in producing civilian products, railroad stations and commercial airports, but bridges, tunnels, laboratories, radio and television stations and any installations or items remotely connected with the military were strictly forbidden. Likewise the taking of pictures while flying, the purchasing of noncommercial maps and the securing of detailed development plans for industrial cities were all prohibited.[79]

In the early fifties the U.S. Post Office added its own restrictions, using the power of a 1940 Justice Department ruling relating to postal distribution of foreign mail to destroy without notice certain Soviet publications, while simultaneously allowing others to receive those same publications. Universities of known standing using the material for study purposes and certain researchers who provided proof of the nature of their work, postal authorities explained, were not denied the publications, which, according to their estimates, comprised only a small part of the propagandistic material coming from Soviet Bloc nations.[80] And in July, 1952, the State Department, arguing that the Soviets had unofficially but effectively reduced the circulation of the magazine so low that it served no useful American purpose, stopped publishing *Amerika*, ordering Moscow at the same time to stop distributing its *Information Bulletin* in the United States.[81]

Both the official measures coming from Washington and the atmosphere of fear and repression spreading across the country disturbed many Americans. Those in the academic community particularly denounced the

McCarran Acts, pointing out that their wording prevented many of their foreign counterparts – including those who were noncommunist and even anticommunist as well as those from Soviet dominated areas – entering the country and thus having a deleterious effect on international scientific cooperation; the same international cooperation, they pointedly observed, that had contributed so much to the winning of World War II and American advancement in general.[82] The October, 1952 issue of the *Bulletin of the Atomic Scientists* devoted itself entirely to the matter, carrying critical comments by America's most eminent scientists. "The very crime against freedom with which the Soviet Union is rightly charged," wrote special editor Edward A. Shils, "is one which we, too, in a less thorough fashion, are committing."[83] Such petty behavior on the part of a powerful country, Albert Einstein added, "is only a peripheral symptom of an ailment which has deeper roots."[84] Eight days after the 1952 act went into effect the President's Commission on Immigration and Nationality issued a 307 page report strongly condemning the measure, charging that it violated America's principles, handicapped its economic development, endangered its foreign policy and weakened its security, but to no avail.[85] The McCarran Acts became law of the land, providing strict controls over "subversive" groups within and guarding the gates against the enemy without. Nor did the American Civil Liberties Union succeed in its efforts against postal discrimination in the distribution of Soviet publications or win many official converts with its argument that the fundamental issue was not the small amount of material involved but Washington's right to decide which Americans could read material not officially approved.[86]

While some Americans waxed indignant over the Soviet theatrical portrayal of their country, others looked first to the nation's own transgressions in the same area. In the spring of 1948 some three hundred Americans signed a letter protesting the release of Twentieth Century Fox's "The Iron Curtain," charging that the film, which they described as designed "to incite anti-Soviet sentiment by falsely presenting the Russian people as enemies of the American people, bent on destroying us by atomic warfare," could only increase "the atmosphere of hysteria leading us down the road to war."[87] Even Ambassador Kirk in Moscow indirectly acknowledged the validity of the point. While he would like to lodge a formal protest over the "grossly insulting" treatment of President Truman in "The Mad Haberdasher," he wired, "such a protest would present the Soviets with an undesirable opportunity for ... protesting in turn against the United States theatrical representations of Stalin." Consequently, he concluded, "I reluctantly recommend that no protest be made."[88]

Americans who either protested too vigorously or indicated a particular interest in maintaining contacts with Soviet institutions and individuals ran at least some risk of official disfavor, or worse. The American Council of Learned Societies was the object of at least a cursory investigation by a special agent who, after noting in his report that the organization received five copies of the *Moscow News* in August, 1944, made the sage observation that the Council was a "club" whose members were "reported to be of high standing and well known in educational circles."[89] And even the private individuals who had earlier received appreciative and encouraging responses when approaching the State Department for information pertaining to cultural relations or volunteering their services in that direction could no longer be sure of the same treatment. Indeed, those who wrote ran the risk of having their names placed in the files of either the Federal Bureau of Investigation, military intelligence, or both.

While Department officials usually replied to the letters of the late forties in a perfunctory manner, in some instances they forwarded the inquiries to investigating agencies. There seems to have been no particular pattern in doing so, for the letters forwarded provided no more reason to suspect the loyalty and motives of the inquirers than did any of the others. In May, 1947, for example, a chemist with a graduate degree, having read about Ambassador Smith's efforts toward cultural relations in the *New York Times*, asked about the possibilities regarding an exchange of chemists. The Department replied politely, expressing appreciation for the writer's concern and explaining that it was doing everything possible to cooperate in the cultural field—and then sent the letter to J. Edgar Hoover.[90] In February of the same year an army private wrote to promote a plan for sending Russian speaking coaches to the USSR to teach football to the Soviets, whereupon the Department sent his letter to both the FBI and military intelligence.[91] And when the following February a Purdue University civil engineering graduate sought instructions as to how he could establish a correspondence with a Soviet counterpart in order to discuss common professional problems, the Department forwarded his letter as well. "While there is no evidence to show that the writer has any subversive intentions," an official wrote in an accompanying note to the FBI, "it is thought that this request might be of interest to you at some future date."[92]

If those who made such seemingly innocent inquiries ran the risk of becoming a file number in an investigative agency, those who continued to actively promote cultural contacts with the Soviets could be sure that their names occupied prominent places in those files.

At the end of World War II the two principal organizations devoted to furthering the cause of American-Soviet cultural relations felt proud and secure. Their goals had become Washington's goals as well; their functions praised and encouraged, their position seemingly secure. Both the American-Russian Institute in New York City and the National Council of American-Soviet Friendship confidently envisioned the possibilities ahead.

But not for long. As early as August, 1945, the Hearst press in New York charged that both were "communist-front" organizations using their in-service courses for public school teachers to inject pro-Stalinist propaganda into the school system. The papers particularly attacked the National Council, charging that the communists were using it to secure a foothold for their literature in schools and colleges throughout the nation.[93] The attacks succeeded. Despite the fact that highly competent professionals conducted the courses, the New York City Board of Education cancelled the program.[94]

The press campaign and the steep decline in the wartime interest in Soviet affairs forced the American-Russian Institute to reduce its staff and to eliminate many of its functions during 1947. In March the Institute employed 30 people; in December only four.[95] In May, 1948, Attorney General Clark dealt a further blow by inadvertently placing the Institute on the list of subversive organizations.[96] New board chairman Ernest C. Ropes corrected the error during a meeting with Clark, but shortly thereafter the Internal Revenue Service crippled the Institute by removing the tax-exempt status it had enjoyed since 1937.[97] In April, 1949, the Attorney General again placed the Institute's name on the subversive list, this time for real, though no specific accusations were made against it.[98] And since its name was on the list, Internal Revenue officials informed ARI officers, its tax-exempt status could not be restored.[99] The difficulties proved too much. In September, 1950, the New York American-Russian Institute, an organization that had served an enormously valuable function in a highly competent and admirable manner, closed its doors; a victim, as an Institute spokesman put it mildly and with great restraint, "of the temper of the times."[100] The National Council of American-Soviet Friendship suffered even greater problems, but refused to bow to the same fate.

On November 12, 1945, two days before President Truman, General Eisenhower and other top government officials sent messages of support and encouragement to the huge Council-sponsored rally at Madison Square Garden, and two days before Under Secretary of State Dean Acheson made his noted speech on the importance of American-Soviet cultural amity at the same rally, the House Un-American Activities Committee ordered the Council to turn over the names of its donors and account for its expenditures over the past twelve months. Was the Council, the Committee wanted to know, a "loyal" organization?[101]

The Council's board of directors unanimously refused the order, pointing out that the organization's 200 directors and sponsors included

some of the nation's most eminent and respected citizens, including
several congressmen, that in the past it had collaborated with the U.S.
Army, the OWI, the State Department and other government agencies, and
that the highest ranking officials in the land had been its speakers, guests
and well-wishers. If the Council were subversive, board chairman Corliss
Lamont wrote, the United States government must face the same
charges.[102]

Lamont's letter touched off a chain of legal battles that embroiled the
Council for over ten years. In April, 1945, the Committee cited Lamont
and Richard Morford, the Council's executive officer and thus the person
responsible for its records, for contempt, and in March, 1948, Morford
was convicted.[103] The United States Supreme Court remanded the decision to the lower courts on a technicality, but in 1950, the case having
worked its way to the top again, upheld the verdict.[104] In August, 1950,
Morford entered a federal prison to begin a three month term.[105]

Morford's trial and imprisonment constituted only a part of the
Council's problems. In November, 1947, the Attorney General placed the
Council on the list of subversive organizations, where it remained despite
appeals.[106] Because the Council was on the subversive list, and because the
Un-American Activities Committee was investigating the activities of Edward Condon, director of the National Bureau of Standards and former
member of the Council's Executive Committee, the Treasury Department
removed the tax-exempt status it had earlier granted the Council's Science
Committee. Having lost its tax-exempt status, the Science Committee
lost a $25,000 Rockefeller grant; having lost the grant it was no longer able
to continue its work of translating and publishing Soviet articles for the
scientific community. Shortly thereafter the committee ceased to function.[107]

The Council's problems were still not over. In April, 1953, the Attorney General asked the Subversive Activities Control Board to require
the Council to register as a "communist-front" organization.[108] The Council again appealed, and, following a year of preliminary battles, won a
full-scale hearing before SACB member David J. Coddaire.[109] Upon the
conclusion of the hearing, which lasted from May to December, 1954, the
Council felt optimistic about the outcome, but early the following year
Coddaire recommended that registration be required, and the full board
agreed.[110] The Council, it ruled, was a "communist-front" organization
and must register as such.[111]

Despite its difficulties the Council continued to function, taking the
offensive against the various federal agencies questioning its loyalty;
sponsoring dinners, rallies, exhibits and programs to promote the cause of
American-Soviet cultural friendship.[112] Admittedly its criticism of America's foreign policy grew more strident as the cold war deepened and its

own problems grew, but criticism is far from subversion. In the final analysis it is difficult to disagree with the assessment of the *Washington Post* regarding the organization's nature and its activities. "Whether wisely or mistakenly," the paper editorialized in praising the Council for challenging the arbitrary right of the Attorney General to place the names of organizations on the subversive list, "it has sought to promote friendly relations between this country and the USSR — certainly not a subversive purpose in itself — and has pursued its objectives by wholly lawful and peaceful means."[113]

By late 1952 the chances for active cultural contacts between the American and Soviet people seemed remote. Moscow's attitude precluded the possibility on the Soviet side, while both the political climate and the legal barriers had much the same effect on the American. Only a change in the official relationship between Washington and Moscow, it was apparent, could permit a return to even the limited level of cultural interaction that existed prior to the late forties. Stalin's death provided at least the possibility of such a change, but official America was far from enthusiastic about pursuing that possibility.

X

Moscow Takes the Initiative, 1953–1955

From early 1953 through the middle of 1955 the United States and the Soviet Union slowly repaired the lines of cultural communication cut during the darkest days of the cold war. American students, journalists, farmers and officials traveled to Moscow, while Soviet skiers, scholars, chess players and agriculturists visited the United States. Though minute in comparison to the pre-World War II period, the numbers involved represented a significant step away from the cultural estrangement of the preceding years.

Moscow took the initiative in restoring the contacts. Whether doing so because it deemed renewed relations advantageous in securing American technology, as some believed, or because it wanted to reduce the level of international tensions, as it claimed, Moscow made the first moves. In some instances the Soviets took their cue from individual American requests and suggestions, but nonetheless were the ones who acted concretely to turn those suggestions into policy.

Washington did not rush to embrace the overtures. By the early fifties, both official America and a large part of the American public had become so afraid of communism, so convinced of its constant and evil designs, that they largely viewed the changing Soviet attitude as a new form of threat, albeit a more subtle one. *Life* succinctly expressed a widely held opinion regarding Moscow's larger motives while assessing its reasons for allowing a small American delegation to enter the USSR in early 1953. Why the Americans were permitted entry, the magazine suggested, was "part of the bigger question of why the glowering Russia of yesterday had suddenly become mild." One likelihood was that the Soviets "were trying to divide the West and lull it into repose." Another possibility was that the Kremlin wanted a rest on the cultural front while its leaders fought over Stalin's powers. But the least likely answer, *Life* assured its readers, was "that Russia was ready for an enduring peace."[1]

While the American and Soviet people grew increasingly alienated during the late forties and early fifties, Moscow, like Washington, carried on an ever-widening program of cultural contacts with the rest of the world. Concentrating on the Soviet bloc in the late forties, the effort extended itself beyond the satellites at the turn of the decade. As early as 1951, Soviet exhibits advertised their nation's achievements at international festivals and Soviet technicians took their talents to the underdeveloped. And Moscow received as well as gave, welcoming students, tourists and delegations from around the globe.[2]

Stalin's death hastened the process, producing changes both in the internal workings of Soviet cultural life and in its relations with countries abroad. Like a springtime Minnesota river that slowly comes to life with great moaning and groaning, as Harrison Salisbury wrote, life in the Soviet Union began slowly moving again.[3] And as Soviet artists shook off the freeze of Zhdanovism, they became more outspoken in their criticism of the regime. Ilya Ehrenburg told Soviet politicians that artistic works could not be turned out like factory products, and Aram Khachaturian told them that creative problems could not be solved by bureaucratic means. "I think," wrote the acclaimed composer, decrying recent works "written without creative elan with a cautious glance over the shoulder," that the time has come "to give up the wrong practice of interfering with the creative process."[4] The Stalinist approach to art, added an anonymous writer in *Pravda*, obliterated individualism, bred triteness and imitation, and deprived the artist of the joy of exploration.[5] Taking his cue from the *Pravda* article, Shostakovich joined the protestors, criticizing particularly the bureaucratic vices of the Union of Soviet Composers.[6] Others voiced similar criticisms, heralding a new degree of artistic freedom and earning for the period the label adopted from Ehrenburg's new novel, *The Thaw*. The thaw was neither long lasting nor complete, as bureaucratic controls over cultural expression went on and off during the remainder of the decade, but for the moment at least, Soviet artists enjoyed a freedom not known for many years.[7]

Some went beyond criticizing bureaucratic controls to suggesting the resumption of contacts with the United States. In March, 1954, Shostakovich suggested that exchanges between the two nations might help them become better friends, and when the *New York Times* tentatively agreed in an editorial blaming the Soviets for the lack of such exchanges, the composer replied that his country intended to broaden its relations with all countries, including the United States.[8] Shortly thereafter Khachaturian wrote in a similar vein. "It is our duty," he stated in an appeal for American-Soviet friendship, "to do everything in our power to promote normal cultural relations between our countries, to strengthen respect, confidence and friendship among our peoples."[9] Both countries, Ilya Ehrenburg added in a *New Republic* article, had much to learn from each other.[10]

At the same time the Soviets indicated by their actions that they were ready, at least on a small scale, for renewed contacts. Americans applying for visas to enter the USSR suddenly and surprisingly found their applications approved and their visits arranged. For whatever reason, whether as a part of a "cultural offensive" against the West, as suggested by some writers, or as an indication of a genuine desire to lessen the terrible tensions of the time, Moscow took a new course shortly after Stalin's death.[11]

Even at the height of the cold war, cultural communication between the two countries never ceased entirely. Scientific and scholarly institutions continued to exchange publications and materials, though deliveries on both sides were erratic and unpredictable, and each continued supplying meteorological information, drawn from scores of weather stations scattered across both nations, to the other.[12]

On rare occasions there were personal contacts as well. In 1950 the Soviets invited the United States womens' chess cochampions to participate in a Moscow match and one, to the dismay and dire predictions of family and friends, accepted. Despite the warnings the Soviet hosts treated the chess champion cordially, and, as far as she was concerned, conducted the tournament altogether fairly.[13] In 1952, Moscow invited 200 American business leaders, including such well known corporate figures as Charles Wilson, Marshall Field and James T. Warburg, to an international economic conference in the Soviet capital, and twelve accepted despite State Department denunciations of the conference as a ploy to pierce the West's front against communism. Flamboyant, self-styled "spokesman for capitalism" Oliver Vickery, wrangling his own invitation, spoke and acted freely in Moscow — one might add even add adolescently and overbearingly — conducting himself generally in a manner that probably would not have been permitted a Soviet "spokesman for communism" in the United States in 1952.[14] But such personal glimpses remained rarities and the Soviet Union such a forbidden bastion that Newsweek deemed it newsworthy to give space to the impressions of a few American merchantmen who had been allowed to go ashore at Odessa to sneak a peak behind the dreaded iron curtain.[15]

The first indication of a significantly changing Soviet attitude in deed as well as word came in April, 1953, when ten small town newspapermen and radio station owners traveling in Europe unexpectedly received visas to enter the Soviet Union. During their subsequent visit the Americans found both friendly treatment and a surprisingly large degree of freedom to ask questions, take photographs and move about in an unrestricted manner. And, like many others who followed, they found much about life in the USSR that failed to fit their preconceptions.[16]

The April visit touched off a round of similar trips. In September, three college newspaper editors, representing Oberlin and the Universities of Colorado and Minnesota, visited Moscow, Leningrad and Kiev. Like those who went earlier, the three, in their words, "traveled freely, or seemed to," filmed largely as they pleased, even inside the Kremlin, and debated with Soviet students, encountering lively discussions but no hostility.[17] Later in the year seven more students spent three weeks traveling between Moscow and Baku, managing along the way to engage their Soviet counterparts in sandlot basketball games.[18] Marshall MacDuffie, who had served with a United Nations mission in the Ukraine seven years earlier, secured permission to make a long trip through the country, as did a number of United States senators and representatives.[19] In May, 1954, James Wicks, the spokesman for the original group that entered the USSR in April of the previous year, accompanied a second delegation numbering sixteen members, finding treatment and conditions similar to the first visit.[20] Nationally known political commentator, presidential speech writer and presidential aide Emmet John Hughes made the trip earlier in 1954, to be followed by feature writer Clifton Daniel at the end of the year.[21]

While some Americans went to the Soviet Union, others approached Washington with suggestions for cultural projects and organized enterprises. Movie producer Darryl Zanuck suggested one of the earliest projects, seeking the assistance of presidential press secretary Sherman Adams to secure permission to film a day in the lives of the new Soviet leaders. Specifically, Zanuck told Adams, he wanted the State Department to arrange an agreement guaranteeing that he could film in the Kremlin, in various Moscow churches, and in other specified places. While such a proposal might have seemed fantastic only a few months earlier, Zanuck wrote, the trend seemed to be in that direction.[22]

Shortly after Zanuck made his proposal, national radio commentator Leon Pearson asked his listeners to express their opinions on the subject of American-Soviet exchanges. Noting the trips made by various groups and individuals, Pearson suggested that it might be well for the United States to make a more formal effort to expand its contacts with the Soviets. Would the American people, he asked, welcome a ballet or choir group, or would it just create another international incident, complete with pickets and rotten eggs?[23] Having made the inquiry of his listeners, Pearson turned to Sherman Adams, asking Washington's attitude toward such contacts, particularly toward exchanging an American symphony orchestra for the Bolshoi Ballet.[24]

Neither Adams nor the State Department was enthusiastic or optimistic about the proposals. Responding that Zanuck's desire to film the Soviet leaders was "striking and a little shocking," Adams sent the producer's letter to Department officials who, though replying that with proper safeguards such a project "probably" would not conflict with

Department policy, refused to promote it or enter into correspondence concerning it. Rather, they suggested, Zanuck should contact the Soviet Embassy concerning the matter.[25]

Adams replied in the same vein to Pearson's inquiry. Personally, he wrote, he favored the idea of exchanging an American orchestra for a Soviet ballet, but past efforts in that direction promised little hope. "The conclusion that one must draw from the Soviet opposition to an exchange of students, professors, exhibitions and exponents of the fine arts," he stated, "is that the Soviet government fears exposure of its people to ideas and ambassadors from democratic nations."[26]

Acting Secretary of State Walter Bedell Smith, to whom Adams passed Pearson's note, said much the same thing, explaining his unsuccessful attempts toward such contacts while ambassador to the USSR and adding, in seeming disregard of the facts of Stalin's death, increasing Soviet contacts with western Europe and at least some indications of a desire to renew contacts with the United States, that there was no evidence to indicate that the Kremlin had changed its mind. Moreover, Smith continued, there now existed a new hurdle in the form of congressional legislation requiring that all persons applying to enter the United States from communist countries be personally approved by the Attorney General, and, like all foreign visitors, be fingerprinted. Those requirements, the former ambassador wrote, posed an almost insuperable obstacle to exchanges under existing conditions.[27]

Pearson answered Adams and Smith publicly. The efforts alluded to, he told his audience, had been made several years ago. There was now a new set of rulers in Moscow and a new administration in Washington. It was time, he insisted over national radio, to try again.[28]

Despite Washington's restrictions, a handful of Soviet citizens visited the country in 1954, though a 1953 attempt ended in refusals and verbal reprisals. In May, 1953, a Soviet chess team of fifteen players, responding to an American invitation to attend a New York City match, applied for visas to enter the country.[29] After a delay of several weeks Washington approved the visit, and the Soviet team flew to Paris en route to the United States.[30] Immediately before its departure from Paris, however, the State Department announced that the team would be confined strictly to New York City and could not, as it planned, stay at the Glen Cove residence of the Soviet United Nations delegation, located some thirty miles from downtown and twelve miles beyond the city limits.[31] After strong Soviet protests the Department relented somewhat, agreeing that the team could visit Glen Cove, but could neither stay there nor travel back and forth between the residence and the site of the match.[32] Despite the slight concession, Moscow, accusing the United States of "intolerable measures violating all rules of hospitality and courtesy," cancelled its participation.[33]

The following year a few Soviet representatives did enter the country. In February, a Soviet skier arrived to present a trophy to the American Ski Association on the occasion of its fiftieth anniversary, in May two Soviet scholars participated in Columbia University's bicentennial celebration, in September a Soviet surgeon attended a medical conference in the nation's capital, and in June the Soviet chess team finally arrived to play its long delayed match.[34] Since they were still limited to a 25 mile radius and allowed to only visit Glen Cove, the team members traveled under largely the same restrictions as those rejected the previous year, but whatever their feelings about the limitations the Soviets conducted themselves in an ingratiating manner. "Quite self-consciously spreading goodwill," *Newsweek* wrote, "they dutifully enthused over the Empire State Building, big town traffic jams, and hot dogs."[35] But when a group of Soviet student editors applied for visas to visit the country in response to an invitation from a reputable American student organization, the State Department denied them admission, and, *Pravda* complained, denied permission as well to a delegation of Soviet radio engineers invited to attend a technical conference in the United States.[36] If indeed a new attitude existed in Moscow, Washington demonstrated little enthusiasm in responding to it.

The year 1955 was pivotal in American-Soviet cultural relations. As the year progressed the contacts begun during the previous months became more widespread and increasingly accepted as individuals and delegations entered the country of the other in growing numbers. And in July, the Geneva Conference gave the entire matter of cultural contacts an importance previously lacking by placing it alongside the questions of disarmament and German unification as one of the three major items on the Geneva agenda.

A growing number of Americans traveled to the Soviet Union during the first half of the year. A three man ice skating team performed in Moscow, William Randolph Hearst, Jr., and a number of associates talked with top officials in the Soviet capital, two Columbia professors returned the Soviet visit of the previous year by attending Moscow University's bicentennial celebration, a Harvard law professor spent a month conferring with Soviet colleagues, and Supreme Court Justice William O. Douglas, traveling most of the way in the company of Robert F. Kennedy, made an extensive tour of the Soviet hinterlands.[37] A delegation of American journalists visited with Soviet editors, the chairman of the Chicago city planning commission studied Soviet practices in an area of his expertise, and an army physician, whose visit was instrumental in arranging a formal exchange of medical films, toured dozens of Soviet hospitals and clinics.[38]

As the individual contacts continued, efforts toward more formal and organized exchanges proceeded apace. In the fall of 1954 the Soviet student editors who had earlier been denied entry to the United States again applied for visas, but by early 1955 the State Department still had not approved the applications. In late February William Randolph Hearst, Jr., speaking before the National Press Club in Washington, criticized the delay, pointing out that the issue had been broached to him everywhere he traveled in the Soviet Union and that Soviet propagandists were making capital out of Washington's hesitations.[39] Two weeks later, on March 10, Attorney General Herbert Brownell approved the visas.[40]

The announcement that the student editors were coming to America touched off a spate of activity and excitement throughout the nation. At the State Department's request the Institute of International Education began contacting a number of universities to arrange an itinerary, but quickly found its initiative unnecessary as offers poured in from across the nation. Over ninety colleges and universities scattered across 34 states extended invitations and offers to the editors, as did business organizations, labor representatives and congressmen.[41] Minnesota Senator Edward J. Thye, for example, personally appealed to President Eisenhower to point the editors in his direction, pointing out the benefits to both the United States and the USSR of a visit to his state.[42]

Newspapers across the country provided editorial support for the visit. If the Soviets were willing to expose their student editors to a close-up view of the country, the New York Times wrote, it would be wise to accept the challenge.[43] The Philadelphia Enquirer reasoned that the Republic would not totter because the Soviets spent a few days here, and the Louisville Times argued that since the country was its best spokesman, we had to let people come and look if we wanted to convince them of its virtues. The Hearst papers editorialized that, despite some reservations about the matter, much good could come from the visit.[44]

The itinerary as finally decided was based on visits to a dozen campuses, carefully selected to represent a cross-section of higher education from large state universities to smaller private schools, located from New York to California. The National Student Association arranged dinners and forums, while students and teachers rearranged schedules and classes to take advantage of the editors' presence, going to great lengths to provide activities and seminars for that purpose.[45] And all of this for eleven student editors whom the nation wanted to welcome and impress.

The editors never arrived. On April 17, two days before their scheduled arrival, Moscow announced that the State Department had informed the editors that they must submit to the fingerprinting requirement of the Immigration and Nationality Act of 1952, and that they refused to do so on the grounds that fingerprinting was a process fit only for criminals. The editors had not anticipated such a demand, the Soviets claimed, because the skiers and the chess team visiting the United States in 1954 had not been required to comply with that provision.[46] Moscow, the State Department admitted, was correct; through "administrative inadvertence" the earlier visitors had been allowed into the country without being finger-printed. Nevertheless, it insisted, the editors must fulfill the requirement.[47] The Soviets continued to refuse, and the project was cancelled.

The cancellation had repercussions in a number of areas. A veterans' organization composed of participants in the World War II Elbe link-up had invited a number of its Soviet counterparts to a reunion in Washington and nine had indicated they would attend, but six days after the editors' cancellation the Soviet veterans cabled that they would celebrate the occasion in Moscow instead, and invited the American veterans to their country. Subsequently, nine of those invited traveled to the Soviet capital for that purpose.[48] And for awhile it appeared that the fingerprinting clause would doom a project that had attracted even more attention and favorable publicity than had the proposed visit of the editors.

On January 25, 1955, First Secretary of the Communist Party, Nikita Khrushchev, speaking before the Party Central Committee, recommended that his country increase eight fold the amount of land that it devoted to growing corn, doubling thereby its capacity to produce pork for Soviet consumption. The United States had greatly expanded its grain production through the cultivation of corn, he pointed out in an example to prove his point, and the Soviet Union must do the same.[49]

An Iowa newspaper editor read Khrushchev's speech and took advantage of the opportunity that it offered. The Soviets, Lauren Soth wrote in the February 10 edition of the *Des Moines Register*, should send a delegation to his state to see how Iowans did it; to learn how they raised corn, cattle, hogs, sheep, chickens and other agricultural products. "Everything we Iowans know about corn, other feed grains, forage crops, meat animals and the dairy and poultry industries," he editorialized, "will be available to the Russians for the asking. We promise to hide none of our 'secrets.' We will let the Russians see how we do it ... we ask nothing in return. We figure that more knowledge about the means to a good life in Russia can only benefit the world and us."[50]

Three weeks later the Soviets accepted the offer. Soviet farmers, replied *Selskoye Khozyaistvo*, the daily publication of the Soviet Ministry of Agriculture, were ready to go to Iowa to study its farming methods, provided of course that Washington would allow them to enter the country.[51]

The response surprised and pleased the Iowa newspaper. Frankly, it responded on the second of March, it was surprised at the reaction to its little "essay into diplomacy," but was completely sincere in its offer and hoped that the State Department would not turn down the Russians out of hand. Even if the Soviet government thought it had something to gain from the venture, the United States and the free world could also gain from it. "This great and powerful country," it concluded, "would appear to be overcome by silly fears if it refused admittance to a few agricultural technicians ... let the Russians come to Iowa, and let an Iowa delegation go to Russia. Nothing but good could come of it for both countries."[52]

Soth's suggestion and the Soviet acceptance received favorable comments from the President down to the Iowa farmers whose methods and products stood to be scrutinized and perhaps copied. The day after the Soviet reply was printed and Soth responded in the above editorial, President Eisenhower, "his eyes lighting up," according to a *New York Times* report, approved the idea. A dozen different difficulties stood in the way, including that of admitting communists barred by law, Eisenhower remarked while recollecting the avid curiosity about American methods among the workers on the collective farms he visited after World War II, but if those difficulties could be overcome, "good and only good" would result from such a visit.[53] *Business Week* agreed with the President's assessment. We couldn't lose, the magazine suggested, for "how are they going to keep them down on the collective after they've seen Des Moines?"[54]

Iowans, a cursory *Newsweek* survey indicated, seemed to favor the idea overwhelmingly. "There are too many hungry people in the world," one native responded, "to think about keeping our farming methods to ourselves." Another replied that, with old Abe Lincoln, he believed that the best way to destroy an enemy was to make a friend of him.[55] And when *Nation* phoned Soth to learn the direct reaction to his proposal, it found that the newspaper had been inundated with communications from individuals and organizations promising assistance and cooperation.[56]

Other publications also approved Soth's suggestion, some urging Washington not only to act upon that particular opportunity but to take a more positive attitude toward contacts in other areas as well. *Nation* lauded the *Des Moines Register* for restoring America's reputation for being good natured and hospitable, and the Hearst papers not only endorsed the idea but wondered why it was necessary for private citizens to take the initiative; why the administration did not attempt to lift the iron curtain by proposing more such visits.[57] The *Wall Street Journal* likewise urged greater exchanges, arguing that while reciprocal visits of farmers, editors, doctors and tourists would not by themselves ease our relations with the Soviets, there would be one less avenue to understanding if Washington insisted on keeping lowered the iron curtain that Moscow was willing to lift a little.[58] The *New York Times* was even more critical of Washington's attitude. We had become so preoccupied with reproaching the Soviets for their iron curtain, the paper asserted, that we had provided them with the material to throw the reproach back upon us; had created an unfavorable impression by obstructing the exchange of persons and ideas at the very time that Moscow was permitting more Americans to visit the Soviet Union. The contrast, it concluded, did the country no credit.[59] But *Commonweal* was the most critical. Our official obduracy regarding fingerprinting and the resulting cancellation of the student editors' visit, it asserted, provided the Soviets with a striking propaganda victory and an "unparalleled opening" in the unrelenting cold war. The world now wonders, it surmised, "whether it was not the United States itself that was opposed to the Soviet editors coming here in the first place." And apparently *Commonweal*, as were many others, was beginning to have its own doubts as to Washington's desire for cultural contacts. "Does this nation, which finds the idea of an Iron Curtain so reprehensible," it asked while observing that the State Department apparently intended to apply the fingerprinting requirement to the agriculturists as well as to the student editors, "really want to increase personal contacts between the peoples of the Soviet Union and the United States or not?"[60]

On March 10, the day that Washington announced that it would allow the Soviet student editors to enter the country, Moscow formally approached the State Department concerning the agricultural visit. Noting the favorable attention given the matter, including that by President Eisenhower, the Soviets expressed their official approval. They were prepared to both send and receive specialists in the area, their note read, and would "like to know how the United States Government regards the question of exchanging agricultural delegations between the United States of America and the USSR."[61]

The State Department initially replied in a noncommittal manner, publicly indicating that it would give the matter serious consideration in view of the President's expressed interest and approval, but noting also that the ultimate decision would be based on such questions as how many would want to come and what they would want to see.[62]

It had still not made the decision, however, when Moscow, one week later, cancelled the planned trip of the student editors because of the fingerprinting requirement, dooming, it appeared, the farm exchange as well. The Soviets bitterly denounced the American stand, leveling the same accusations against the United States that Washington had been hurling at Moscow. On the first of May, *Pravda* featured a five panel cartoon titled "Behind the Iron Curtain," depicting the United States erecting barriers against foreign contacts. At the entrance to the country stood a sign reading "Entrance Prohibited to Cultural and Agricultural Delegations, War Veterans and Editors of Student Newspapers of the

Socialist Camp." One panel depicted an armed guard watching over a stalk of corn growing behind a barbed wire fence; another portrayed Lincoln being fingerprinted. An accompanying verse proclaimed that "henceforth entry is prohibited to sports champions, workers, peasants." Columbus himself would be denied entrance today, and even the peaceful corn state of Iowa is forbidden, *Pravda* ended on a jesting note; "it makes the cows laugh."[63]

Despite the Soviet indignation and the fears of some Americans that Washington's regulations would doom the project, Washington and Moscow continued discussing the matter and eventually worked out a compromise which, by designating the Soviet delegates as "official" visitors, allowed the State Department to surmount the fingerprinting clause by issuing them official visas free from the requirement.[64] Moscow in turn authorized visas for twelve American farm specialists, and both sides proceeded to make final arrangements for the exchange.[65]

From mid-July to mid-August, 1955, the respective delegations gathered information across vast areas of each other's farmlands. The Soviet visitors inspected farms, machine factories and processing plants from Iowa to California and back to Washington, while the Americans visited similar facilities and agricultural installations from the Ukraine to Siberia.[66] Press coverage on both sides was full and preponderantly favorable. The *New York Times Index* listed three pages of articles devoted to the exchange, and reporters from numerous publications followed the Soviet delegation by the busloads.[67] Soviet papers and magazines likewise reported extensively on the visits, including in their coverage both the Soviet delegation's praise of American achievements and the American delegations's criticisms regarding Soviet practices and shortcomings.[68] Minor incidents flawed the visits on occasion, but caused no real problems. A few demonstrators picketed the Soviets, and the Americans saw some anti-American signs in a Soviet park, but the incidents had no repercussions.[69]

Beyond their specific function of gathering information, both delegations acted as ambassadors of goodwill. The Soviets ingratiated themselves by playing touch football, eating hot dogs, making an awkward attempt at golf, and, to the astonishment of all, attending Sunday services at the First Presbyterian Church at Jefferson, Iowa.[70] One observer noted that the leader of the Soviet delegation, First Deputy Minister of Agriculture Vladimir Matskevich, acted more like an American political candidate than a Soviet delegate, and Matskevich certainly made no enemies in Texas by comparing its size to that of his country and telling the natives that they deserved to brag even more than they did.[71] But perhaps more important than the deliberate attempts at amiability were the small acts that revealed essential similarities long obscured by ideological differences. Watching one Soviet delegate test the quality of oats by rubbing the grains in his palms seemed, for example, a revelation to one Iowan. "Look at him," the farmer remarked to a neighbor, "that's the same way I do it."[72]

No one assumed of course that exchanging two dozen farmers was going to bridge the ideological gap separating the two nations, but it was a start, and a promising one. *Collier's* eloquently expressed both the possibilities and the limitations in such exchanges. While the Big Four powers were facing each other across the table at Geneva, the magazine wrote, "a lower level of exchange was taking place in the pigsties and haymows of Iowa and other Midwestern states." While it would be foolish to assume that the "folksy rapprochement" would greatly affect the hard issues at the summit, they could have a profound and cumulative meaning; could

> be a continuing reminder that beneath the high question of national policies lie simple human goals; that on either side of the iron curtain millions of plain folks share an overwhelming bond of humaness — of hope for a more tranquil world. The friendly talk among ordinary people about ordinary problems, the American delegate playing with Russian children, the Russian expert rubbing oat kernels in his palm on an Iowa farm — all these can help create the climate of goodwill for the patient negotiations to come. They are the images of the aspirations of all men, the small coin that passes from hand to hand, from nation to nation. They are the pennies of peace, and pennies can add up sometimes.[73]

Such expressions might of course be considered well meaning and well sounding, but of little practical value. Only the diplomats and statesmen who deal with the hard issues of international existence, some might argue, have the full grasp of reality that allows for the ordering of human affairs. But from the evidence presented at Geneva concerning cultural matters, the diplomats might well have learned something from the farmers.

XI
Geneva Conference:
Contest over Contacts

On the same day that the Soviet farm delegation landed in Des Moines, Soviet and western statesmen gathered at Geneva to apply their expertise to the problems plaguing the relationship between the communist and capitalist worlds. The weighty issues of disarmament and German reunification occupied center stage, but just slightly to the rear the question of East-West contacts held a position all its own, confirming and increasing thereby the role of cultural diplomacy in world affairs.

If those who went to Geneva had titles and expertise, they lacked wisdom sufficient to surmount their differences. In the area of cultural contacts each side had a purpose to serve, and neither was willing to compromise to the point of consent. The United States, England and France wanted access to Soviet minds; the Soviets to increased western trade and technology. In the push to fulfill those fundamental demands the more commonly considered forms of cultural intercourse — exchanges of artists, athletes, scholars and scientists — were largely treated as intruders.

Neither side got what it wanted, for as the conference progressed the high minded rhetoric of international accord degenerated into acrimonious arguments and insistent efforts to cast the other in the role of villain. The delegates left Geneva still leveling accusations, but beneath the dealings of the diplomats the process of exchange and interaction steadily grew.

The four nations represented at the summit conference formally began their discussions on July 18. For five days President Eisenhower, British Prime Minister Anthony Eden, French Premier Henri Faure and Soviet Premier Nikolai Bulganin delienated the issues, stated their positions, and, by the simple fact of their presence, indicated the importance they attached to the proceedings.

Each of the leaders alluded to the importance of increased contacts between East and West, but none stated the case as fully and emphatically

146

as did Eisenhower. The American people, the president stated in his opening address, wanted to be friends with the Soviet people. No natural
differences, territorial conflicts or commercial rivalries separated them,
and traditionally they had lived in peace. But that was not enough: friendly understanding could grow and develop only when the artificial barriers
that restricted free movement and communication were removed. All cur-
tains, whether or guns or laws or regulations, must come down.[1]

Four days later the President returned to the same theme, this time
with specific suggestions to offer. Since restrictions of all kinds caused
mutual distrust, he remarked, concrete steps should be taken to

(1) lower the barriers which now impede the interchange of information and ideas between peoples.

(2) lower the barriers which now impede the opportunities to travel
anywhere in the world for peaceful, friendly purposes, so that all will
have a chance to know each other face-to-face.

(3) create conditions which will encourage nations to increase the exchange of peaceful goods throughout the world.[2]

Bulganin responded to Eisenhower on the same day, expressing gratitude for his comment that the American people wanted to be friendly
with the Soviet people, and assuring the delegates of his complete agreement with the President's suggestions. "We have been and still are in
favor," the Soviet leader stated, "of broad development in the field of
culture and science and the removal of obstacles to intercourse among
nations." But, he added in a qualifying note, his government believed that
in trying to improve relations among themselves, the countries at the conference should "pay due attention to the problem of strengthening economic ties between them, and in particular to the development of trade."
The artificial controls placed on the sale of goods to the Soviet Union,
he concluded, posed a serious threat to the relaxation of international
tensions.[3]

Bulganin's pointed comments concerning trade, aimed essentially at
the American-inspired regulations that controlled the shipment of western
goods to the Soviet bloc nations, introduced an argument that became
increasingly important in the matter of cultural contacts. For without
normal trade relations, the Soviets insisted, there could be no normal contacts in other areas of cultural concern.

From the early postwar period the United States had embargoed war
material to Soviet bloc nations and had controlled the export of other
items through a complicated system of licenses.[4] The Mutual Defense
Assistance Control Act of 1951, popularly known as the Battle Act, regu-
larized and extended the system and its procedures, and, significantly,
established a degree of control over the trade relations between the USSR
and America's allies as well. Any nation that either sold war material to

the Soviet bloc powers or refused to cooperate with the United States in controlling the sale of goods not specifically listed as war supplies automatically forfeited American military, economic and financial assistance, and even those countries that received no assistance were invited to join in the common effort to control exports to communist states.[5] It was to these controls that Bulganin objected.

On the 23rd the leaders of the four nations, having stated their positions on the various issues in general terms, issued a directive to guide their foreign ministers in detailed consideration of the broad questions that they had defined. The third item in the directive dealt with East-West contacts. The foreign ministers of the four powers, it read,

> should by means of experts study measures   which could (a) bring about a progressive elimination of barriers which interfere with free communication and peaceful trade between people and (b) bring about such freer contacts and exchanges as are to the mutual advantage of the countries and the peoples concerned.[6]

The directive having been issued, the heads of state adjourned the conference and returned to their respective capitals, leaving it to their subordinates to interpret and implement its phrases.

The foreign ministers returned to Geneva on October 27, and four days later turned to the topic of East-West contacts. After each of the ministers reiterated his nation's goals and solutions, French Foreign Minister Antoine Pinay submitted a draft proposal on behalf of the western nations, and Molotov did the same for the Soviet Union. Both the introductory speeches and the draft proposals indicated a wide divergence in emphasis and ambition between the Soviets and their western counterparts. Once past the generalities marking the first stages of the conference, the foreign ministers quickly discovered, they faced obstacles that belied the easy optimism of July.

Molotov immediately returned to the matter of trade and economic ties. The refusal of some countries to sell certain goods to the USSR and the violation of normally accepted practices in the field of credit, he contended, created mistrust which imperiled economic and other relations. Therefore in accordance with the directive, the committee of experts established to deal with the question of contacts should, "in the first instance ... examine the question of liquidating existing measures which hinder the development of contacts and ties between states," because removing those restrictions would lead to the "strengthening of confidence between countries and the development of contacts and ties between peoples." It is our view, Molotov concluded in words that left no doubt as to the way in which the Soviets looked at the issue, "that the development of contacts between East and West will be successful only if it is based on the development of economic relations between states, which is unthinkable without the normal development of trade between them."[7]

Only after dealing at length with the matter of trade did Molotov mention other forms of contacts, and then he first emphasized interaction in such areas as industry, agriculture, medicine and technology. Though calling for increased exchanges in tourism, literature and other fields of cultural endeavor, Moscow's primary concern, his address indicated, lay in the areas of practical benefit.[8]

The proposal that Molotov submitted to the committee of experts for formal consideration followed closely the pattern of his speech. The first two provisions called for removing restrictions on international trade and for application of the most favored nation principle, the third suggested measures "to broaden international scientific and technical relations," and the fourth alluded to cooperation with the United States. The fifth, divided into several parts, called for increased exchanges of delegations, but again placed primary emphasis on "reciprocal visits of representatives of industry, agriculture, and trade," in order to exchange experiences and to learn of the achievements of other countries in these fields. At the end of his proposal, Molotov called for exchanging publications between "institutions of scientific research, libraries, scientific and cultural associations, cultural organizations and individuals," for increased tourism and for "sports relations."[9] But while expressing a willingness to engage in contacts of the latter sort, the real concern lay in the areas of trade and technology.

The western statesmen were not interested in trade, but in removing the obstacles that barred the Soviet population from access to "ideas and information" coming from the West. For as Secretary of State John Foster Dulles implied at Geneva and stated repeatedly during the months afterward, Soviet exposure to western ideas could hasten the changes already underway in the Soviet Union and could ultimately result in a regime more acceptable to western nations. Like the Soviets, the western powers were willing to discuss other types of cultural contacts, but the core of their proposals lay in the realm of exchanging what they consistently referred to as "ideas and information."

Both Dulles' opening remarks and the formal proposals submitted by the French delegation on behalf of the western states indicated the thrust of western aims. Dulles began by dividing the subject of East-West contacts into separate areas, and then noting the problems and preferred solutions in each. In the area of exchanging information and ideas, he remarked, the western nations immediately encountered basic obstacles, among them the "systematic jamming of radio broadcasts" to the Soviet Union, and an "all-embracing Soviet censorship of press and radio." Moreover, the artificial ruble exchange rate posed a barrier to increased travel and the exchange of persons. "We hope," Dulles emphasized, "that steps will be initiated at this conference looking forward to the removal of these obstacles."[10]

Turning to the matter of trade, Dulles injected a new term into the argument. The third aspect of the directive, he insisted, related to *peaceful* trade, and not to that aspect of *strategic* trade pertaining to goods which the United States embargoed to the Soviet Union.[11] Strategic trade was a matter of security concern, and thus outside the purview of the directive. Nor could the Soviets blame the embargo for the low level of trade, he continued, for the goods placed in that category represented only a minute portion of the products in which trade could be maintained. The restrictions, Dulles asserted, were a consequence rather than a cause of tensions; Soviet practices and policies, not American regulations, were responsible for the low level of trade.[12]

On the same day that Dulles outlined his country's position, the French delegation submitted a list of western proposals for formal consideration. The seventeen points on the list, following closely the line of reasoning espoused by Dulles, are worthy of enumeration because they formed the framework of the American concept of cultural relations with the Soviets both at Geneva and during the months following.

The first of the seventeen proposals called for measures to facilitate a freer exchange of information and to remove the obstacles hampering "the free flow of full factual information and varied comment" between the western and Soviet nations. The second called for each of the four powers to open "information centers" in the capital cities of the others, with all citizens guaranteed the right to use those centers without disturbance or hindrance by their governments. Points three through five proposed the reciprocal distribution of official publications, books, newspapers and periodicals, to be "available for general and unimpeded sale in the Soviet Union on one hand and the western countries on the other." Numbers six through ten condemned the jamming of radio broadcasts, and proposed greater access by western journalists in the Soviet Union to "normal sources of information." Proposals eleven through fifteen dealt with more personal and individual forms of cultural interchange in professional, cultural, scientific and technical fields, for meetings of outstanding scientists at "reputable" international congresses, for sporting exchanges, exchanges of students, and increased tourism. The latter, the proposal noted, would require more liberal Soviet procedures regarding travel restrictions and administrative practices, and, above all, more reasonable rates of currency exchange. The last two points in the western list called for greater freedom of movement for diplomatic personnel in the USSR and for agreement in principle regarding direct air transport between Soviet and western cities.[13]

After enumerating the specific points, the western draft proposal dealt briefly and in broad terms with the matter of trade. "So far as trade is concerned," it stated, "the western powers sincerely desire to see an improvement in commercial relations between the countries of Eastern Europe and themselves," and were prepared to "consider sympathetically any proposals which seem likely to lead to a mutually beneficial development of trade."[14]

By the time the opening speeches were finished and the draft proposals introduced it was obvious that the two sides were far apart in what they considered vital to the creation of closer contacts. Both mentioned areas in which they might possibly have found some basis for agreement, but both emphasized areas in which they had most to gain and in which, at the same time, they were most unlikely to compromise.

From November 2 through the 10th, the committee of experts established to study the details of the various proposals held eighteen meetings to discuss the measures submitted by both sides.[15] Following the meetings both sides submitted draft proposals of official declarations to be adopted by the conference concerning the matter of East-West contacts.[16] Both drafts reflected the original arguments and proposals, for no common ground was found during the committee sessions.

Exactly what transpired during the meetings is impossible to determine, for official records are unavailable and public references few and obscure.[17] But an analysis of the speeches made by the foreign ministers when they resumed their discussions following the meetings provides a reasonably good idea of the tenor and direction of those proceedings.

The debate held in the committee of experts followed the line of reasoning laid down by the foreign ministers of the respective sides. The western powers refused to compromise on the matter of trade and the Soviets rejected the western requests for exchanges in the area of information and ideas. Both professed an interest in the type of cultural contacts that seemingly afforded the opportunity for agreement, but by the time the foreign ministers took up the matter again both sides seemed more interested in casting blame than in reaching agreement. The western powers, and particularly Secretary of State Dulles, seemed especially bent on proving that the Soviets rejected all the suggestions that they offered.

British Foreign Secretary Harold MacMillan succinctly stated the general tenor of the committee meetings. The longer the sessions continued, he observed, the clearer it became "not merely that the western and Soviet representatives had a radically different point of view of what subjects it would be important to discuss, but a radically different approach to those subjects on which it might have been thought that we would have something in common. Even when we were talking about the same thing, we did not mean quite the same by it."[18]

But MacMillan had no doubt as to where the blame lay. The only barriers that the Soviets thought important to discuss, he charged, were those that levied controls on strategic goods, which, he claimed, "were clearly excluded from the directive." Out of eighteen meetings the Soviet experts could be persuaded to devote only two to matters such as censorship and controls on individuals, and except for the matter of trade, "where they harped continually on the strategic controls," he concluded, "they sought to avoid a discussion on subjects which they said were not common ground between us."[19]

Dulles was even more determined to prove that the Soviets were to blame for the lack of agreement. On November 14 he accused the Soviets in general terms of blocking progress with their selfish attitude, and on the following day specified Soviet objections to particular items in the seventeen point western proposal. The Soviets, he enumerated, rejected item one, calling for a freer exchange of ideas and information, as they did number two, requesting the establishment of information centers on a reciprocal basis. Likewise, he asserted, they rejected points three and four, asking for reciprocal distribution and sales of books and periodicals, "seemed" to reject item five, stipulating the exchange of government publications, and refused to accept number six, which dealt with the exchange of commercial films at normal prices and on normal terms. They also, he continued, rejected items eight through ten, dealing with jamming, censorship and journalistic freedom. Concerning tourism, he stated in relation to point eleven, they allowed the possibility but denied the actuality by refusing to change the ruble exchange rate. Dulles said nothing about objections to points twelve through fifteen, suggesting that perhaps the Soviets raised none, but concluded by accusing them of rejecting points sixteen and seventeen, calling for freedom of movement by members of diplomatic missions and for direct air transport between western and Soviet cities.[20] The Soviet delegation, he summarized, "seems to have picked out of our proposals only four or five suggestions which it deems to its interest, and to have rejected all the others, without any spirit of give and take, and with a complete omission of anything of substance in the realm of the exchange of ideas."[21] The Soviet stand on the matter of East-West contacts therefore did not adequately fulfill the requirements of the directive in that it contained "nothing, or practically nothing, designed to permit an exchange of ideas and information."[22]

The Soviets did not deny Dulles' charges. Rather they defended their position and in turn leveled their own accusations against the western stand on the matter of trade and economic ties.

The western proposals to which the Soviets objected, Molotov stated on the 15th, were unacceptable because they interfered with the internal affairs of the Soviet state. In the matter of censorship and jamming, he remarked, for example, "we in the Soviet Union do not disguise the fact that we never in the past nor will in the future picture to ourselves such a 'freedom in the exchange of ideas' which would consist of 'free war propaganda' or the misanthropic propaganda of atomic attack...." As for allowing foreign radio stations to broadcast directly to his country, "nobody who is a supporter of democratic principles can ... argue that radio stations, even though they are disguised by false slogans such as 'Free Europe' really serves the interests of peoples." Rather they served that "black reaction which fans the flames of enmity between peoples, is harmful to peace, and makes for war." As for the opening of "information centers," he continued while noting in an aside that it had been explained that such centers were aimed precisely at his country, "we cannot allow this to pass unchallenged." Similar centers created in Czechoslovakia, Poland, Hungary and Rumania had been closed because they had been used for espionage, and, he emphasized, "in so far as the Soviet Union is concerned, it has no intention of opening such centers." Regarding tourism, the Soviet spokesman continued, western demands went far beyond the simple question of tourist travel to an unacceptable insistence that his country amend its administrative regulations and change its rate of ruble exchange. And as for direct air transport, he concluded, his government by no means opposed the principle; indeed, it had an air agreement with France and was beginning negotiations with England on the matter. But it was impossible, as the western delegation demanded, to work out an immediate agreement at Geneva, for "without the necessary specialists one cannot discuss such a proposal at a meeting."[23]

On the other hand the Soviets had their own complaints. It was no accident, Molotov insisted, that the directive gave prime importance to removing barriers to trade by mentioning that topic first, and his delegation had formulated its proposals accordingly. But the western representatives had shifted the question to last place and then obscured its meaning by talking about "strategic trade," which, he correctly observed, the directive did not even mention. His country was not proposing anything specific in the area of trade, but only asking that the western nations recognize the necessity of eliminating barriers to its normal development, for, the foreign minister reiterated, unless those barriers were eliminated there could be no normal development of contacts between East and West.[24]

Despite the charges and counter-charges, there were still areas in which the two sides could have agreed had they been determined to do so. The accusations they made against each other largely concerned areas in which each had a specific interest and hopes for advantage. On the other hand there was little discussion of the type of contacts normally considered cultural in nature. In their formal proposals both sides called for exchanges of artists, athletes, scholars and scientists, but there is little evidence that those areas received serious consideration at the working level. Nor is there any indication that the Soviets objected to such artistic and scholarly exchanges. In enumerating the Soviet objections to specific items in the seventeen point western proposal, Dulles, significantly, skipped points twelve through fifteen, which were precisely those that dealt with increased interaction among persons engaged in professional, cultural, scholarly, scientific and athletic pursuits.[25] That Dulles skipped those points, given the lengths to which he went to prove Soviet recalcitrance in other areas, seems to indicate that the Soviet delegation raised no fundamental objections regarding those particular proposals.

The Soviets, moreover, went to some lengths to profess a specific interest in precisely the type exchanges that Dulles omitted in his enumeration of their objections. The original Soviet draft called for such exchanges, and Molotov repeatedly claimed during the course of the conference that his country favored them. On the 15th, moreover, the Soviet Foreign Minister stated that his country was willing to accept as a basis for agreement a draft proposal submitted by French Premier Faure at the Heads of Government Conference in July. The majority of Faure's points, which dealt almost exclusively with the type of artistic and scholarly exchanges mentioned in the above paragraph, were acceptable, Molotov stated, and his country was ready to use them as a basis for agreement provided the western nations were willing to do the same.[26]

But, the Soviet spokesman contended, the western delegations might not now be willing to accept the French proposal, for since its formulation the western demands had assumed a new direction. Whereas Faure's nine points were at least filled with the spirit of agreement, the seventeen point program formally submitted by the western powers was permeated with an entirely different spirit and did not, Molotov suggested, really aim at achieving accord. "One gets the impression," he continued in a vein that incensed the western representatives and edged the discussions toward a lower and more personal level, "that the proposals of the Three Powers of October 31 were formulated as if the authors thereof did not wish to reach an agreement."[27] And western rhetoric at the conference, the Soviet official implied, was aimed at accomplishing — or failing to accomplish — the same thing. "For purposes of burying the proposals submitted on the question of contacts," he stated in the same speech, "it seems to me that we do not need any more artful speeches than those we have just heard."[28]

Molotov's implied accusations brought a swift rejoinder from Secretary of State Dulles. To suggest that the seventeen point proposal was deliberately drawn so as to be refused, he emphatically replied, "is a charge that I reject in the most categorical manner." Molotov had made many statements of a similarly frivolous nature to which he would like to reply in kind, Dulles remarked as the debate grew more rancorous, but he would deny himself that pleasure.[29]

If willing to deny himself that particular pleasure, he permitted himself another. He had thought, he commented to Molotov in a rather taunting tone, that socialism was so fully established that it would not topple perchance some contradictory ideas found their way into the Soviet Union. But apparently that was not the case, and the West must reconcile itself to the position taken by the Soviet delegation that it was dangerous to permit entry to any ideas that did not precisely conform to Moscow's. "That nervousness on behalf of the Soviet Government for its own future," Dulles concluded, "was something which we will have to take into account and evaluate when we consider the possibility of other contacts."[30]

Dulles was being coy, for he had well taken into account that supposed nervousness and fear long before coming to Geneva. Indeed, the western effort to introduce "ideas and information" into the USSR was not only a considered effort at the conference to capitalize on perceived possibilities within the Soviet Union, as Dulles was to make abundantly clear, but was to remain the basis for Washington's cultural relations policy vis-à-vis the Soviets for the following two years as well.

XII
Continued Contacts and
Formal Agreement, 1955–1958

Despite the failure at Geneva, the individual contacts begun before the summit continued on an increasing but sporadic basis for the following two years, culminating in a formal exchange agreement in early 1958. As was the case prior to the conference, Moscow and private American citizens took the initiative in arranging personal exchanges and human contacts, while official America remained reticent. Washington's goal remained that of injecting "ideas and information" into the USSR, not the exchanging of individuals and delegations on a reciprocal basis. Indeed, a State Department proposal to exchange radio and television broadcasts became the immediate catalyst for the 1958 agreement regularizing contacts, but that pact, ironically enough, gave the United States little that it sought while granting to the Soviet Union much of that which it had long been pursuing.

The contacts begun before Geneva continued even while the diplomats debated at the conference. Delegations of Soviet housing specialists, newsmen and engineers toured the length and breadth of the United States during the latter half of 1955, and the following year Soviet visitors attended conferences, studied scientific advances, examined food preparation practices and conferred with American church leaders. By September some one hundred Soviet visitors, all traveling as "official" delegates to obviate the fingerprinting requirement of the 1952 immigration act, had arrived in the United States.[1]

Most of the visitors drew scant notice, but three internationally known musicians drew widespread attention and critical acclaim. Pianist Emil Gilels, violinist David Oistrakh and cellist Mtsislav Rostropovich, appearing in the winter of 1955 and the spring of 1956, proved enormously successful with at least a portion of the American public. Capacity audiences applauded their performances, critics praised their talents and music companies vied for the right to record their renditions.[2] The same

156

Musical America that only months earlier had criticized the direction of Soviet culture neatly captured the comments of a number of publications regarding the visits, and in doing so unwittingly illuminated the continuing estrangement between the American and Soviet people. Noting the "great anticipatory excitement" caused by their coming, the "sensational character of their reception" and the universal admiration of the men as artists, the magazine discerned a deeper meaning in the matter. Though it was unlikely that any listener left the concerts converted to communism, it reasoned, audiences did leave aware that the Soviets loved and supported great music, and that fact both rehumanized them and made Americans aware that they were "just people like us."[3] That *Musical America's* comment was so strikingly similar to that of the critic who in 1924 applauded the visit of the Moscow Art Theatre because it would show Americans that the Soviets, despite government innuendo, had neither horns nor tails, well illustrates the depth and span of the estrangement between the two peoples.[4] Despite the prewar and wartime contacts, and despite the increased American academic study of the USSR in the postwar period, most of the people in the United States and in the Soviet Union knew little more about each other in 1955 than had an older generation in 1925.

During late 1955 and most of 1956, some 25 hundred Americans returned the Soviet visits.[5] Writers, educators, religious leaders, entertainers, scientists and tourists traveled to various locations throughout the USSR, and so many Congressmen made the trip that *Time* complained that Moscow had become Congress's favorite vacationing spot.[6] The direct flow of books, periodicals and newspapers between American and Soviet institutions likewise increased as a result of an agreement negotiated by Harvard professor Martin Malia on behalf of the Library of Congress and a number of major universities. If the Soviets were unwilling to deal with Simmons regarding such matters in 1947, they proved agreeable to similar suggestions in 1955.[7]

As was true in the reverse instance, the most visible Americans in the USSR were musicians and stage performers. In late 1955, the Everyman Opera Company's production of "Porgy and Bess," playing to wildly enthusiastic audiences in Leningrad and Moscow, became America's first theatrical production in the Soviet Union.[8] The Soviets, as *Life* noted, lionized the play's cast both on and off stage, and Moscow, despite State Department fears, refrained from using the play to propagandize the plight of American blacks.[9] In May, Isaac Stern received the same kind of welcome during a tour of six Soviet cities, and opera star Jan Peerce followed with similar success.[10] The Boston Symphony Orchestra's September visit was the crowning appearance. Like the others, the Boston orchestra, which had been trying to go to the Soviet Union for over a year, received rave reviews for its performances and appreciative words for its presence.[11]

While the State Department continued its emphasis on supplying "information and ideas" to the Soviet people, President Eisenhower provided at least verbal support for increased contacts in other areas as well. The long impenetrable iron curtain which had prevented us from sharing the arts and sports of the communist countries, he told a 1956 Cow Palace audience while accepting his party's nomination for the presidency, was showing signs of giving way to a friendly intercourse; to an interchange of ideas, books, magazines, students, artists, radio programs, technical experts, religious leaders and governmental officials. We must, he urged, try "to bridge the great chasm that separates us from the peoples under communist rule...," because the alternative was "more misunderstanding and an ever deepening division in the world."[12]

Three weeks later the President reiterated the message in phrases worthy of quoting because of the manner in which they captured some of the more worthy reasons for maintaining officially sponsored international cultural relations. "Every bomb we can manufacture, every plane, every ship, every gun," he told a September People to People Conference, "in the long run has no purpose other than negative." The "truest path to peace" lay in another direction. The nation must, the President stated,

> widen every possible chink in the Iron Curtain and bring the family of Russia, or of any other country behind the Iron Curtain ... closer into our circle, to show them how we do it, and then to sit down between us to say 'Now, how do we improve the lot of both of us?'
> In this way, I believe, is the truest path to peace. All the other things are mere palliatives or they are holding the line while constructive forces of this kind can take effect.[13]

The reciprocal appearances of American and Soviet performers, the growing American tourist traffic to the Soviet Union and Eisenhower's expressed interest all seemed to portend a friendlier era in the realm of cultural relations, promising relief in at least one area from the terrible tensions pervading other aspects of American-Soviet relations. Increasing numbers in the United States seemed interested in promoting such contacts, and Moscow appeared willing to accommodate that interest.

The promise was premature. In the fall of 1956, Hungarian nationalists rebelled against Soviet domination, Moscow replied with tanks and troops, and the hopes for expanded contacts momentarily vanished. The State Department cancelled its efforts toward official contacts through reciprocal exchanges of information, and discouraged contacts by private citizens.[14] For the following several months, cultural contacts between the two nations practically ceased to exist.

If Moscow's actions in Hungary diminished the chances for contacts in late 1956 and early 1957, its attitude and actions in large part accounted for the burgeoning cultural interaction between Geneva and the Hungarian eruption. For Moscow continued to take the lead in the matter of individual contacts, expressing a desire for more intimate cultural relations with both the American people and those of other western nations.

Even as the formal conversations continued at Geneva, American entrepeneurs negotiated in Moscow for the right to present Gilels, Oistrakh and Rostropovich in the United States, and only the American fingerprinting requirement prevented the appearance of the 100 member Moiseyev Dance Ensemble, signed by Hurok to appear in the fall of 1956.[15] At the same time the Soviets invited the Philadelphia Symphony Orchestra to appear in their country, and verbally signalled a willingness to arrange other forms of contacts.[16] In late 1955 Moscow indicated that it favored a week long film festival, featuring the exchange of films and film stars, and in August of the following year Deputy Minister of Culture Vladimir Surin, in Hollywood to examine the possibility of film purchases and exchanges, stated that his country was willing to consider any American projects for expanding exchanges on a reciprocal basis.[17] In April, the Counselor of the Soviet Embassy in Washington told a Columbia University audience that his country considered the time appropriate for all types of exchanges, and another Embassy staff member, referring to the enthusiastic reception given "Porgy and Bess," wrote that his country hoped such exchanges would be broadened in the future.[18] French Foreign Minister Christian Pineau, just returned from negotiating in Moscow, told an American audience much the same thing. Though not willing to make concessions on major international issues, he remarked, the Soviets were willing to raise the iron curtain to escape their cultural isolation and it would be maladroit for the United States to try to maintain it.[19] Washington was aware of and acknowledged Moscow's readiness to allow more intimate interaction with the United States. "Today," Vice-President Nixon commented in June, 1956, "we can have such contacts for the asking."[20]

In January, 1956, the Kremlin provided even more concrete evidence of its desire for increased connections by proposing a 20 year treaty of friendship and cooperation, the heart of which lay in the area of artistic and scientific contacts.[21] Recalling Eisenhower's Geneva statement regarding the historical friendship between the two countries, pointing to past examples of their cooperation and expressing regret over the deterioration of American-Soviet relations, Bulganin personally appealed to the President to approve the treaty. "I am sure," he wrote, "that you, like myself, are convinced that the social differences of the United States and the USSR should not prevent our countries from maintaining the political, economic and cultural relations in which our people are interested."[22]

A skeptical Washington, remembering the discrepancy between Soviet words and deeds in the late forties, was justified in treating the Soviet suggestions and overtures warily, but a number of considerations called for examining their sincerity. In the post-Stalin years the Soviets were increasingly opening their country to at least certain kinds of contacts, and that openness was becoming even more marked as Moscow carried on ever-widening contacts with England, France, Belgium, Japan and numerous other countries during the months following Geneva. Washington had little to lose in encouraging similarly expanded contacts, and perhaps much to gain. Increased interaction on the cultural level could hardly have weakened the nation's capacities on the military and the diplomatic, and would have involved the nation's pride and prestige only if Washington chose to have it so; chose to treat such broadened relations as extensions of the competition with Moscow, complete with winners and losers. And if Washington feared that increased exposure to Soviet citizens would somehow weaken America and its institutions, it had less faith in the nation and its people than did those that were asking for increased interchanges. By the mid-fifties the danger of mass destruction had become too great to ignore any kind of contacts that might lessen international tensions and reduce the danger of war. Perhaps an increased level of interaction would have done little to ease the immediate diplomatic difficulties, but the contacts would have had an intrinsic value in themselves, and at the minimum would have provided Washington and Moscow with the means to cooperate in one area while competing in others. Communism existed, the Soviet state existed, and neither, despite the optimistic predictions of some in the United States, showed signs of fading away. Washington should have recognized that fact and dealt with it more realistically: disliking the reality would not make it go away, any attempt to change it by force would have invited nuclear retaliation, and attempts to change it by more subtle means, as some in Washington were trying to do, could only prove futile. It was precisely at this time of high tensions that increased contacts on the human level, removed from the realm of national pride and prestige, could have served a valuable national purpose, for they could have allowed Washington and Moscow to maintain the level of communication and cooperation that is so essential to powerful nations of opposing ideologies, without, at the same time, opening officials to accusations of appeasement; to charges of, in the vernacular of the day, being "soft" on communism. Had Washington really wanted broadened contacts, it could have at least pursued the possibilities raised in the Soviet offers and intimations, and could have taken a minimum measure of initiative itself.

But Washington was little interested in increasing formal exchanges between individuals and delegations. Though it cooperated in permitting small scale contacts arranged between Moscow and individual Americans, it did nothing to promote them, and in instances involving large numbers actively discouraged them. Anyone looking to Washington to take the lead in opening the iron curtain to human traffic could only be disappointed.

Secretary of State Dulles left little doubt as to his lack of enthusiasm for personal exchanges. When queried as to his opinion of the 1955 agricultural exchange, for instance, the Secretary replied that the reciprocal visits were, on the whole, "probably" desirable, but expressed reservations about many aspects of the matter, particularly the emotionalism surrounding it.[23] Nor did his comments immediately prior to Isaac Stern's Soviet tour constitute a ringing endorsement. While exchanges of "genuine" artists was probably a good thing, he remarked, "if the artists are spies in disguise that's another matter."[24] Moreover, Dulles cautioned, America had to be careful lest its example have an adverse effect on smaller nations, for while the United States could withstand whatever harmful consequences might accompany cultural exchanges, weaker countries following our lead might be susceptible to subversion.[25]

Washington revealed its reluctance in a number of other ways. Immediately after Geneva the State Department, apparently uncertain as to its own policy, afraid that the Soviets would gain more than they gave, and piqued at the Soviet attitude at Geneva, cancelled the scheduled arrival of a second Soviet agricultural delegation. The delay infuriated the Iowans who invited the Soviets; the Department, they claimed, was less than candid in its remarks concerning the matter.[26] Likewise the Department frowned on the suggested exchange of the Bolshoi Ballet for an American symphony orchestra, and threw sufficient cold water on the planned visit of a Soviet track and field team, as diplomat Chester Bowles expressed it, to cause its cancellation.[27] Even Dr. Paul Dudley White, Eisenhower's personal heart specialist, found little encouragement for a planned trip to Moscow at the invitation of the Soviet Ministry of Health. While the Department would not prevent his going, White wrote in an appeal for aid to presidential assistant Sherman Adams, he would prefer making the trip with its blessings and approval.[28]

Department officials were even more reluctant to encourage or assist the appearance of large American groups in the Soviet Union. Upon receiving invitations to perform in the USSR, the managers of both "Porgy and Bess" and the Philadelphia Symphony Orchestra approached Washington for assistance from funds designated for overseas cultural appearances, and both, despite having been subsidized on earlier occasions when appearing in other countries, were turned down. Such appearances in the Soviet Union, Department officials reportedly told the "Porgy and Bess" managers, would be politically inapt at the time.[29] Consequently the

Philadelphia Symphony never made the 1956 trip, and the Soviets themselves reaped a large part of the propaganda benefit inherent in the Porgy performances by providing the financial guarantees requisite to the venture.[30]

One reason for the reluctance to assist such groups became evident in the attempts by the Boston Symphony Orchestra to travel to Moscow. Despite diligent efforts since the summer of 1955 by both the orchestra's managers and by presidential aide C.D. Jackson, a trustee of the orchestra, the Boston musicians had made little progress by the spring of 1956. In early March of that year Jackson explained the lack of success to Henry Cabot, president of the orchestra's board of trustees. "I had an unofficial visit from USIA on the subject of the Russian trip," Jackson wrote,

> and find that the basis for the State Department's foot-dragging is really quite practical. They are really terrified that if a U.S. cultural organization—numbering a lot of people, like a symphony orchestra, were to be allowed to perform in Russia, the immediate counter would be a request for a similarly large number of Russian artists to come here. Then the complications would immediately begin—fingerprinting, McCarran Act, etc. So long as the exchange is limited to one man affairs like Gilels and Oistrakh they feel they can handle it, but they dread the prospect of large numbers.[31]

If less than enthusiastic about large scale personal exchanges, Washington remained ready to provide "ideas and information" to the Soviet people. The American attitude toward contacts with the Soviets remained the same as at Geneva, President Eisenhower told a May, 1956 press conference, and in late June the President proclaimed that policy more explicitly. In keeping with a National Security Council recommendation regarding the matter, an official press release stated on the 29th of that month, it was the policy of the United States to seek exchanges with the Soviets "along the lines of the seventeen point program" put forward at Geneva.[32] According to columnist Arthur Krock, during 1956 the State Department particularly pursued points eight, nine and ten, dealing with radio and television exchanges, and according to Secretary of State Dulles, that pursuit extended into 1957 as well.[33] Throughout the eighteen months following Geneva, Dulles stated in June 1957, the United States had pressed the Soviets "off and on, with consistency," for reciprocal rights to discuss contemporary concerns through regularly scheduled broadcasts and telecasts.[34] Exchanging "ideas and information," not people, remained the principal concern of Washington's policy.

The State Department took one step in that direction even while the negotiations were proceeding at Geneva. In September 1955, Washington approached the Soviets with a proposal to resume the distribution of an uncensored *Amerika* in the Soviet Union, and offered similar rights for a Soviet magazine in the United States. The Kremlin consented, and according to a subsequent agreement each nation received the right to circulate 50,000 copies per issue.[35] The first copies of the rejuvenated *Amerika*, appearing in July, 1956, featured a two page spread displaying Detroit's newest models in full color, undoubtedly accomplishing thereby at least a part of the purpose of supplying "ideas" to the Soviet public.[36] The Soviet magazine *U.S.S.R.* countered with Moscow's latest passenger plane, but since few people dream of owning a four motored flying machine, *Amerika* undoubtedly took the first round in the new competition.[37]

In the fall of 1956, Washington provided the Soviets with information through a different means. In September the State Department invited Moscow to send election observers to witness the quadrennial process of picking a president and the Soviets promptly accepted.[38] In late October three delegates arrived for that purpose, but some greeted even this type activity with skepticism. The "election observers," the *Saturday Evening Post* suggested, were really spies in disguise.[39]

Washington was less successful in its efforts to convey information via the air waves. Despite American indignation and protests, Moscow continued jamming the Voice of America and the liberation stations, and refused reciprocal exchanges of broadcasts. Given Washington's repeated pronouncements regarding its aims, the Soviet attitude was by no means illogical. For one of America's principal goals vis-à-vis the USSR, Dulles made clear, was to reform the Soviet state; to, as he explained it, make it a "normal" rather than an "abnormal" member of the society of nations.

Dulles explained his thinking on a number of occasions during the post-Geneva months. While Moscow had made many changes in its foreign policy after Stalin's death, his line of reasoning began, those changes had not been voluntary nor had they altered its ultimate goal of world conquest. Rather, the determined free world resistance to communist expansion had forced the Kremlin to either abandon its aims or alter its methods, and it had opted for the latter. Thus the new look in foreign policy.

But the new friendliness and apparent accommodation in international affairs, Dulles' reasoning continued, necessarily required a relaxation of the rigidity and controls within the USSR, and that fact provided possibilities. As the Soviet people experienced a slight taste in personal freedom they were sure to demand more, and that demand could force significant changes in the Moscow regime. Thus when Soviet policy began to shift in the spring of 1955, Dulles told a Philadelphia audience in February, 1956, "we determined to do all that we safely could to make that change a first installment toward a Russian state that would be a normal, not an abnormal, member of the society of nations." One major step in that direction was "to join hands with Britain and France to invite the Russian rulers to a Conference of the Heads of Government."[40] And the success of that conference, Dulles recalled having remarked, depended in large part upon whether or not "it set up within the Soviet Union forces that might become irreversible."[41]

In February Dulles was not convinced that the irreversible trend had begun, but by May Khrushchev's revelations concerning Stalin made him more positive. The events inside the USSR, he stated at a May 15 news conference, were a barometer measuring the demand for increased personal freedom, security, goods and a government "more responsive to the basic wishes of the Soviet people." And that demand, he reasoned, must be strong and deep, for to destroy Stalin and some of the sacred creeds of communism was a dangerous thing; once such forces were unleashed, they were difficult to control. If those forces continued to gather momentum, "we can, I think," Dulles predicted, "reasonably hope ... within a decade or perhaps a generation, that we will have what is the great goal of our policy, that is, a Russia that is governed by people who are responsible to the wishes of the Russian people ... and who conform to the principles of civilized nations."[42]

By the following summer, Dulles was even more convinced that the trend existed. The struggle between "modernists" and "fundamentalists," he stated in reference to the Khrushchev shake-up in the Kremlin, again proved how strong were the forces for change and how difficult it must be for the Soviet rulers to simultaneously cope with those forces and maintain their absolute power. And, he remarked significantly, "I think we have done quite a bit to promote this trend." The "big beginning," he asserted, was made at Geneva and afterward, when the State Department sent out a circular letter "explaining that conference and indicating that we felt there was such an irreversible trend which we had begun and suggested various ways we might improve it."[43] Though Dulles did not on that occasion specifically link the injection of "ideas and information" into the USSR with the effort to promote the trend, the idea was implicit throughout his statements relating to the matter. As the Soviet people become better educated, he remarked on one occasion, "their minds become more inquiring. They get, sometimes through underground channels, literature which is otherwise officially denied to them, and there are quite a few processes going on which we believe Americans can, to some extent, help."[44]

Assistant Secretary of State for Policy Planning Robert R. Bowie made explicit that which Dulles implied. Since the United States must, "as a final objective" do what it could to foster the evolution of communist states toward more liberal patterns, the Department official wrote, its first aim must be "to try to create a set of conditions to which the Soviet

Union will have to adjust its conduct." And one modest means toward that goal was exchanging information, for such exchanges acted to "open up the communist world to ideas and influences from abroad and to strengthen the forces for change within."[45]

Moscow, of course, had its own goals in promoting contacts, and it could be argued that Washington was only replying in kind. But in pursuing its larger ends, Moscow at least had the perspicacity to emphasize the mutual benefits of cultural interaction and to refrain from announcing that its purpose was to drive a wedge between Washington and the American people. The Soviets were well aware of the American statements, and resented them.[46] It was not particularly astute, to say the least, to tell the Soviet leaders that we desired to exchange ideas and information with them in order to encourage the Soviet People to rise against their leaders.

In one sense Dulles was correct. Moscow's relaxed attitude did encourage dissent and rebellion, but the outward expression came not in the USSR but in Hungary. Moscow replied with force, dashing, since the two nations had not progressed to the point of separating cultural matters from those political and diplomatic in nature, any immediate hopes for increased American-Soviet cultural interaction. From the fall of 1956 to the summer of 1957, cultural activity between the two powers became virtually nonexistent.

The contacts so precipitously terminated by the Hungarian crisis slowly resumed during the summer of 1957. In June, a Soviet delegation traveling on official visas attended Oklahoma's 50th anniversary celebration, while in Moscow Sol Hurok contracted for a number of Soviet artists to appear in American cities.[47] In addition to Gilels and Oistrakh, Hurok signed violinist Lenoid Kogan, composer Aram Khachaturian, ballerina Galina Ulanova, and, for its first American appearance, the Bolshoi Ballet. The Moiseyev Dance Ensemble, prevented from making its scheduled American appearance the previous fall by the Soviet position regarding fingerprinting, again agreed to come. While anticipating no fingerprinting problems in bringing solo performers and small groups, Hurok arranged the contracts to span a two year period on the assumption that Congress would shortly amend the troublesome clause to permit entry to larger ensembles as well.[48] Soviet willingness to arrange favorable financial and transportation terms, the impresario reported of his experience in the Soviet capital, indicated that Moscow was more eager than ever to engage in large scale contacts.[49]

As the individual contacts slowly resumed, CBS television sent a crew to Moscow to tape an interview with Nikita Khrushchev. On the 2nd of June an estimated five million Americans watched the Soviet leader on a "Face the Nation" appearance that was to have important consequences for the development of American-Soviet contacts.

The interview touched on a number of topics, but when asked what he considered to be the "most pressing points that must be solved between the two countries," Khrushchev replied that the "main thing" was to normalize relations through eliminating trade barriers and increasing the level of cultural exchanges. "There must be," he responded, "more contacts between our peoples, between businessmen. That is the main thing." But, he contended, the United States was placing obstacles in the way of contacts and discriminating against his country in the matter of trade. "You must," he remarked in a statement that surely must have surprised many of his listeners, "do away with your Iron Curtain...." As for his country's jamming of the Voice of America, the Soviet leader replied to another question, it was done only when the broadcasts ceased to truly be the voice of the American people, when it stopped playing pretty music and began to "cut on the ear."[50]

Four days after Khrushchev's appearance on American television, Moscow submitted a broad-scale proposal calling for more extensive cultural exchanges between the two countries. Under its terms, Soviet ballet groups, technical delegations and scientists would tour the United States, while similar American groups would visit Soviet cities and installations. Particularly, the Soviet note indicated, it would like the Philadelphia Symphony, with which Gilels had performed while in the United States, to appear in the Soviet Union.[51]

The Soviet moves seem to have caught Washington unprepared. President Eisenhower initially dismissed Khrushchev's telecast by remarking that CBS was simply looking to its profits, and Dulles responded that while he favored exchanges along the lines of the seventeen point Geneva proposal, he did not necessarily approve of such contacts along the lines that Moscow suggested.[52]

In the absence of either a positive administration response or a counter-proposal to the Soviet suggestions, Senate Majority Leader Lyndon B. Johnson responded with a suggestion of his own. Quoting the Bible and Thomas Jefferson, the Texas politician called for a new kind of curtain, an "open curtain" through which the truth would flow freely — by implication in one direction only — and through which ideas would "cleanse evil just as fresh air cleanses the poisoned, stagnant mass of a long-closed cavern." The United States, Johnson told a United Jewish Appeal audience in New York City, should turn Khrushchev's appearance back upon him by insisting that the USSR provide radio and television facilities through which American spokesmen could speak weekly to the Soviet people on matters of contemporary concern. Washington would of course be obligated to reciprocate, but that posed no problem to a nation too wise to succumb to Soviet blandishments. "No demagogue is going to lead the lean spare Texan who runs my cattle ranch," proclaimed the

Jefferson-leaning Johnson, "and Nikita Khrushchev is not going to convert him to a Communist. He's just plain got too much sense.... I believe that most Americans are like that." And if Americans were too wise to be fooled by propaganda, the Soviet people were equally astute when provided the opportunity. "The Russian people," the senator assured his listeners while citing the Biblical maxim that men shall know the truth and it shall make them free, "are capable of recognizing the truth when it is offered to them." The United States should not let a day go by without raising the issue of broadcast exchanges, Johnson concluded; indeed, "should insist upon it every time a Russian representative is within earshot."[53]

Calling Johnson's speech the most intelligent that he had heard in a long time, Arkansas Senator J. William Fulbright inserted it into the *Congressional Record*, while numerous others identified themselves with it and quoted local editorials to prove the popularity of its reception. Though most of the senators and the editorial writers who praised Johnson's suggestions saw no possibility that Moscow would agree to them, they deemed it just as well, for Soviet refusal would mean an American propaganda victory.[54] But if by some miracle the Soviets did accept the overture the results would be even better, for, as the *Waco News Tribune* stated in an editorial that expressed directly what others said more subtly, such an exchange of opinion could be used "as a springboard to put some pressure on the Commies."[55]

Two weeks after Johnson's speech, Washington formally proposed such an exchange. In order "to promote a freer exchange of information and ideas on important world developments," a tersely worded three-sentence State Department message to the Kremlin read, the United States "proposes that the Soviet and United States Governments reach an agreement in principle at an early date for the regular exchange of uncensored radio and television broadcasts."[56]

Three days later Vice-President Nixon strongly attacked the Soviet position regarding cultural contacts, labeling as "hypocritical double-talk" Khrushchev's accusations that the United States was blocking broadened exchanges and challenging the Soviet leader to back his words with deeds. To prove its good faith, the vice-president stated in a speech that illuminated the continuing American concept of cultural contacts, Moscow should, in addition to accepting the American proposal on broadcast exchanges, stop jamming and censoring, remove all travel restrictions within the USSR, allow Soviet citizens to freely visit the United States, and permit them to freely purchase foreign publications, including American newspapers and magazines. Taking those steps, Nixon asserted, would prove that the Soviets were sincere in their expressed desire to reduce tensions and promote better understanding between the communist and capitalist worlds, but refusing would "place the responsibility on the Soviet leaders alone for blocking the road to peace."[57]

Moscow replied to Washington's overture in late July. It was willing to discuss the question of radio and television exchanges, the Soviet message read after reciting its own version of initiative and rejection in the matter of contacts, but only "in conjunction with other problems in the development of broad ties between the Soviet and American peoples." Particularly, the note made clear, fingerprinting posed a problem that must be solved. But if the United States was ready to discuss the development of "contacts and ties in their entirety," the lengthy Soviet response said in essence, Moscow was likewise prepared.[58] Despite the fact that the State Department's initial public response made it appear that Moscow had accepted its overture without reservations, the Department agreed to the Soviet conditions, thus setting the stage for the first formal bilateral negotiations on American-Soviet contacts.[59] But there was little chance for success as long as the fingerprinting requirement remained law.[60]

The requirement to which the Soviets so adamantly objected had begun drawing American criticism as well. The *Washington Star*, noting that the United States was taking a propaganda flogging over the matter, urged its repeal, as did a *Newsweek* commentator who observed that while the Soviets had opened a door in the iron curtain, we had placed a bar across our side.[61] And even President Eisenhower, pointing out that some countries viewed the procedure with disfavor and that it did not significantly add to either our national safety or security, twice urged Congress to amend the law so as to allow either Secretary of State or the Attorney General to waive it in the case of temporary visitors.[62] But by mid-summer, 1957, Congress had still failed to act on such an amendment submitted by Senator Dirksen of Illinois.[63]

In light of the new developments and the pending bilateral talks, New York Senator Jacob Javits, who had already been pushing for increased American-Soviet contacts, introduced in early August both a bill to amend the immigration law and a concurrent resolution urging that the Secretary of State begin exchanging persons with the Soviet Union under the auspices of the Information and Educational Exchange Act of 1948.[64] Early the following month, Congress finally amended the immigration law, and on October 10 the Secretary of State and the Attorney General, acting under the authority conferred upon them by Congress's actions, authorized the waiving of the fingerprinting requirement in the case of most nonimmigrant aliens who planned to stay in the country less than a year.[65] That authorization provided at least the possibility of success in the negotiations that began in Washington two weeks later.

The opening speeches at the conference left no doubt as to the positions and priorities of the two sides. Neither had forsaken its Geneva proposals or altered the object of its aims. The United States still wanted to exchange ideas and information and the Soviets, despite a reduced emphasis on the importance of trade and a marked willingness to engage in intellectual and artistic exchanges, still placed a premium on contacts in industry, science and technology.

Assistant Secretary of State for East-West Affairs William S.B. Lacy, leader of the American delegation, quickly got to the point in a rather brusque and accusatory address. His country, he stated in no uncertain terms, still considered the exchange of ideas and information to be the "necessary ingredient" to better understanding and reduced tensions; progress toward removing obstructions to such exchanges, he emphasized while quoting Dulles' Geneva remarks and citing examples of Soviet intransigence since the summit, was an important American objective in the negotiations. Even in those instances in which the Soviets had been somewhat cooperative, such as allowing the distribution of *Amerika* and exchanging the ruble exchange rate to encourage tourism, Lacy complained, the results had been less than satisfactory, for the circulation arrangements for the magazine were inadequate and foreign visitors to the USSR were still restricted as to where they could travel.[66]

If the American delegation had any specific aims or proposals other than those in the area of radio and television broadcasts, they did not appear in Lacy's remarks. Soviet Ambassador Zaroubin on the other hand came prepared with both a different approach and a sweeping array of specific suggestions Emphasizing the areas of agreement and accord since the summit in a diplomatic and conciliatory address, the Soviet spokesman dwelt on the importance which his country assigned to the talks as a step toward normalizing Soviet-American contacts and reducing international tensions. One could surmise of course that Zaroubin's ingratiating style masked self-serving goals, but taken at face value his approach placed the Soviet delegation in a positive position while making Lacy's comments sound negative and carping.

The wide ranging Soviet proposals dwelt first on exchanges in the fields of industry, engineering and technology. Specifically, Zaroubin stated, Moscow desired exchanges in such fields as metallurgy, mining, chemistry, radio, electronics, plastics, automobile manufacturing and various types of construction, including bridge and industrial design. In agriculture, his country wanted exchanges in animal-husbandry, horticulture, vegetable farming and in other specified areas. And, he continued, Moscow attached "great importance" to establishing "close connections and cooperation between Soviet and American scientists," including those whose expertise lay in the field of medicine.

Zaroubin's proposals went far beyond the technical and practical. For the artistically, athletically and scholarly inclined, Zaroubin outlined broad suggestions for exchanging artists, performers, writers, composers, actors, singers, symphony orchestras, teachers, professors, students, athletes, social and women's organizations, tourists and others. In the political realm the Soviets suggested exchanges between members of the USSR Supreme Soviet and the United States Congress, for such an exchange, Zaroubin commented, "would contribute to the establishment of useful contacts between these legislative bodies and promote visits of that kind in the future." As for exchanging radio and television broadcasts, Zaroubin approved the idea, but was careful to specify broadcasts in such fields as science, technique, sports, industry, agriculture, music and the artistic fields while omitting mention of political topics. His country was also prepared to discuss "the question of concluding a convention on cultural cooperation," the Soviet leader stated in conclusion, and would like to know the United States position regarding the same.[67]

The negotiations following the introductory addresses, lasting from October 28 to January 27, covered almost every imaginable area of exchange.[68] If, as Lacy later claimed, the Soviets arrived hostile but underwent a palpable change and left friendly, they had sufficient reason for the reversal, for almost all of Zaroubin's suggestions as outlined in his initial remarks were written into the final agreement.[69]

As finally formulated, the agreement called for reciprocal visits of scientists, industrialists, agriculturists, students and scholars; for reciprocal performances by theatrical, artistic and musical groups; for athletic competitions; for visits by cultural, civic and youth groups, and for exchanges of publications and exhibits. Both sides accepted the principle of direct air flights with specific negotiations to follow, agreed to promote tourism, and consented to pursue the possibility of exchanging members of Congress and the Supreme Soviet. With the exception of those areas in which final arrangements were left to the future, the agreement specified dates, numbers, destinations and similar details.[70]

If the Soviets got much of that which they suggested at the beginning of the negotiations, the United States received little of that which it had publicly pursued. While calling for exchanges of radio and television broadcasts "on the subjects of science, technology, industry, agriculture, education, public health and sports," and for similar exchanges of filmed musical, literary and theatrical productions, the agreement provided few opportunities to provide "ideas and information" of a political or economic nature to the Soviet people.[71] For the purpose of "strengthening mutual understanding and developing friendly relations," it specified, the two nations were to "organize from time to time an exchange of broadcasts devoted to discussion of such international political problems as may be agreed upon by the two parties," but even that opening was largely neutralized by an exchange of letters of understanding signed by both and attached to the completed agreement. The texts of all broadcasts, both sides agreed in the letters, were to be exchanged in advance and discussed at the working level; should either party consider that the effect of a broadcast would not "contribute to the betterment of relations," the broadcast would be cancelled.[72] The letters of understanding thus protected the American public from Soviet propaganda, but they also precluded the possibility of reaching the Soviet public with what many in the United States considered "the truth." And in agreeing to such a limitation, Washington automatically relinquished an important part of its post-Geneva policy regarding American-Soviet contacts. On the other hand, the United States and the Soviet Union now had, for the first time, a sweeping and significant relationship in the area of cultural exchange.

XIII
Conclusion

The 1958 agreement dramatically changed the nature of American-Soviet cultural relations. During the following two years, thousands of American and Soviet citizens passed through the now porous iron curtain, taking their knowledge, skills and curiosities to a brief exposure on the other side. By the end of the first eighteen months, 1,674 Americans comprising 107 delegations had traveled to the USSR under the terms of the agreement, while 1,637 Soviets connected with 100 projects had visited the United States.[1] Approximately seventy-five per cent of the projects specified in the agreement had been completed by the end of the two year period covered by the pact.[2] A comprehensive publications exchange program had been set in motion, the film industries of the two nations had negotiated their own reciprocal arrangements, and the U.S. National Academy of Sciences and the Soviet Academy of Sciences, operating under the auspices of the larger agreement, had drawn up their own program of scientific activities.[3] "The future of the program," State Department officials wrote at the time, "seems assured, probably on an increasing basis."[4]

Most of the exchange agreements were fulfilled without fanfare, but a few captured the attention of both nations. Bob Hope found an appreciative audience in the Kremlin, proving to skeptical Americans that communists could laugh, and prompting *Christian Century* to wonder whether it was tragic or ludicrous that it should so surprise us that the Soviet people could enjoy a joke.[5] Van Cliburn's success at the Tchaikovsky Music Festival brought both fame to himself and heightened appreciation to his art, while the Philadelphia Symphony Orchestra won affection in Soviet cities and Leopold Stokowski, the first American to conduct a Soviet symphony, proved a popular figure in the USSR.[6] But the biggest American attraction was the fair that it staged in Moscow, which proved a huge success despite Kremlin complaints that it over-emphasized American consumer goods and an American Congressman's attacks upon its art as being communist-inspired.[7] Almost three million people pushed

172

through the gates of the Moscow Fair during the late summer of 1959, and many more would have done so had time and tickets permitted.[8]

The Moiseyev Dance Ensemble, on the other hand, proved a smashing success in the United States, and the long awaited Bolshoi Ballet an even larger one.[9] Like the Moscow Art Theatre some thirty-five years earlier, the Bolshoi sold out all performances weeks before its arrival, even at prices that — at $50 for opening nights and $15 for subsequent ones — prompted pundits to sympathize with Soviets who complained that it was easier to get out of the Lubianka Prison than into the Bolshoi Ballet.[10] Shostakovich returned to a far different welcome than that which had greeted him ten years earlier, and in New York City the Soviets staged their own exhibition which, though smaller than the American extravaganza in Moscow, drew large crowds as the first such Soviet exhibit to appear in America since the 1939 World's Fair.[11]

But the 1958 agreement was only a beginning. Since that time the two nations have signed similar pacts every two years, providing at least one relatively stable element in an uneasy relationship that on occasion has become volatile. Despite minor problems with the exchanges themselves and regardless of diplomatic difficulties over the U-2, Berlin, Cuba, Vietnam and a host of lesser episodes, the exchanges have continued, keeping open at least one avenue of awareness to tens of thousands of people in both countries. Though the agreements have not solved the great problems separating the two nations, the human interaction under their auspices has at least told the two peoples much more than they formerly knew about each other.

For one fact clearly emerges from the accounts of those who traveled to the USSR during the period between Stalin's death and the signing of the 1958 agreement: if the travelers reflected American knowledge and perception as a whole, the American people knew very little about the realities of everyday life in the Soviet Union. What the visitors found was not what they expected, and they said so. They expected to find rigid inspections at the borders, and, once within, anticipated surveillance, propaganda, controls, grimness, isolation, suspicion and perhaps hostility. Those who had been there in the thirties expected to find the same country that they had left two decades earlier, and those who had not been there at all expected Moscow, as Clifton Daniel observed, to appear as Tolstoy described it and Napoleon first saw it.[12]

They found the opposite. Customs officials treated them courteously, checked their bags cursorily, and other surprises quickly followed.[13] Instead of Tolstoy's Moscow they found subways, boulevards, and a surprising number of automobiles. The transformation since the thirties, wrote Merle Fainsod, Harvard professor of government and author of knowledgeable books about the Soviet Union, was astounding. "Then," he he observed, "Moscow seemed like a sprawling village. Today it looks like a world capital."[14] Instead of beaten and downtrodden people, they found a relatively relaxed and prosperous population that talked back to policemen, complained like humans everywhere, and even, as Alabama Senator John Sparkman told Americans in what apparently was a revelation to him, "seemed well fed."[15] Nor did the visitors find the anticipated controls on travel and communication. While some complained that they were not allowed to visit places that they requested, most commented on the freedom they had to wander freely, to ask questions, to take photographs and to purchase whatever they could afford.[16] National political commentator, presidential speech writer and Eisenhower assistant Emmet John Hughes, for example, found himself surprised not only that his bags were not opened at the border, but that, once in Moscow, he could walk alone for hours while taking detailed notes on prices and other aspects of Soviet life.[17] A 1956 Quaker delegation found much the same freedom. "With only a few exceptions," the delegates reported in an observation that typified many others, "we were able to wander at will and alone around the cities, observing without interference the showplace and the slum, the old and the new, the rich and the poor."[18] The expected propaganda devices were likewise conspicuously absent, as Hughes and many others noted. Instead of signs, slogans and loudspeakers the visitors found, as one observer commented, "only the inconspicuous and remarkably uniform signs advertising state institutions and stores, theatres and concerts."[19] One understands at once, wrote scholar Frederick L. Schuman after alluding to the changes in the country since his last visit and noting the disparity between reality and American preconceptions, "why many American tourists call on the tall Embassy building on Tchaikovsky Boulevard to ask why everything is wholly different from what they had been led to expect."[20] *Los Angeles Times* owner Norman Chandler and his wife found many of their preconceptions so erroneous, in fact, that upon returning to the United States Mrs. Chandler urged Washington to engage in more extensive artistic exchanges with the Soviets, to remove the fingerprinting requirement, and to encourage more Americans to make the trip to Moscow.[21]

But by far the most widely noted discovery made by the visitors was the warmth and friendliness which the Soviet people displayed toward America and Americans. Few failed to comment on the fact, including those severely critical of the Soviet regime and its machinations. The Soviet people, they repeatedly wrote in one form or another, expressed a genuine friendliness toward them, a curiosity about them, and an ardent desire to live in peace with them.

It is to be expected of course that people of a particular persuasion would find favorable things to say about the Soviet Union. But those who went in the fifties — and particularly those whose comments have been considered for present purposes — were not of that persuasion. Indeed, most were careful to be sufficiently critical to establish their credibility. Nor is the purpose here to praise Soviet life. But it is to suggest that if the visitors were surprised at what they found, the average American would have been much more so, for presumably the presidential assistant, the Supreme Court Justice, the radio and television station owners, the scholars, religious leaders, businessmen, congressmen and the others who went were in a position to know more about the realities of everyday Soviet life than was the ordinary citizen. It is also to suggest that if Americans knew so little about the USSR, the Soviet masses knew no more, and probably much less, about the realities of American life. And while recognizing the limited role of such intangible entities as mutual understanding and cultural friendship in international affairs, and while acknowledging that policy is made in Washington and Moscow, not in public places, there is still little to be said for the people of two great nations knowing so little about the day to day existence of the other.

The exchange agreements have undoubtedly improved the degree of mutual knowledge, but there is still much to be learned, as illustrated by a personal experience. In the spring of 1976 the writer attended a Houston reception honoring a Soviet delegation headed by Georgi Arbatov, then Director of the Institute on U.S. Studies of the Soviet Academy of Sciences, and nowadays one of the Kremlin's senior authorities on American affairs. Immediately ahead in the line to meet the Soviet official was the proverbial little gray haired lady with a kindly countenance who, upon being introduced to Arbatov, asked a question that brought a twinkle to his eyes and indulgent smiles to all within hearing. When, she earnestly asked, are you communists going to get to where you have to sleep only one hour a night?

Amusing, perhaps, but even though most Americans know that communists sleep much like capitalists, do we, on a different plane and in a different context, still think that the Soviet aim is to sleep only one hour a night? And do the Soviet people think the same about us? The answer in both instances appears altogether too often to be yes — and that fact alone constitutes a powerful argument for continued and expanded contacts between the American and Soviet people.

The stakes are too high to follow any other course. The American and Soviet people can no longer afford to know so little about each other; can no longer unquestioningly accept the stereotyped images propagated on both sides. The possibility of total war and nuclear annihilation provides both with an intimate common interest in the most fundamental of all human endeavors — survival — and that common interest demands that both sides increase their efforts to know more about the other. Though many find the fact reprehensible, both nations exist, both ideologies exist, and neither, despite the musings of some who live in fantasy land, show signs of ceasing to exist. The choice, then, is mutual destruction or continued coexistence, and if the latter, as reasonable men agree that it must be, coexistence based either on fear and confrontation or on increased understanding and acceptance. Both sides must recognize that while friendly contacts do not imply approval or admiration of the other's ideology and actions, their mutual interest in preserving peace requires that they find ways in which they can agree and cooperate. While both sides have depended on the threat of massive retaliation to maintain peace in the past, and must continue to do so to an extent in the future, the danger of destruction through misunderstanding and mistake makes it imperative that all possible measures be taken to broaden the basis of coexistence. Cultural relations have played a limited role toward that end in recent years — in incidental ways prior to 1958 and through more deliberate designs since that date — but they must play an even greater role in the future. Washington and Moscow must maintain the level of interaction established by the successive exchange agreements signed since the late fifties, and must intensify their efforts in that direction. Though it would be foolish to assume the ability of increased contacts to alone resolve the deep and fundamental differences dividing the two nations, they do offer possibilities that statesmen cannot afford to overlook while dealing with those deep divisions.

Foremost among these is the assumption that peoples who know something about each other on the personal level are more tolerant of each other on the impersonal; are more willing to make reasonable concessions and to accept necessary compromises than are those who live in isolation and ignorance, who view each other as nothing more than the embodiment of an alien and hostile system. Nothing is more dangerous to peace between the two powers than the mutual perception of the other as an implacable enemy, ready to strike at the opportune moment of advantage; and nothing is more conducive to such perceptions, as the American visitors in the USSR discovered during the fifties, than cultural estrangement between their societies. The visitors' surprise at finding that the Soviet people feared a war with the United States and fervently desired to live in peace with the American people says a great deal about the dangers of cultural isolation, for while Americans overwhelmingly held the same fear of war and desire for peace, they undoubtedly found it difficult to perceive of themselves as being considered dangerous; as occupying the same role of villain in which they cast the Soviets. Yet Soviet fears of "capitalist encirclement" and other supposed anti-Soviet designs in the West, while scoffed at by Americans, were apparently no less real that were western fears of Soviet advances throughout the world, knocking dominoes right and left. As the Soviets repeatedly remarked, they had only to look a little beyond their borders to see the American military presence, and the rhetoric of American cold warriors could hardly have been less unsettling and inflammatory than that streaming to the United States from the USSR. Had contacts been as full and free during the late forties and early fifties as even during the twenties and thirties, perhaps the level of tension, fueled by fears and tensions bottled up behind the barriers on both sides, would not have reached the dangerous heights to which it climbed. The two peoples must never allow themselves to become so estranged again, for the world has become an even more dangerous place than it was three decades ago.

But broad-scaled contacts provide possibilities of an even more practical and immediate nature. Nurtured for their own sake and pursued for their own purposes during times of relative relaxation, they can provide Washington and Moscow with the means to maintain precisely the kind of communication and cooperation so essential during times of increasing ideological alienation; can offer the means to sustain a friendly dialogue in one area even while officials maneuver for advantage or accord in others. For while it is not reasonable to expect disputes over ideological and national issues to soon disappear, it is not unreasonable to expect national leaders to keep those disputes within limits; to maintain the necessary perspective to accurately assess the importance of long range human concerns relative to the significance of immediate problems and transistory issues. By providing a neutral arena in which statesmen can confer during times of crisis as well as conciliation, carefully cultivated cultural contacts help provide that perspective; can help preserve the proper sense of proportion in balancing the long term requirements of human existence against the short term necessities stemming from the struggle over matters of national and ideological import.

To effectively serve such a purpose, cultural relations must be pursued in the proper manner and for appropriate purposes. They must be removed from the realm of national and ideological competition, must be isolated from issues involving provincial pride and honor, and must be maintained through bad times as well as good; through danger as well as detente. They must be freed from being pawns in a larger game, used to signal displeasure over noncultural developments. They must be maintained on the level of simple human interaction that recognizes that individuals have interests and aspirations that go beyond national and ideological concerns; that understands that all men, beneath their acquired beliefs and prejudices, share fundamental human hopes and fears. To do otherwise reduces cultural relations to being a part of the problem rather than a possible solution; to being a part of the continuing competition that emphasizes differences rather than similarities.

Some may well object to the idea of living in harmony with an ideological opponent, but the alternatives are only two: living in an uneasy coexistence permeated by fear and punctured by crises, or abandoning that uneasy coexistence in favor of solutions bordering on the unthinkable. Viewed from that perspective, the idealism inherent in the concept of cultural cooperation becomes the essence of practicality. Americans cannot, of course, dictate Soviet policies and practices, but they can encourage their own government to seek an increasing level of cultural interaction, and hope that Moscow reciprocates the effort. Though the record is ambiguous on the American side, and even more so on the side of the Soviets, past performance provides no reason to be altogether pessimistic about the possibilities.

Chapter Notes

NOTES TO CHAPTER I

1. The term "historic friendship" is used here in the same sense as employed by T.A. Bailey, i.e., to denote the lack of overt conflict, not the presence of common goals or ideological intimacy. See Thomas A. Bailey, *America Faces Russia: Russian-American Relations from Early Times to Our Day* (Ithaca: Cornell University Press, 1950), pp. 1–4.

2. Eufrosina Dvoichenko-Markov, "The American Philosophical Society and Early Russian-American Relations," *Proceedings of the American Philosophical Society*, XCIV (December, 1950), pp. 1–4.

3. *Ibid.*, 549, 552, 610.

4. Nikolai N. Bolkhovitinov, *The Beginnings of Russian-American Relations, 1775–1815*, trans. by Elena Levin (Cambridge: Harvard University Press, 1975), pp. 334–338.

5. Dvoichenko-Markov, "The American Philosophical Society," pp. 556–563.

6. Bolkhovitinov, *Russian-American Relations*, pp. 139–144.

7. Dvoichenko-Markov, "The American-Philosophical Society," pp. 566–567.

8. *Ibid.*, pp. 557–558.

9. *Ibid.*, pp. 579–582.

10. For a particularly interesting article concerning American literature in both pre- and postrevolutionary Russia, see Robert Magidoff, "American Literature in Russia," *Saturday Review of Literature*, XXI (November 2, 1946), pp. 9–12. Much the same information appears in the same author's *In Anger and Pity: A Report on Russia* (Garden City, New York: Doubleday and Doubleday, Inc., 1949), pp. 223–235. See also Bailey, *America Faces Russia*, pp. 136–140.

11. Herbert Weinstock, *Tchaikovsky* (New York: Alfred A. Knopf, 1959), p. 333. See also pp. 107, 215, 323–343.

12. Feodor Ivanovitch Chaliapine, *Pages From My Life: An Autobiography*, trans. by H.M. Buck (New York: Harper and Brothers Publishers, 1927), pp. 254–255; Christine Edwards, *The Stanislavsky Heritage: Its Contributions to the Russian and American Theatres* (New York: University Press, 1965), pp. 214–216.

13. Sergei Bertensson and Jay Leyda, *Sergei Rachmaninoff: A Lifetime in Music* (New York: New York University Press, 1956), pp. 156–167; S.L. Grigoriev, *The Diaghilev Ballet, 1909–1929*, trans. by Vera Bowen (New York: Dance Horizons, 1953), pp. 109–119. For Nijinsky in particular, see Anatole Bourman, *The Tragedy of Nijinsky* (Westport, Connecticut: Greenwood Press, 1970), pp. 246–266.

14. State Department Records, National Archives, Washington, D.C., Record Group 59, Decimal File 811.42761/2. Consul General Snodgrass to Secretary of State Knox, December 15, 1912; and Decimal File 811.42761/4, Snodgrass to Secretary of State Bryan, April 16, 1914. NOTE: Unless otherwise indicated, all State Department sources cited are located in Record Group 59 at the National Archives in Washington, D.C. Subsequent citations will not repeat "National Archives," "Record Group 59," or "Decimal File."

15. J.A. Posin, "Russian Studies in American Colleges," *Russian Review*, VII (Spring, 1948), p. 62; Paul V. Harper, ed., *The Russia I Believe In: The Memoirs of Samuel N. Harper* (Chicago: University of Chicago Press, 1945), pp. 8–9, 52; Robert F. Byrnes, "The Academic Labor Market: Where Do We Go From Here?" *Slavic Review*, June, 1977, p. 286.

16. U.S. Department of State, *Foreign Relations of the United States*, 1919, Vol. IV (Washington: Government Printing Office, 1937), p. 161. Cited hereafter as *FR*. *Ibid.*, 1920, III, p. 717. See also Joan Hoff Wilson, *Ideology and Economics: U.S. Relations with the Soviet Union, 1918–1933* (Columbia, Missouri: University of Missouri Press, 1974), pp. 33–36. For more concerning the immigration law of 1918, see p. 186.

17. *FR*, 1920, III, pp. 436–438.

18. For documentation concerning those arrested and deported, see *FR*, 1920, III, pp. 687–700. For a general description of the Red Scare, see Robert K. Murray, *Red Scare: A Study in National Hysteria, 1919–1920* (New York: McGraw Hill Book Company, 1964).

19. There is no intention here to enter the argument concerning Hoover's motives. The essential fact for present purposes is that the Soviet people gratefully received American relief, and that it favorably affected their attitude toward the United States.

20. Benjamin M. Weissman, *Herbert Hoover and Famine Relief to Russia, 1921–1923* (Stanford, California: Hoover Institution Press, 1974), p. 130.

21. *Ibid.*, p. 117.

22. *Ibid.*

23. *Ibid.*

24. H.H. Fisher, *The Famine in Soviet Russia, 1919–1923: The Operations of the American Relief Administration* (New York: The Macmillan Company, 1927), pp. 457–468.

25. *Ibid.*

26. *Ibid.*

27. *Literary Digest*, XCI (November 20, 1926), p. 37.

28. Edgar Rickard, "Engineers Work in Russia Through the Relief Administration," *Mining and Metallurgy*, III (November, 1922), p. 34; *New York Times*, February 10, 1924, sec. 4, p. 3. Cited hereafter as *NYT*.

29. These letters are contained in Box no. 6, Folder no. 1, Herbert Hoover Archives, A.R.A., Russian Operations, Hoover Institution on War, Revolution and Peace, Palo Alto, California. Cited hereafter as Hoover Archives.

30. J.F. Taylor, "Russian Actors under Soviet Rule," *Theatre Magazine*, V (May, 1922), p. 298.

31. *NYT*, March 28, 1922, p. 17. See also Weissman, *Hoover and Famine Relief*, p. 116.

32. *NYT*, March 28, 1922, p. 17.

33. *Ibid.*, April 10, 1922, p. 18.

34. Edwards, *Stanislavsky Heritage*, p. 226.

35. *Ibid.*, p. 227. See p. 29.

36. Oliver M. Sayler, *Inside the Moscow Art Theatre* (Westport, Connecticut: Greenwood Press Publishers, 1970), pp. 20–21. Originally published by Brentano's, New York, 1925. See also Edwards, *Stanislavsky Heritage*, pp. 220–226. *Theatre Magazine* particularly noted the activities of the MAT. See, for example, Oliver M. Sayler, "Europe's Premier Playhouse in the Offing," *Theatre Magazine*, XXXVI (October, 1922), p. 215.

37. Edwards, *Stanislavsky Heritage*, p. 226.

38. Sayler, *Inside the Moscow Art Theatre*, p. 18. During its second season the MAT played nine weeks in New York City, three in Chicago, and one each in Boston, Philadelphia, Pittsburgh, Detroit and Cleveland. See Edwards, *Stanislavsky Heritage*, p. 228. For specific examples of favorable comments, see "Those Amazing Moscow Players," *Literary Digest*, LXXIX (December 22, 1923), pp. 26–28; "The Muscovites Return," *Nation*, CXVII (December 5, 1923), p. 15; and Edmund Wilson, "The Moscow Players," *Dial*, LXXIV (March, 1923), pp. 319–320.

39. Edwards, *Stanislavsky Heritage*, pp. 227–229.

40. Sayler, *Inside the Moscow Art Theatre*, pp. 31–32. The MAT, according to *Theatre Magazine*, earned $47,500 during its first week in New York, slightly more in the second. In contrast, an American-produced Gorki play had earned only $200 per night the previous season. *Theatre Magazine*, XXXVII (March, 1923), p. 39.

41. Sayler, *Inside the Moscow Art Theatre*, p. 32.

42. *Ibid.*

43. Jerome Lachenbruch, *Nation*, CXVI (February 7, 1923), p. 156.

44. *NYT*, December 26, 1922, p. 5.

45. *Ibid.*, December 27, 1922, p. 10.

46. *Ibid.* See also Sayler, *Inside the Moscow Art Theatre*, p. 218.

47. *Literary Digest*, LXXVI (February 3, 1923), p. 30. Some of the MAT's valuable stage sets were lost in a warehouse fire, but there was no suggestion that this was anything other than an accident. *NYT*, April 16, 1923, p. 1.

48. Edwards, *Stanislavsky Heritage*, pp. 239–280.

49. *Ibid.*, p. 261.

50. *Chaliapine*, Pages From My Life, pp. 321–328. See also, "Chaliapin—Another Three," *Literary Digest*, LXXI (December 31, 1921), pp. 24–25.

51. Sol Hurok, *Impresario* (Westport, Connecticut: Greenwood Press Publishers, 1946), pp. 89–118.

52. See, for example, Anatole Bourman's comments in Bourman, *Tragedy of Nijinsky*, pp. 70–72. Bourman was Nijinsky's fellow dancer and accompanist. See also Ivan Narodny, "American Jazz and Russian Ballet: The Rhythmic Reformers of Russia and America," *Theatre Magazine*, XLIII (October, 1925), p. 12.

53. *NYT*, March 6, 1924, p. 17. See also, *Ibid.*, January 15, 1924, p. 3; *Ibid.*, March 9, 1924, sec. 1, part 2, p. 5; and *Ibid.*, April 18, 1924, p. 19.

54. Hibben was the person who originally suggested the exhibition to the All-Russian Central Relief Committee. *NYT*, April 6, 1924, p. 5.

55. See, for example, *NYT*, March 2, 1924, sec. 4, p. 11; *Ibid.*, April 6, 1924, p. 5; and *Ibid.*, April 18, 1924, p. 19.

56. See p. 40.

57. *NYT*, June 29, 1923, p. 20.

58. Ruth Epperson Kennell, *Theodore Dreiser and the Soviet Union: A First Hand Chronicle* (New York: International Publishers, 1969), pp. 230–234. Kennell, who had gone to the Soviet Union in the early twenties as a member of the Kuzbas Colony (see p. 34), was Dreiser's guide and interpreter during the Soviet tour, and upon returning to the United States, his friend and correspondent.

59. *Ibid.* See also *NYT*, June 2, 1929, sec. 8, p. 9.

60. Sol Hurok presented most of the ballet stars. See Hurok, *Impresario*, pp. 186–236; and the same author's *S. Hurok Presents: A Memoir of the Dance World* (New York: Hermitage House, 1953), pp. 105–182.

61. For examples, see *Science*, XLIX (June 27, 1919), pp. 613–614; *Ibid.*, LI (March 26, 1920), pp. 322–323; and *Ibid.*, LIV (November 25, 1921), pp. 510–511.

62. *Science*, LIV (November 25, 1921), pp. 510–511.

63. *Ibid.*, LV (June 23, 1922), pp. 667–668.

64. Among the largest contributors were the Smithsonian Institution, the American Society of Mechanical Engineers, the American Chemical Society, the Carnegie Institute and United States Geological Survey. Fisher, *Famine in Soviet Russia*, p. 468. See also *Science*, LVI (November 3, 1922), pp. 504–505; and *Science*, LVIII (October 5, 1923), p. 264.

65. *Science*, LVI (November 3, 1922), pp. 504–505.

66. Fisher, *Famine in Soviet Russia*, p. 466.

67. *Science*, LVI (September 8, 1922), pp. 279–281.

68. For Gorki's appeal, see *Science*, LVI (October 8, 1922), pp. 389–390.

69. Walter Bradford Cannon, *The Way of An Investigator: A Scientist's Experiences in Medical Research* (New York: W.W. Norton Company, 1945), pp. 184–185.

70. Hoover Archives, Box 319, Folder titled "Relief Organizations-Student Friendship Fund."

71. Letter from Nikolai Borodin to Harvey B. Peairs, Lawrence, Kansas, December 21, 1921, Papers of the Haskell Institute, "Correspondence of a General Nature, 1917–1942," No. 53-A224-161, Federal Records Center of the National Archives, Kansas City, Missouri. See also *Science*, XLIX (June 27, 1919), pp. 613–614; and Herman J. Muller, "Observations of Biological Sciences in Russia," *Scientific Monthly*, XVI (January–June, 1923), p. 552.

72. Cannon, *The Way of an Investigator*, pp. 185–186. See also B.P. Babkin, *Pavlov: A Biography* (Chicago: University of Chicago Press, 1949), pp. 105–107. While in New York City, Pavlov was accosted and robbed on a station platform, whereupon Cannon persuaded him to accept a Rockefeller Institute offer to replace the stolen money. To the surprise of Americans accustomed to reading of the dangers in Soviet Russia, Pavlov remarked that he wanted to return home where it was safe! Both Cannon and Babkin relate the incident.

73. Muller, "Observations of Biological Science in Russia," pp. 539–552.

74. *Ibid.*, p. 552.

75. *Ibid.*, p. 539. The published list is in *Science*, LVII (April 20, 1923), p. 472.

76. T.D.A. Cockerell, "A Journey in Siberia," *Scientific Monthly*, XIX (Oct., 1924), p. 416.

77. *Ibid.*, pp. 415–433.

78. H.J. Muller, *Man's Future Birthright: Essays on Science and Humanity*, ed. by Elof Axel Carlson (Albany: State University of New York Press, 1973). See introduction by Bentley Glass, p. xi. See also *Science*, LXXXIV (December 18, 1936), pp. 555–556.

79. For some of the more prominent travelers, see Lewis S. Feuer, "American Travelers to the Soviet Union, 1917–1934: The Formation of a Component of New Deal Ideology," *American Quarterly*, XIV (Summer, 1962), pp. 118–149. For an interesting article concerning the activities of those who went to the Soviet Union very early, see Lewis S. Gannett, "Americans in Russia," *Nation*, CXIII (August 17, 1921), pp. 167–169. According to Gannett, fifteen thousand Russian-Americans returned through Libau alone between December, 1920, and March, 1921, after which the Soviets allowed only cooperative groups to enter. For an example of a Soviet appeal to organized groups of workers, agricultural and industrial cooperatives, etc., see the advertisement placed by the American representative of the Supreme Council of the National Economy of the RSFSR, in *Nation*, CXIV (January 4, 1922), p. 17.

80. Robert M. LaFollette, "What I Saw in Europe," *LaFollette's Magazine*, XVI (January, 1924), pp. 4–6.

81. Feuer, "Travelers to the Soviet Union," pp. 129–132; Lillian D. Wald, "Public Health in Soviet Russia," *Survey*, LIII (December 1, 1924), pp. 270–274. See also Lillian D. Wald, *Windows on Henry Street* (Boston: Little, Brown and Company, 1934), pp. 255–271.

82. Donald Day, *Will Rogers: A Biography* (New York: David McKay Company, 1962), pp. 188–190.

83. Magidoff, "American Literature in Russia," p. 45.

84. Maurice Hindus, "American Authors in Russia," *Saturday Review of Literature*, I (August 16, 1925), p. 50.

85. Louis Fischer, "What They Read in Russia," *Nation*, CXXI (November 11, 1925), pp. 538–539. See also Brent Dow Allison, "From the Cultural Front in Russia," *Dial*, LXXXV (September, 1928), pp. 239–245.

86. Fischer, "What They Read in Russia," pp. 538–539.

87. State Department, 811.42761/11, Legation at Riga, Latvia, to State Department, September 16, 1924.

88. Hindus, "American Authors in Russia," p. 51.

89. Kennell, *Dreiser*, p. 65. These figures were cited by the president of the Soviet State Publishing House at a Moscow dinner attended by Dreiser.

90. Franz Horst, "Eugene O'Neill in Soviet Russia," *Poet Lore*, XCIX, pp. 242–247. See also letter from the associate editor of *Russky Golos* to the editors on *Nation* on the popularity of "Anna Christie" in the USSR. *Nation*, CXX (March 4, 1925), p. 125.

91. Paxton Hibben, "The Movies in Russia," *Nation*, CXXI (November 11, 1925), pp. 539–540; *NYT*, July 28, 1926, p. 33.

92. Hibben, "Movies in Russia," p. 539.

93. *NYT*, December 19, 1926, sec. 7, pt. 2. Letter from Leon S. Zamkovov, general director of Soviet film activities in the U.S. to the editors of the *NYT*.

94. See p. 29. The interest was also reflected in the fact that Americans wrote more about the Soviet film industry, and in the writings of Soviet producers in American publications. For two examples, see Sergei Mikhailovich Eisenstein, "Mass Movies," *Nation*, CXXV (November 9, 1927), pp. 507–508, and Joseph Wood Krutch, "The Season in Moscow: Eisenstein and Lunacharsky," *Ibid.*, CXXVI (June 27, 1928), pp. 716–717.

95. Juri Jelagin, *Taming of the Arts*, trans. by Nicholas Wreden (New York: E.P.

Dutton and Company, 1951), pp. 254–256. Jelagin was the concertmaster of the USSR State Jazz Band during the thirties. After being freed from a German prisoner of war camp at the end of World War II he made to the United States, and at the time of publication was a violinist with the Houston Symphony Orchestra. See also Sidney Bechet, *Treat it Gentle* (New York: Hill and Wang, 1960), pp. 147–148; Time, LXXVII (March 10, 1961), p. 34; and R. Blum, "Letter from Leningrad," *New Yorker*, XXXVII (July 14, 1962), pp. 81–82.

96. Jelagin, *Taming of the Arts*, pp. 256–257.

97. *Ibid.*

NOTES TO CHAPTER II

1. This information taken from a letter written by Boris Skirvsky to the editors of *Nation. Nation*, CXX (June 17, 1925), p. 692.

2. *Ibid.* See also *Nation*, CXX (January 20, 1925), p. 53.

3. *FR*, 1921, p. 750.

4. State Department, 811.42761/13, editor of *Safety Engineering* to Secretary of State Hughes, March 2, 1925. See attached circular.

5. State Department, 811.42761/14, Skirvsky to editors of *Oil Engine Power*, March 4, 1925; State Department, 811.42761/17, Russian Information Bureau to American Book Company, April 18, 1925; and State Department, 811.42761/13, Skirvsky to editors of *Safety Engineering*, March 11, 1925.

6. State Department, 811.42761/13, Evan B. Young to editors of *Safety Engineering*, March 11, 1925.

7. State Department, 032 American Society for Cultural Relations with Russia. (This document has no further identifying numbers. It is located in Box no. 303, from 032AM32 to 032 Armstrong. The document itself consists of a report submitted by Francis Ralston Welch to the Division of Eastern European Affairs, dated May 18, 1928). See also *NYT*, April 24, 1927, p. 2.

8. *NYT*, April 27, 1929, sec. 11, p. 5.

9. *Ibid.*, January 27, 1929, sec. 3, p. 7; and State Department, 811.42761/42, Osgood Field to Lawrence Duggan, December 5, 1934.

10. Files of the Library for Intercultural Studies, located in the Bobst Library, New York University. Cited hereafter as LICS Files. NOTE: The Library for Intercultural Studies contains the papers and records of what was originally the Society for Cultural Relations with Russia, subsequently the New York American-Russian Institute. Some of the files are contained in marked folders; others, particularly those containing scattered information about the original society, in unmarked containers. When possible the folder title will be identified along with specific documents. Mr. Bernard Koten, an early member of the American-Russian Institute and long the director of its language school, is the director of the Library. For a published account of the holdings and activities of the Library for Intercultural Studies, see Bernard Koten, "Library for Soviet Research," *Library Journal*, LXXXI (November 15, 1957), pp. 2874–2875.

11. For examples of specific exhibits and activities, see pp. 30–31.

12. Toby Cole, "A Library on the Soviet Union," *Library Journal*, LXX (May 15, 1945), pp. 476–479. The same article appears in shortened form in *Wilson Library Bulletin*, XX (November, 1945), p. 20. Cole was the librarian for the American-Russian Institute.

13. Especially during World War II. See pp. 63–65. The clipping file is still located at the LICS, though not in the same indexed form as earlier.

14. *NYT*, January 27, 1929, sec. 3, p. 7.

15. *Ibid.*

16. State Department, 811.42761/64, plus enclosure No. 1, Charge d'Affaires Loy Henderson to Hull, August 15, 1936.

17. *Ibid.*

18. *Ibid.*

19. *Ibid.*

20. State Department, 811.42761/18, enclosure No. 2, American Legation at Riga,

Latvia, to Secretary of State Kellog, July 12, 1925. For Duggan's role in founding the IIE, see Stephen P. Duggan, *A Professor at Large* (New York: Macmillan Press, 1943), pp. 1–87. For his trip to Moscow, see pp. 191–201.

21. "Soviet-American Cultural Relations: A Review Since 1917," *Institute of International Education News Bulletin*, XXXII (October, 1956), pp. 17–18.

22. *Ibid.*

23. *Ibid.*

24. *NYT*, September 9, 1925, p. 27; State Department, 811.111 Russian Students/17, Simpson, Thacher and Bartlett to American Consul, Berlin, July 1, 1931. See also State Department 811.111 Russian Students/48, State Department to Consul at Berlin, transmitting Labor Department authorization for students to enter the United States, September 16, 1931; and State Department, 811.42761/64, Henderson to Hull, August 15, 1936.

25. See pp. 54–57.

26. Harriet G. Eddy, "Beginnings of United Library Services in USSR," *Library Journal*, LVII (January 15, 1932), pp. 61–67. See also *Libraries*, XXXVI (April, 1931), pp. 158–159.

27. Eddy, "Library Services in USSR," pp. 66–67.

28. *Ibid.*

29. "Libraries in Soviet Russia," *Literary Digest*, XCIII (April 9, 1927), p. 28.

30. *FR*, 1922, II, pp. 825–834.

31. *NYT*, August 5, 1928, sec. 2, p. 13.

32. *Ibid.*, May 2, 1926, sec. 2, p. 4; *Ibid.*, October 23, 1927, sec. 2, p. 13; and *Ibid.*, September 6, 1928, p. 6.

33. *Ibid.*, July 15, 1932, secs. 2&3, p. 7. For groups from Bates College and Syracuse University, and for a report of approximately one hundred delegates representing the Student Council of New York, see *Ibid.*, June 25, 1927, p. 15, and *Ibid.*, April 3, 1927, sec. 2, p. 1.

34. See Chapter III.

35. Feuer, "American Travelers," pp. 123–125.

36. *Ibid.*, pp. 119–149. See also Peter G. Filene, *Americans and the Soviet Experiment: 1917–1933* (Cambridge: Harvard University Press, 1967).

37. *NYT*, December 15, 1927, p. 31.

38. State Department, 032 American Society for Cultural Relations with Russia/1, Kellog to Coleman, May 26, 1928; and State Department 032 American Society for Cultural Relations with Russia/7, Sussdorf to Kellog, transmitting letter written by Dewey to Commissar of Education Lunacharsky upon the delegation's departure, September 19, 1928.

39. Lunacharsky particularly admired Dewey and promoted his ideas, as did the eminent Soviet educator, A.P. Pinkevitch. For Dewey's influence in the Soviet Union see William W. Brickman, "John Dewey's Foreign Reputation as an Educator," *School and Society*, LXX (October 22, 1948), pp. 257–265. Dewey first published his impressions in five installments in the November and December, 1928 issues of the *New Republic*, and later in his *Impressions of Soviet Russia and the Revolutionary World* (New York: New Republic, Inc., 1929), pp. 3–133. For some of his comments upon returning from the USSR, see *NYT*, December 16, 1928, sec. 2, p. 6.

40. *NYT*, July 22, 1928, p. 6.

41. *Ibid.*, June 21, 1928, p. 8.

42. State Department, 032 American Society for Cultural Relations with Russia/3, Kolbe to Kellog, January 13, 1928. For the State Department's reaction, see p. 31.

43. *NYT*, July 2, 1928, p. 19.

44. *Ibid.*, June 24, 1928, sec. 3, p. 4.

45. For examples of Soviet tourist advertising, featuring several different companies and types of tours, see *Nation*, CXXIX (November 27, 1929), p. 641; *Ibid.* (December 4, 1929), p. 672; *Ibid.*, CXXXII (May 13, 1931), p. 451; and *Ibid.* (May 27, 1931), p. 594.

46. *NYT*, May 11, 1928, p. 51; Joseph Barnes, "Cultural Recognition of Russia," *Nation*, CXXXVI (May 18, 1932), pp. 565.

47. "Russia Bids for the Tourist Trade," *Review of Reviews*, LXXXIV (August, 1931), pp. 94–96. See also Amy S. Jennings, "How to Travel in Soviet Russia," *Nation*, CXXXVI (May 19, 1933), pp. 528–529.

48. Barnes, "Cultural Recognition," p. 565.

49. Figures vary somewhat according to source, but are generally consistent. Barnes states that 2,800 went in 1929, 5,000 in 1930, and 9,000 in 1931. Barnes, "Cultural Recognition," p. 565. *Review of Review* cites the figures as 2,200 in 1929, 5,000 in 1930, and 10,000 anticipated in 1931. "Russia Bids," *Review of Reviews*, p. 94. *Fortune* states that 10,000 went in 1931. "Russia, Russia, Russia," *Fortune*, V (March, 1931), p. 57.

50. Jennings, "Travel," pp. 528–529; "Russia Bids," *Review of Reviews*, p. 94.

51. Filene, *Americans and the Soviet Experiment*, p. 224. Corliss and Margaret Lamont, *Russia Day by Day: A Travel Diary* (New York: Covici-Friede Publishers, 1933), pp. 24–25. According to the Lamonts, the Soviets purchased the Lincolns in connection with the Ford contract to build an automobile plant at Nizhni-Novgorod. See pp. 35–36.

52. Filene, p. 60. See also *NYT*, July 18, 1929, p. 9.

53. Filene, p. 60.

54. Oswald Garrison Villard, "Russia from a Car Window," *Nation*, CXXXIX (November 6, 1929), pp. 515–517.

55. Kennell, *Dreiser*, and Theodore Dreiser, *Dreiser Looks at Russia* (New York: Horace Liverwright, 1928). Dreiser's opinions and comments are scattered throughout both books.

56. Barnes, "Cultural Recognition," p. 565.

57. Albert Parry, "Soviet Writers View America," *Bookman*, LXXIII (August, 1930), p. 580. For further treatment of the United States in Soviet literature, see Vera Alexandrova, "America and Americans in Soviet Literature," *Russian Review*, II (Spring, 1943), pp. 19–25; and Ina Telberg, "Heroes and Villains in Soviet Drama," *American Sociological Review*, IX (June, 1944), pp. 308–311.

58. Tansey McNab, "The Soviet Invasion of America," *Nation*, CXXV (August, 1930), p. 529; *NYT*, May 13, 1926, p. 10; Oliver Sayler, "The Lyric Daughter of the Sober Russians," *Theatre Magazine*, XLII (September, 1925), pp. 12–13; Paul Bechert, "Habima — A Theatre for Jewish People," *Theatre Magazine*, XLIV (November, 1926), pp. 20–21; *Theatre Magazine*, XLIII (June, 1926), p. 34; and Chaliapine, *Pages from My Life*, pp. 329–345.

59. Parry, "Soviet Writers," p. 380; Norman Swallow, *Eisenstein: A Documentary Portrait* (London: George Allen and Unwin, 1976), pp. 58–59, and Edmund Wilson, "Eisenstein in Hollywood," *New Republic*, LXVIII (November 4, 1921), pp. 320–322.

60. Swallow, Eisenstein, pp. 85–89; and Wilson, "Eisenstein in Hollywood," pp. 320–322.

61. For an interesting and detailed account of subsequent efforts by Upton Sinclair and Eisenstein to produce a film in Mexico, see Harry M. Geduld and Ronald Gottesman, *Sergei Eisenstein and Upton Sinclair: The Making and Unmaking of "Que Viva Mexico"* (Bloomington: Indiana University Press, 1970).

62. See Chapter III.

63. *NYT*, August 1, 1927, p. 36. See also McNab, "Soviet Invasion," p. 529.

64. Cannon, *The Way of an Investigator*, p. 187; and Dvoichenko-Markov, "The American Philosophical Society," p. 529.

65. McNab, "Soviet Invasion," p. 529.

66. Press Releases, LICS Files, unmarked folder. See also *NYT*, May 29, 1927, sec. 2, p. 1.

67. LICS Files, unmarked folder. See also *NYT*, January 29, 1928, sec. 2, p. 5; *Ibid.*, January 30, 1928, p. 18; and *Ibid.*, January 31, 1928, p. 7.

68. Amtorg was the official Soviet trading agency in the United States.

69. Robert Littell, "Soviet Arts and Handicrafts," *New Republic*, LVIII (February 20, 1929), pp. 16–17; *Literary Digest*, C (February 23, 1929), pp. 22–23.

70. *NYT*, February 11, 1929, p. 11.

71. *Ibid.*, February 1. 1929, p. 16.

72. State Department, 811.42761/42. Osgood Field to Lawrence Duggan, December 5, 1934. See attached, unmarked enclosures, including pamphlet. For the protest mentioned above, see "Icon Exhibit Draws Protest," *Art News*, XXIX (January 10, 1931), p. 7. For other examples and comments, see Lee Simonson, "Exhibition of Russian Icons," *Metropolitan Museum Bulletin*, XXVI (January, 1931), pp. 2–6; H.S. Francis, "Exhibitions of Russian Icons Circulated by the ARI," *Cleveland Museum Bulletin*, XXIX (February, 1932), pp. 25–26; and

M.S. Dimand, "Exhibitions of Russian Icons," *Parnassus*, CXI (February, 1931), pp. 35–36. Dozens of such articles appeared in trade magazines, particularly in *Art News* and *Art Digest*.

73. State Department, 811.42761/42, Field to Duggan, December 5, 1934; LICS Files, press clippings, unmarked folders. See also *NYT*, June 16, 1932, p. 23; and *Ibid.*, June 19, 1932, sec. 9, p. 8.

74. *NYT*, May 19, 1932, p. 18. New York architect Hector O. Hamilton shared first place in a competition to design the proposed Palace of the Soviets, to be the largest building in the world. The building was started but never completed. See *Architecture*, LXV (April, 1932), pp. 203–204; and *Architectural Record*, LXXI (April, 1932), p. 278.

75. Frederick C. Barghoorn, *The Soviet Cultural Offensive: The Role of Cultural Diplomacy in Soviet Foreign Policy* (Princeton: Princeton University Press, 1960), p. 32.

76. State Department, 032 American Society for Cultural Relations with Russia/4, Kelley to Kolbe, January 28, 1928.

77. State Department, 811.42761/23, State Department of Microbiology and Epidemiology, Saratov, USSR, January 8, 1930. See enclosure also.

78. *Ibid.*, Treasury Department to State Department, February 7, 1930.

79. *Ibid.*, Cotton to Mellon, March 6, 1930.

80. State Department, 811.42761/24, Mellon to State Department, March 12, 1930; *Ibid.*, Cotton to Mellon, March 24, 1930.

81. State Department, 861.01 B11/50, State Department to Agriculture Department, June 11, 1930.

82. State Department, 811.111 Russian Students/24, Consul at Berlin to State Department, August 10, 1931; and State Department 811.42761/48, State Department to Consul at Berlin, September 16, 1931. The State Department instructed the consul, who suggested rejecting the student visa applications on the grounds that the students believed in and worked for communism, and were therefore ineligible to enter the country under the immigration law of 1918, to grant the necessary visas under the Ninth Proviso of Section 3 of the Immigration Act of 1917. The 1918 law excluded from the country aliens "who are anarchists ... who believe in or advocate the overthrow by force or violence of the Government of the United States ... who are members or are affiliated with any organization that entertains a belief in, teaches, or advocates the overthrow by force or violence of the Government of the United States or all forms of law...." *An Act to Exclude and Expel from the United States Aliens Who are Members of the Anarchistic and Similar Classes*, *Statutes at Large*, XL, sec. 1, p. 1012 (1918). Proviso Nine of the 1917 act stated that "The Provisions of this law applying to contract labor shall not held to exclude professional actors, artists, lecturers, singers, nurses, ministers of any religious denomination, professors for colleges or seminaries, persons belonging to any recognized learned profession, or persons employed as domestic servants." *Immigration Act of 1917*, Statutes at Large, XXXIX, sec. 3, pp. 877–878 (1917).

NOTES TO CHAPTER III

1. *FR*, 1944, IV, p. 973.

2. Bernard Knollenberg, "American Business in Russia," *Nation's Business*, VIII (April, 1930), p. 266.

3. The part of this chapter outlining America's technical contributions to Soviet development draws heavily from Anthony C. Sutton's admirable and massively documented study, *Western Technology and Soviet Economic Development*. To admire Sutton's work is not, however, necessarily to agree with the argument carried throughout its three volumes that the Soviets turned to the United States and other western nations because their socialist system was incapable of fostering and maintaining technological advancement. One could just as easily argue that, entering the technological era late, the Soviets saw no reason to duplicate the long process of self-development, choosing instead to buy the best hardware and knowledge that the West had to offer. See Anthony C. Sutton, *Western Technology and Soviet Economic Development* (3 vols.; Stanford: Stanford University Press, 1968–1973).

4. Sutton, *Western Technology*, I, pp. 49–52. For a personal description of the Kuzbas colony, see Ruth Epperson Kennell, "Kuzbas Tells Its Own Story," *Nation*, CXVII (August 8, 1923), pp. 145–147, and the same author's "Kuzbas in 1924," *Ibid.*, CXIX (November 26, 1924), pp. 566–568.

5. Sutton, *Western Technology*, I, pp. 126–127.

6. *Ibid.*

7. *Ibid.*, pp. 226–231.

8. *Ibid.* For text of agreement, see *Nation*, CXIV (June 22, 1922), p. 728.

9. Armand Hammer, *The Quest of the Romanoff Treasure* (New York: Payson, 1932), pp. 32–44. Sutton, *Western Technology*, I, pp. 126–127.

10. Sutton, *Western Technology*, I, pp. 18–34. See also *NYT*, February 10, 1924, sec. 4, p. 3, and *NYT*, April 19, 1928, p. 5.

11. Sutton, *Western Technology*, I, p. 37.

12. J. Stalin, *Voprosy Leninisma* (Moscow, 1945), p. 373.

13. Allan Nevins and Frank Ernest Hill, *Ford: Expansion and Challenge, 1915–1933* (New York: Charles Scribner's Sons, 1957), p. 673.

14. *Ibid.*, p. 676.

15. Sutton, *Western Technology*, I, p. 245.

16. Nevins and Hill, *Ford: Expansion and Challenge*, p. 677.

17. *Ibid.*, pp. 677–681.

18. *Ibid.*, pp. 678–681.

19. *Ibid.*

20. *Ibid.*

21. *Ibid.*, p. 683.

22. Henry Ford, "Why I am Helping Russian Industry," *Nation's Business*, XVIII (June 1930), pp. 20–23.

23. Sutton, *Western Technology*, I, p. 141.

24. *Ibid.*

25. *Ibid.*, p. 137.

26. Sutton, *Western Technology*, II, p. 185.

27. *Ibid.*, p. 187.

28. George Nelson, *Industrial Architecture of Albert Kahn, Inc.* (New York: Architectural Book Publishing Company, 1939), pp. 17–18.

29. Sutton, *Western Technology*, II, p. 249.

30. Nelson, *Industrial Architecture of Albert Kahn*, p. 19.

31. Sutton, *Western Technology*, I, p. 72; *Ibid.*, p. 75.

32. Sutton, *Western Technology*, II, p. 62.

33. *Ibid.*, pp. 63–77.

34. *Ibid.*, p. 63.

35. *Ibid.*, p. 61.

36. Sutton, *Western Technology*, I, pp. 51–52.

37. *Ibid.*

38. *Ibid.*

39. V. Karmashov, "Non-Ferrous Metal Industry in Soviet Russia," *Engineers and Mining Journal*, CXXX (July 24, 1930), pp. 67–68.

40. Sutton, *Western Technology*, I, pp. 106, 108.

41. John D. Littlepage and Demaree Bess, *In Search of Soviet Gold* (New York: Harcourt, Brace and Company, 1937), pp. 68, 87–88.

42. Sutton, *Western Technology*, I, p. 54.

43. *Ibid.*, p. 198.

44. Sutton, *Western Technology*, II, p. 163.

45. Sutton, *Western Technology*, I, p. 250.

46. *Ibid.*

47. *Ibid.*, pp. 195–200.

48. *Ibid.*, pp. 219–235.

49. Sutton, *Western Technology*, I, p. 120.

50. *Ibid.*

51. Sutton, *Western Technology*, II, pp. 34–35.

52. Sutton, *Western Technology*, I, pp. 37, 222; Sutton, *Western Technology*, II, p. 184.

53. *NYT*, September 26, 1926, p. 9; State Department 811.42761/65, Henderson to Hull, transmitting statement by the Moscow representative of International Business Machines, December 12, 1936. See also State Department 811.42761/66, Henderson to Hull, December 25, 1936, with enclosure no. 1.

54. Sutton, quoting Soviet sources, places the number at 1700. Sutton, II, p. 11; Andrew Steiger puts the number at 1500 between 1928 and 1932. Andrew Steiger, *American Engineers in the Soviet Union* (New York, 1944), p. 4. In addition, a large number of technicians and workers went to the USSR in the early thirties. According to *Business Week*, Amtorg received over 100,000 applications for 6,000 positions which it filled in 1931. See *Business Week*, September 2, 1931, pp. 36–37, and *Ibid.*, October 7, 1931, pp. 32–33. For a listing of the American companies holding technical assistance contracts in 1930, and a map locating their projects, see *Business Week*, July 16, 1930, pp. 24–25.

55. Maurice Hindus, "Pinch-Hitter for the Soviets," *American Magazine*, CXIII (April, 1932), pp. 31–33. For a particularly interesting and informative article concerning American engineers in the USSR, see William Henry Chamberlin, "Missionaries of American Technique in Russia," *Asia*, XXXII (July, 1932), pp. 422–427.

56. Telberg, "Heroes and Villains," p. 311; Hindus, "Pinch-Hitter," p. 31. For Nikolai Pogodin's play, "Tempo," see Eugence D. Lyons, *Six Soviet Plays* (New York: Houghton-Mifflin, 1934), pp. 157–224.

57. State Department, 811.42761/2, Consul General Snodgrass, Moscow, to Secretary of State Knox, transmitting articles by Professor Ozerov, Moscow University, December 25, 1912.

58. State Department, 811.42761/4, Snodgrass to Secretary of State Bryan, April 16, 1914. Zemstvos were units of local administration that supplemented the actions of the rural peasant communes which developed in Russia following the emancipation of the serfs in the mid-1800's.

59. Hammer, *Quest*, p. 62.

60. *Ibid.*

61. Rene Fuelop-Miller, *The Mind and Face of Bolshevism: An Examination of Cultural Life in the Soviet Union*, trans. by F.S. Flint and D.F. Tait (New York: Harper and Row, 1965), p. 49. First printed in the German language in 1926; first published in the U.S. in 1927 by G.P. Putnam's Sons.

62. *Ibid.* Oblomov, the central figure in Ivan A. Goncharov's novel, *Oblomov*, epitomized the laziness, lack of will and dreamy inefficiency that characterized a portion of the Russian landed nobility.

63. Joseph Stalin, *Foundations of Leninism* (Moscow: Foreign Languages Publishing House, 1954), p. 158.

64. Emil Ludwig, *Nine Etched from Life* (New York: Robert M. McBride Company, 1934), p. 376. But Stalin also made it clear that the admiration did not extend to all parts of American life. We never forget, he further remarked to Ludwig, "that it is a capitalist land." In 1932 Stalin also stated that "we observe the United States with interest, since this country ranks high as regards science and technique. We should be glad to have American scientists and technicians as our teachers and in the technical field to be their pupils." See Z. Suchkov, "Soviet Industry and the U.S.," *Review of the Soviet Union*, February 2, 1934, p. 45.

65. Nevins and Hill, *Ford: Expansion and Challenge*, p. 604. State Department, 811.42761/22, reference to Rykov's comments before the Fifth Congress of Soviets, July 19, 1929.

66. Frederick C. Barghoorn, *The Soviet Image of the United States: A Study in Distortion* (Port Washington, New York: Kennikat Press, 1969), p. 35.

67. *Ibid.*

68. By 1930 the Society for Cultural Relations with Russia was referring to itself as the American-Russian Institute, though it did not incorporate under that name until 1936.

69. Speech by Ambassador Alexander A. Troyanovsky at an ARI dinner honoring Troyanovsky and U.S. Ambassador to the Soviet Union William Bullitt, January 24, 1934, Brown Folder, LICS Files.

70. Sutton, *Western Technology*, II, p. 195.
71. *NYT*, May 29, 1927, sec. 2, p. 1.
72. State Department, 711.61/525, Bullitt to Hull, June 6, 1935.
73. *Ibid.*, enclosure no. 1. Bogdanov gave lengthy examples in his article to illustrate how each of these principles was applied in America.
74. *Ibid.*
75. *Ibid.* Underlined in the original.
76. *Ibid.*
77. State Department, 711.61/527, Bullitt transmitting Bogdanov's remarks, June 22, 1935, with enclosure no. 1.
78. *Ibid.*
79. *Ibid.*
80. Joan Hoff Wilson, *Ideology and Economics: U.S. Relations with the Soviet Union, 1918–1933* (Columbia: University of Missouri Press, 1974), p. 8.
81. For examples, see Nevins and Hill, *Ford: Expansion and Challenge*, p. 681, and Sutton, *Western Technology*, II, p. 347.
82. Barghoorn, *Image*, p. 30.
83. Sutton, *Western Technology*, II.
84. Barghoorn, *Image*, p. 53.
85. Fleming speech at ARI dinner, May 16, 1945, Folder FR/US, 1945, Organizations-General, LICS Files.
86. Speech by B.G. Skramataev, Soviet Purchasing Commission, at ARI dinner, October 19, 1944, Folder Organizations-General, 1944, LICS Files.
87. See p. 33.
88. Barghoorn, *Image*, p. 240.
89. *Ibid.*
90. *NYT*, February 10, 1924, sec. 4, p. 3.
91. *Ibid.*
92. Eugene Lyons, *Assignment in Utopia* (New York: Harcourt, Brace and Company, 1937), p. 63.
93. Knollenberg, "American Business in Russia," p. 266.
94. *Ibid.* For further comments concerning Soviet admiration of America and the "Amerikansky tempo," see Walter Arnold Rukeyser, "I Work for the Soviets: The Worker at Work," *Nation*, CXXXII (May 27, 1931), pp. 577–579, and Rukeyser, "Do Our Engineers in Russia Damage America?" *Scribner's Magazine*, XC (November, 1931), pp. 521–523. Rukeyser was one of the engineers in the Soviet Union.
95. Barghoorn, *Image*, pp. 30–37.
96. See p. 90.
97. Maurice Hindus, "Ford Conquers Russia," *Outlook*, CXLVI (June 29, 1927), p. 281.
98. Nevins and Hill, *Ford: Expansion and Challenge*, pp. 604, 673. A succinct Soviet view of Ford and "Fordisimus" is contained in *Bolshaya Sovetskaya Entsiklopediya*, Vol. 58 (Moscow, first Edition, 1936).
99. *Ibid.*
100. *Ibid.*, p. 694.
101. Eric Johnston, *We're All in It* (New York: E.P. Dutton and Company, 1950), pp. 81–82.
102. Hindus, "Ford Conquers Russia," p. 282. "How amazed the sage of Dearborn would be," Lyons wrote, "to realize that he occupied a prominent niche in every young communist's private pantheon." Lyons, *Assignment*, p. 63.
103. Nevins and Hill, *Ford: Expansion and Challenge*, p. 604.
104. Hindus, "Ford Conquers Russia," p. 283.

Notes to Chapter IV

1. Troyanovsky speech at ARI dinner, January 24, 1934, brown folder, LICS Files.
2. One writer stated in 1939, for example, that cultural contacts had increased "many

fold" since recognition, but the evidence does not support that assertion. See Themistocles Clayton Rodis, "Russo-American Contacts during the Hoover Administration," *South Atlantic Quarterly*, LI (April, 1952), pp. 235–245.

3. John Rothchild, "The Intelligent Traveler: Tours to the Soviet Union," *Nation*, CXXXVII (May 9, 1934), pp. 536–537; and Rothchild, *Ibid.*, CXL (May 1, 1935), pp. 506–508. Rothschild was the director of Open Road. See also, "Seeing Red: Russia Attracts Many Students," *Review of Reviews*, XCII (July, 1935), pp. 70–71; and "Russia Expects Many Tourists," *Literary Digest*, CXVII (June 9, 1934), p. 45.

4. Lyman P. Powell, "A Clergyman Looks at Russia," *Review of Reviews*, XC (October, 1934), pp. 62–63.

5. Rothschild, "Intelligent Traveler," May 1, 1935, p. 507.

6. *Ibid.* See also *NYT*, July 19, 1936, sec. 4, p. 4.

7. For examples of advertising see *NYT*, May 23, 1937, sec. 11, p. 9; *Travel*, LXV (June, 1935), pp. 52, 56; and *Travel*, LXIX (June, 1937), p. 35.

8 *NYT*, February 16, 1936, sec. 10, p. 4.

9. *Ibid.*

10. For directly opposed impressions and conclusions of what they observed, see Matthew Josephson, "From a Russian Notebook," *Travel*, LXIV (November, 1934), pp. 16–19; and J.C. Furnas, "Leningraduates," *Saturday Evening Post*, CCVIII (October 26, 1935), pp. 12–14; *Ibid.*, (November 3, 1935), pp. 32–35; and *Ibid.*, (November 9, 1935), pp. 16–18.

11. *NYT*, July 19, 1936, sec. 4, p. 4.

12. *Ibid.*, April 17, 1936, p. 12.

13. State Department, 032 American Society for Cultural Relations with Russia/4, Robert Kelley to Park Kolbe, January 28, 1928.

14. *Science*, LXXXII (August 16, 1935), pp. 153–154.

15. "The Fifteenth International Congress of Physiology: The Congress and Russian Physiology," *Ibid.*, (September 13, 1935), pp. 240–243; see also Dean Burk, "A Scientist in Moscow," *Scientific Monthly*, XLVII (September, 1938), pp. 227–231.

16. Frank Lloyd Wright, "Architecture and Life in the USSR," *Architectural Record*, LXXXVII (October, 1937), pp. 57–63; see also Simon Breines, *Ibid.*, pp. 63–65.

17. Virginia Hamilton, *Paul Robeson: The Life and Times of a Free Black Man* (New York: Harper and Row, 1974), pp. 54–64.

18. Marian Anderson, *My Lord What a Morning: An Autobiography* (New York: Viking Press, 1956), pp. 174–183; see also Sol Hurok, *Impresario* (Westport, Connecticut: Greenwood Press, 1946), pp. 247–250.

19. Moore, "Five Years of American-Soviet Relations," p. 30; *Time*, XXVII (March 9, 1936), p. 36; Nicholas Slonimsky, "Russia Revisited," *Modern Music*, XIII (November-December, 1935), pp. 21–25.

20. George Antheil, "Good Russian Advice About Movie Music," *Modern Music*, XIII (November-December, 1935), pp. 53–56; *NYT*, September 29, 1935, sec. 10, p. 4; Victor Seroff, *Sergei Prokofiev: A Soviet Tragedy* (London: Leslie Frewin, 1969), pp. 241–255.

21. William H. Standley and Arthur A. Ageton, *Admiral Ambassador to Russia* (Chicago: Henry Regnery Company, 1955), pp. 47–48. See also *NYT*, May 31, 1939, p. 1, for the flag incident, and, for a description of the Soviet pavilion and the tower supporting the red star, *NYT*, May 17, 1939, p. 20.

22. For the popularity of American literature see Magidoff, *In Anger and Pity*, pp. 223–235, and the same author's "American Literature in Russia," pp. 9–13. For Sholokhov, see Moore, "Five Years of American-Soviet Relations," p. 30. For films, see State Department, 811.000B/94, Messersmith to Hull, no date.

23. Jelagin, *Taming of the Arts*, pp. 257–264.

24. *Ibid.*, p. 263. Tsfasman and his band were so popular and independent, Jelagin wrote, that they "constituted the only private enterprise in the Soviet Union." They traveled in the best cars, ate in the best restaurants, wore the best clothes and drew fabulous incomes. "To arrest a general or a member of the Central Committee of the Party," Jelagin stated, "was easier than to arrest a member of the Tsfasman band." *Ibid.*, pp. 263–264.

25. State Department, 811.42761/42, Osgood Field to Lawrence Duggan, December 5, 1934. See attached pamphlet.

26. *Ibid.* See also *NYT*, November 13, 1936, p. 21; and *NYT*, November 22, 1936, sec. 10, p. 9.

27. State Department, 811.42761/42, Field to Duggan, December 5, 1934. See also *NYT*, January 16, 1935, p. 14, and *NYT*, January 20, 1934, sec. 9, p. 4.

28. *Pencil Points*, XVII (November, 1937), p. 24.

29. State Department, 811.42761/42, Field to Duggan, December 5, 1934.

30. "Report on a Dinner Given in Honor of the Soviet Trans-Polar Flyers by the Explorers Club and the American-Russian Institute," brown folder, LICS Files; and State Department 811.42761/42, Field to Duggan, December 5, 1934.

31. *Ibid.*

32. *Ibid.*

33. "The Story of a Long Friendship: The First Twenty-Five Years of the American-Russian Institute of San Francisco." Booklet located in the files of the San Francisco American-Russian Institute. As in the case of the New York ARI, many of the older documents and records possessed by the San Francisco ARI are located in unmarked folders. When possible the folders will be identified along with the documents; when not possible, the material will be cited simply as SF-ARI Files.

34. *Ibid.*

35. *Ibid.*

36. This conclusion is based on the correspondence, promotional literature and related material found in the SF-ARI Files, plus conversations with present and former members of the Institutes in both New York and San Francisco.

37. State Department, 861.40634/1, Bullitt to Kelley, April 20, 1934. Bullitt was able to equip four teams with a dozen balls, six bats, sixteen gloves, bases and other necessary equipment for a total of $170. State Department, 861.40634/3, Spalding Company to Kelley, April 26, 1934. For an interesting account of Bullitt, baseball and the Soviets, see Charles W. Thayer, *Bears in the Caviar* (Philadelphia: Lippincott Company, 1951). In 1934 and again in 1937, University of Alabama coach and athletic director Champ Pickens tried to take football, track, swimming and other athletic teams to the Soviet Union, but problems on both sides prevented him doing so. The 1934 correspondence is contained in State Department 861.40634/6 through /10; the 1937 correspondence in 861.4063/1 through /4.

38. In a letter to President Roosevelt written in August, 1934, Bullitt noted that "polo has brought not only myself but our military leaders into the closest relationship with the Red Army leaders and has been most useful," and that baseball has "helped to bring us into the closest relations with the Moscow Soviet." See Orville H. Bullitt, ed., *For the President, Personal and Secret: Correspondence Between Franklin D. Roosevelt and William C. Bullitt* (Boston: Houghton Mifflin Company, 1972), p. 93. See also Beatrice Farnsworth, *William C. Bullitt and the Soviet Union* (Bloomington: Indiana University Press, 1967), pp. 130-131.

39. Clare R. Reiss, *Composers, Conductors and Critics* (New York: Oxford University Press, 1955), p. 144.

40. Seroff, *Prokofiev*, pp. 213-218.

41. Fuelop-Miller, *Mind and Face of Bolshevism*, p. 291.

42. *Ibid.*, p. 292.

43. Marc Slonim, *Soviet Russian Literature: Writers and Problems, 1917-1977* (New York: Oxford University Press, 1977), pp. 277-291. See also Seroff, *Prokofiev*, pp. 256-265; Fuelop-Miller, *Mind and Face of Bolshevism*, pp. 300-302, and Jelagin, *Taming of the Arts*, pp. 208-212.

44. For a particularly good explanation of the status and treatment of the great composers, see Jelagin, *Taming of the Arts*, pp. 208-212.

45. *Ibid.*, pp. 266-267.

46. U.S. Department of State, *Foreign Relations of the United States: The Soviet Union, 1933-1939* (Washington: U.S. Government Printing Office, 1952), pp. 388-394, 397-400. Cited hereafter as *FR: The Soviet Union, 1933-1939*.

47. *Ibid.*

48. Messages concerning these problems are scattered throughout the volume *FR: The Soviet Union, 1933-1939*. For some of the more relevant messages, see pp. 166, 268, 244-245, 391-400, 446-451, 624-629, 638-663, and 855-857.

49. *Ibid.*, pp. 250–254, 260–262, 624–627, 642–643. Bullitt suggested that in retaliation for the Comintern meeting the United States should strictly apply the 1918 law excluding communists from the country; should "refuse visas to Soviet citizens unless they present ... satisfactory evidence that they are not and never have been members of the Communist Party or Communist International...." *Ibid.*, p. 254.

50. *Ibid.*, p. 6.

51. State Department, X/TVF 811.42761/35, Duggan to Hull, February 16, 1934.

52. *Ibid.*, Hull to Duggan, March 10, 1934.

53. State Department, 811.42761/39, Hanson to Hull, May 16, 1934.

54. State Department, 811.42761/13, Wiley to Hull, transmitting statements by Schapiro, December 28, 1934.

55. *Ibid.*, enclosures no. 1 and no. 3.

56. *Ibid.*

57. *Ibid.*, enclosure no. 1.

58. *Ibid.*

59. *Ibid.*, Wiley to Hull, plus enclosures no. 1 and no. 2.

60. *Ibid.*

61. *Ibid.*, enclosure no. 1.

62. *Ibid.*

63. State Department, 811.42761/45, Wiley to Hull, February 4, 1935.

64. State Department, 811.42761/61, Wiley to Hull, transmitting letter from Harper to Duggan, August 2, 1935.

65. *Ibid.*

66. State Department, 811.42761/62, Disney to Hull, transmitting letter from Hooper, August 31, 1935; *Ibid.*, Hull to Disney, September 17, 1935.

67. State Department, 811.42761/60, Bullitt to Hull, July 20, 1935, with enclosure no. 1, containing Harper's statement to the press; and State Department 811.42761/58, Bullitt to Hull, July 19, 1935.

68. State Department, 811.42761/46, Henderson to Hull, March 7, 1935.

69. *Ibid.*, enclosure no. 1.

70. *Ibid.*, Henderson to Hull.

71. Torgsin stores were special stores in which both Soviet and foreign citizens could purchase goods, but only with precious metals or foreign currency.

72. State Department, 811.42761/56, Henderson to Hull, June 18, 1935.

73. *Ibid.*

74. *Ibid.*

75. *Ibid.* The Soviet authorities discreetly turned their heads while the group disposed of the rubles for $400 cash.

76. *Ibid.*, and State Department 811.42761/59, Mangean to Phillips, July 7, 1935.

77. State Department, 811.42761/50, memorandum relating to press conference held by Phillips, April 19, 1935.

78. State Department, 811.42761/56, enclosure no. 1, transmitting copy of *Billboard* article published on April 27, 1935.

79. State Department, 811.42761/49, Clark to Phillips, April 19, 1935; *NYT*, April 21, 1935, p. 29.

80. State Department, 811.42761/48, Basy to Phillips, April 20, 1935; State Department 811.42761/56, enclosure no. 2, June 18, 1935; *NYT*, April 21, 1935, p. 29.

81. State Department, 811.42761/51, Bullitt to Hull, May 13, 1935.

82. State Department, 811.42761/56, Henderson to Hull, June 18, 1935; and *NYT*, July 14, 1935, sec. 9, p. 2.

83. *Ibid.*, Henderson to Hull, including enclosures no. 3 and no. 4.

84. *Ibid.*, Henderson to Hull, including enclosures no. 3, 4, 5.

85. *Ibid.*, Henderson to Hull, including enclosure no. 5.

86. *NYT*, March 21, 1937, sec. 13, p. 9. For examples of advertising, see *Ibid.*, May 23, 1937, sec. 11, p. 9; *Travel*, LXV (June, 1935), pp. 52, 56; and *Travel*, LXIX (June, 1937), p. 55.

87. *NYT*, March 21, 1937, sec. 13, p. 9.

88. *Ibid.*, May 21, 1937, p. 39.

89. *FR: The Soviet Union, 1933-1939*, pp. 389, 590.

90. *NYT*, July 29, 1937, p. 1; *Ibid.*, July 30, 1937, p. 17.

91. *Ibid.*, August 15, 1937, p. 31.

92. *Ibid.*, August 23, 1937, p. 4.

93. *Ibid.*, July 29, 1937, p. 1; and *Ibid.*, July 30, 1937, p. 17.

94. *Ibid.*, January 14, 1938, p. 2, and *Ibid.*, February 3, 1938, p. 30. For examples of travel articles and features relating to the Soviet Union prior to 1938, see Ralph Fox, "Building a New Siberia," *Travel*, LXV (May, 1935), pp. 45–48; Rena L. Niles, "Old Russia on the Frontier of the New," *Ibid*, LXIX (June, 1937), pp. 22–26; and Albert Parry, "The Cossacks Ride Again," *Ibid.*, LXIX (October, 1937), pp. 5–9.

95. *NYT*, May 27, 1938, p. 9.

96. For an example of Embassy complaint, see *FR: The Soviet Union, 1933-1939*, p. 450. See also *NYT*, September 16, 1938, p. 1.

97. *Science*, LXXXIV (December 18, 1936), pp. 555–556.

98. *Ibid*. See also "The Genetic Furor in the USSR," *Journal of Heredity*, VIII (February, 1937), p. 57.

99. State Department, 811.42761/64, Henderson to Hull, August 15, 1936.

100. State Department, 811.42761/69, Embassy to Secretary of State, August 26, 1939.

101. State Department, 811.42761/34, Graves to Kelley, February 5, 1934.

102. One survey of college catalogues indicated that only seventeen out of 300 colleges offered a course in Russian history. See Dorsey D. Jones and Sol Meltzer, "Colleges Need Russian History," *Journal of Higher Education*, IV (October, 1933), pp. 358–359. See also Kathleen Barnes, "Intensive Study of the Russian Language," *Institute of International Education News Bulletin*, XIII (February 1, 1938), pp. 6–9.

103. Ernest J. Simmons, "Negotiating on Cultural Exchange," in Raymond Dennett and Joseph E. Johnston, eds., *Negotiating with the Russians* (Boston: World Peace Foundation, 1951), p. 243.

104. *Ibid*.

NOTES TO CHAPTER V

1. Byrnes, "Academic Labor Market," p. 286; Posin, "Russian Studies," p. 66.

2. "Annual Dinner of the American-Russian Institute," Folder FR/US, 1948, American-Russian Institute, LICS Files.

3. "Annual Report of the American-Russian Institute, 1945," Folder FR/US Organizations-General, LICS Files.

4. *Ibid*. Among others availing themselves of the ARI's services were *Fortune, Barron's Magazine*, Chrysler Corporation, General Motors and the Army Air Force Tactical School.

5. *Ibid*. Others included Samuel Cross, head of Harvard's Slavic Department, John L. Curtis, vice-president of the City National Bank, New York City, and Joseph Barnes, foreign editor of the *New York Herald Tribune*.

6. "Annual Report of the American-Russian Institute, 1947," Folder FR/US, ARI, LICS Files.

7. "Annual Dinner of the American-Russian Institute," Folder FR/US, 1948, American-Russian Institute, LICS Files.

8. "Annual Report of the American-Russian Institute, 1948," Folder FR/US, ARI, LICS Files.

9. "Annual Report, 1947." The scores of other publications, including books, pamphlets and related materials are listed in "Staff Report on ARI Programs, 1946," Folder FR/US, Organizations-General, LICS Files.

10. "Annual Report, ARI, 1945."

11. *Ibid*.

12. Press releases, Folder FR/US Organizations-General, 1945, LICS Files.

13. *Ibid*.

14. Ralph B. Turner speech, Folder Organizations-General, 1944, LICS Files.

15. *Ibid.*, Gromyko speech.

16. *Ibid.*, E.C. Ropes speech.

17. Folder FR/US, Organizations, NCASF, LICS Files.

18. State Department, 811.42761/3-945, Edwin Smith, Executive Director of the NCASF to Bryan J. Hovde, Chief, Division of Cultural Cooperation, Department of State, March 9, 1945. Smith provided Hovde with lists of several of the committees.

19. *Ibid.*

20. "Books Sought for Soviet Libraries," *Publishers' Weekly*, CXLIV (November 6, 1944), pp. 1789–1790.

21. State Department, 811.42761/3-945, Smith to Hovde, March 9, 1945.

22. *Magazine of Art*, XXXVII (February, 1944), p. 69.

23. Folder FR/US, Organizations, NCASF, 1946, LICS Files. Embassy officer George F. Kennan made a brief speech at the opening of the exhibit, remarking that it provided a window through which the Soviet people could see America and learn some of the thoughts and tastes of its people.

24. State Department, 811.42761/3-1445, Silverstein to Hovde, March 14, 1945; Folder FR/US, NCASF, 1944 1945, LICS Files

25. "American Books Presented for Soviet Libraries," *Publishers' Weekly*, CXLIV (January 15, 1944), p. 207.

26. State Department, 811.42761/3-3045, Smith to Hovde, March 30, 1945. See also L.C. Dunn, "Scientific Interchange between the United States and the Soviet Union," *Science*, CI (February 23, 1945), pp. 200–201.

27. "Architects' Committee for American-Soviet Friendship," *Journal of the American Institute of Architects*, I–II (May, 1944), pp. 250–251.

28. "Exhibit for the USSR," *Architectural Forum*, LXXXI (September, 1944), p. 194. See also *Pencil Points*, XXV (August, 1944), p. 22.

29. State Department, 811.42761/5-1545, Corbett to Stettinius, May 15, 1945, enclosing letter from Soviet Purchasing Commission. For published accounts of the conference, see *Pencil Points*, XXVI (June, 1945), p. 16; and *Architectural Record*, XCVII (June, 1945), p. 20.

30. "Architecture Exhibit Presented to Russia," *Architectural Record*, XCVIII (December, 1945), p. 134.

31. State Department, 811.42761/10-945, Smith to Benton, October 19, 1945; and *Ibid.*, Benton to Smith, November 9, 1945. Relevant material in Folder FR/US, NCASF, 1944–1945, LICS Files.

32. Press releases, flyers, posters, advertisements and memorabilia contained in Folder FR/US, NCASF, LICS Files.

33. *Ibid.*

34. *Ibid.*

35. *Ibid.*

36. *Ibid.*

37. *Ibid.*

38. *Ibid.*, see p. 81.

39. *Ibid.*

40. "The Story of a Long Friendship, 1931–1945: The First Twenty-Five Years of the American-Russian Institute of San Francisco," SF-ARI Files.

41. *Ibid.*

42. Press releases and news clippings, unmarked folders, SF-ARI Files.

43. "Twenty-Five Years of a Long Friendship," SF-ARI Files.

44. SF-ARI Newsletter, September 24, 1946, unmarked folder, SF-ARI Files.

45. Press releases, unmarked folder, SF-ARI Files.

46. "Twenty-Five Years of a Long Friendship," SF-ARI Files.

47. *Ibid.*

48. *Ibid.*

49. Donald Fuller, "New York, '42: Soviet Tribute," *Modern Music*, XXX (November–December, 1942), p. 37.

50. Eleanor Wakefield, "Red Star over the Southwest," *Modern Music*, XXI (November–December, 1943), p. 41. *Modern Music* carried several articles by and about Soviet music and musicians during the war. See, for example, Sergei Prokofiev, "My Cinderella," *Modern*

Music, XXI (January–February, 1943), pp. 67–68; and "Russian and American Season, 1945," 1945," *Ibid.*, XXII (May–June, 1945), pp. 254–255.

51. State Department, 861.4083/3, with attached "Music Assembled by Special Promotions Division, OWI," December 9, 1942.

52. Several people who had occasion to be in Moscow commented on the popularity of certain American songs, particularly "Alexander's Ragtime Band" and "Tavern in the Town." See, for example, Barghoorn, *Image*, p. 81.

53. See pp. 84–87.

54. Press release, Folder FR/US Organizations-Publications, LICS Files.

55. *Ibid.* "Statement by Archibald MacLeish Regarding Library of Congress Interest in Russian Books and Literature."

56. *Ibid.*

57. Frederick E. Brasch, "History and Activities of the USSR Academy of Sciences during the Past Twenty-Five Years," *Science*, XCIX (June 2, 1946), p. 439.

58. Posin, "Russian Studies," p. 64.

59. From remarks made by Verner W. Clapp, Acting Librarian of Congress, at a library conference sponsored by the ARI in New York City in 1945. Contained in "Special Libraries Conference on Russian Materials," November 17, 1945, Folder FR/US, Organizations-General, 1945, LICS Files.

60. *Ibid.* The checklist was completed by Michael Karpovich of Harvard and Serge Yakobsen of the Library of Congress.

61. *Ibid.*

62. *Ibid.* The delegation consisted of Keyes D. Metcalf of Harvard, Paul N. Rice of the New York City Public Library and Charles W. David of the University of Pennsylvania.

63. "Special Libraries Conference on Russian Materials," November 17, 1945, Folder FR/US, Organizations-General, 1945, LICS Files. This fifty page unpublished report covers the conference in detail. For a published summary, see Toby Cole, "A Special Libraries Conference on Russian Material," *Library Journal*, LXXI (May 15, 1946), pp. 31–33.

64. State Department, 811.42761/12-1745, Harriet Moore, ARI Research Director, to William Benton, Assistant Secretary of State, December 17, 1945.

65. State Department, 811.42761/12-1346, Corbett to Huntington, December 13, 1945. For published descriptions of the translation project, see W. Chapin Huntington, "The Russian Translation Project of the American Council of Learned Societies," *Russian Review*, IV (Spring, 1945), pp. 40–48, and the same author's "The Russian Translation Project Three Years Later," *Ibid.*, VII (Spring, 1948), pp. 76–87.

66. Huntington, "The Russian Translation Project Three Years Later," p. 85.

67. Philip E. Moseley, "The Russian Institute of Columbia University," *Proceedings of the American Philosophical Society*, XC (January, 1955), pp. 36–39.

68. *Life*, XIV (March 29, 1943); *American Sociological Review*, IX (June, 1944), pp. 217–311.

69. Both State Department records and the LICS Files contain a great deal of information about the activities of the American-Soviet Medical Society, only a small part of which is cited here. Particularly relevant is State Department 811.42761/7-1346, Leslie to Shimkin, July 11, 1946, which contains a full description of the Society, its publications, functions, etc. See also Stuart Mudd, "Cultural Interchange between the United States and the Soviet Union," *Science*, C (December 1, 1944), pp. 486–487. Mudd was the president of the Medical Society.

70. Stuart Mudd, "Recent Observations on Programs for Medicine and National Health in the USSR," *Proceedings of the American Philosophical Society*, XCI (April, 1947), pp. 181–188; State Department, 811.42761/12-545, Byrnes to Embassy, Moscow, December 5, 1945; State Department 811.42761/4-2645, Mudd to Lebedenko, April 26, 1945; and *Ibid.*, Lebedenko to Mudd, May 7, 1945.

71. A. Baird Hastings and Michael B. Shimkin, "Medical Research Mission to the Soviet Union," *Science*, CIII (May 24, 1946), p. 644.

72. State Department 811.42761/9-346, Interdepartmental Memorandum, September 3, 1946; State Department 811.42761/9-3046, Acheson to Embassy, Moscow, September 30, 1946. For further comment concerning the KR serum developed by Nina Klyueva and Georgi

Roskin, see *Science Digest*, XXI (January, 1947), p. 33.

73. State Department, 811.42761/11-3046, Smith to Acheson, November 30, 1946; State Department 811.42761/12-546, Acheson to Parran, December 5, 1946.

74. See p. 102.

75. State Department, 811.42761/6-745, Moscow Embassy to State Department, June 7, 1945, enclosing list of Soviet institutions receiving and desiring to receive the Academy's publications.

76. Dvoichenko-Markov, "Early Russian-American Relations," p. 583; State Department, 811.42761/9-2346, Acheson to Embassy, Moscow, September 22, 1946.

77. State Department, 811.42761/11-947, Shapley to State Department, November 9, 1947; State Department 811.42761/1-2849, Office Memorandum, January 28, 1949.

78. State Department, 811.42761/12-645, Memorandum from Conant to Byrnes, December 6, 1945. See also James B. Conant, *My Several Lives: Memoirs of a Social Inventor* (New York: Harper and Row, 1970), pp. 484–487.

79. State Department, 811.42761/12-645, Memorandum of Conversation between Grew and Truman, June 8, 1945. Several other scientists evidently would have gone had the State Department not discouraged them because of their military connected duties See, for example, correspondence between University of Chicago physicist Arthur Compton and the State Department, State Department 811.42761/5-2145 and /5-2545.

80. State Department, 811.42761/8-1145, Shapley to Durbrow, August 11, 1945. For published accounts by some of the delegates, see Irving Langmuir, "Science and Incentives in Russia," *Scientific Monthly*, LXVII (August, 1946), pp. 85–92; Harlow Shapley, "Stars over Russia," *Soviet Russia Today* (September, 1945), pp. 11–13; Arthur Upham Pope, "Scientists are Public Heroes," *Ibid.*, pp. 9–11; and "Guests Pay Tribute to Soviet Science," *Ibid.*, p. 22.

81. State Department, 811.42761/8-1145, Shapley to Durbrow, August 11, 1945.

82. State Department, 811.42761/11-145, Shapley to Byrnes, November 1, 1945.

83. *Ibid.*, Durbrow to Matthews, November 14, 1945; *Ibid.*, Byrnes to Shapley, November 15, 1945.

84. *Ibid.*, Durbrow to Matthews, November 14, 1945.

85. State Department, 811.427261/12-445, Jewitt to Byrnes, December 4, 1945; and State Department 811.42761/12-1245, Jewett to Byrnes with attached correspondence from Detlev Bronk, December 12, 1945.

86. State Department, 811.42761/12-745, Bohlen memorandum on visit of scientists to Soviet Union, December 7, 1945.

87. State Department, 811.42761/5-3146, Jewett and Gates to the president of the USSR Academy of Sciences, May 31, 1946.

88. State Department, 811.42761/10-545, Ella Winter to William Benton, October 5, 1945.

89. State Department, 811.42761/2-2646, Cabot to Mravinsky, February 26, 1946.

90. *Ibid.*

91. U.S. Department of State. *Department of State Bulletin*, XVI (March 2, 1947), p. 393.

92. State Department, 811.42761/1-2546, Sloan to Acheson, January 25, 1946; and State Department 811.42761/2-1047, Whalen to Molotov, November 6, 1947.

93. State Department, 811.42761/11-2645, Todd to Acheson, November 26, 1945.

94. State Department, 811.42761/4-946, Snavely to Byrnes, enclosing letter to Andrei Gromyko, April 9, 1946.

95. State Department, 811.42761/8-546, Acheson to Embassy, Moscow, August 5, 1946.

96. State Department, 811.42761/9-2346, State Department to Embassy, Moscow, September 22, 1946; and State Department 811.42761/10-946, Aydelotte to Colligan, October 9, 1946.

97. *Department of State Bulletin*, XVI (March 2, 1947), p. 393; State Department, 811.42761 SE/1-2247, McBain to Hanson, January 22, 1947; and State Department 811.42761/11-3045, Shapley to Byrnes, November 30, 1945. See also Edward L. Young, "An American Surgeon on Soviet Medicine," *Soviet Russia Today* (October, 1946), pp. 12–13.

98. State Department, 811.,42761/9-2346, State Department to Embassy, Moscow,

September 22, 1946. The Rockefeller Foundation expressed hope that the two could spend at least two to three months visiting various campuses, helping thereby to broaden the contacts within the scientific community. See also State Department 811.42761/2-846, J.W. Studebaker, U.S. Commissioner of Education to Vladimir S. Kemenov, President of voks.

99. State Department, 811.42761 SE/3-747, Duggan to Benton, March 7, 1947.

100. *NYT*. March 6, 1946, p. 3.

101. *Ibid.*, March 18, 1946, p. 1. See also Reid Robinson, "A cio Report on the ussr," *Soviet Review Today* (January, 1946), pp. 13–14; and *NYT*, March 9, 1946, p. 28.

102. The various requests, comments and questions, too numerous to cite individually, are located in the State Department files in Decimal File 811.42761.

103. State Department, 861.4063/12-1245, Harriman to Byrnes, December 12, 1945; and State Department FW 811.42761/1-446, Colligan to Pickens, no date, but acknowledges Pickens' letter dated January 4, 1946.

104. *NYT*, August 31, 1946, p. 6; and press releases, Folder FR/US, American-Russian Institute, LICS Files.

105. State Department, 861.40621/1, Gradstein to Hull, November 10, 1942; and *Ibid.*, Hickerson to Gradstein, November 16, 1942.

106. *Ibid.*, State Department to Embassy, Moscow, December 2, 1943.

107. State Department, 861.40621/8-945, Wertheim to Clayton, August 9, 1945.

108. State Department, 861.40621/4-1846, Byrnes to Embassy, Moscow, April 18, 1946; State Department 861.40621/6-146, Smith to Bellquist, June 1, 1946; and State Department FW 861.40621/7-1946, Neal to Poore, August 6, 1948.

109. *NYT*, July 15, 1946, p. 19.

110. *Ibid.*, August 29, 1946, p. 26.

NOTES TO CHAPTER VI

1. State Department, 111.017/260, State Department Order No. 768, creating Division of Cultural Relations, July 28, 1938. For a general description of activities envisioned by State Department officials, see State Department 111.46/13, no date.

2. Ralph B. Turner speech, Folder Organizations-General, 1944, LICS Files.

3. *Ibid.*

4. Charles A. Thompson and Walter H.C. Laves, *Cultural Relations and U.S. Foreign Policy* (Bloomington: Indiana University Press, 1963), p. 43.

5. *Ibid.*, p. 44.

6. *Ibid.*, p. 40.

7. *State Department Bulletin*, I (November 11, 1939), p. 492.

8. Turner speech, LICS Files.

9. Dean Acheson Speech, Folder Organizations-General, 1944, LICS Files. New Mexico's Senator Hatch considered the speech important enough to insert into the *Congressional Record*. See U.S. Congress, Senate, 79th Cong., 1st sess., November 15, 1945, *Congressional Record*, XCI, p. A4886. For Stalin's remarks to Senator Pepper, see *FR*, 1945, V, p. 884.

10. Ernest C. Ropes speech, Folder Organizations-General, 1944, LICS Files.

11. State Department, 811.42761/12-946, State Department to Embassy, Moscow, December 9, 1946.

12. State Department, 811.42761/12-1346, P.E. Corbett to W. Chapin Huntington, December 13, 1946. Yale professor Corbett was effusive in his praise for Embassy staff members, noting that they were working with "diligence and first class ability" on the project, and remarking that if successful the plan would change the nature of Soviet studies in the United States from mere commentary on the letter of the law to a vivid reflection of living and changing reality in the Soviet Union. For Simmons' efforts, see pp. 107–115.

13. State Department, 811.42761/4-346, Kennan to Acheson, transmitting list of publications secured for Yale University Library, April 3, 1946; *Ibid.*, Acheson to James T. Babb, Yale University librarian, May 10, 1946. For efforts to implement the library program, see pp. 99–101.

14. State Department, 811.42761/3-546, Kennan to State Department, March 5, 1946;

and State Department 861.4036/12-1245, Kennan to Secretary of State, December 12, 1945.

15. *Ibid.*, Harriman to Secretary of State, December 12, 1945.

16. *NYT*, October 9, 1946, p. 30. In April, 1942, Congress amended the Foreign Agents Registration Act of 1938 to more closely regulate the distribution of propaganda in the United States (56 Stat. 248). The subsequent negotiations on the matter with O.A. Lambkin, president of Four Continents Bookstore, were long and complicated, involving personnel from both the Justice and State Departments. Because Moscow would not certify Four Continents Bookstore as an agent of Mezhdunarodnaya Kniga — though it was willing to certify Mezhdunarodnaya Kniga as an agent of Moscow — it was necessary for Four Continents to comply with the filing and labeling provisions of the FARA as amended in 1942. Generally speaking, those provisions required that all propaganda be labeled as such and that a certain number of copies of each item be supplied to various government agencies. The State and Justice Departments reduced those requirements to a minimum — even implied some could be ignored — and assured Lambkin that if he violated the act he would first be so informed and simply asked not to do it again. Within the latitude permitted by the act, officials from both departments appeared to be making, at least in 1945, a sincere effort to reduce its burdens. Though the discussions took place on several occasions and at a number of locations, the essentials are related in State Department FW 811.42761/11-2345, memorandum of conversation held in Justice Department, November 28, 1945, and in another memorandum with the same file number dated December 6, 1945.

17. The replies were too numerous to cite by number, but each was tailored to the individual inquiry and demonstrated thought and consideration. None were standardized, though the information given was necessarily similar.

18. State Department, 811.42761/12-845, State Department to Charge d'Affaires, USSR Embassy, Washington, D.C., December 8, 1945.

19. State Department, 811.42761/6-845, Durbrow to Davenport, June 8, 1945.

20. *Ibid.*

21. See above, pp. 110–111.

22. State Department, 811.42761/7-945, Library Committee to Byrnes, July 9, 1945.

23. State Department, 811.42761/7-945, Department memorandum, July 14, 1945. For Harriman's comments, see State Department 811.42761/7-745, Harriman to Byrnes, July 7, 1945.

24. State Department, 811.42761/7-945, memorandum of conversation on interchange and acquisition of Russian publications, July 27, 1945.

25. *Ibid.*

26. State Department Records, 811.42761/11-1745, Charles David to Eugene Anderson, Division of Cultural Relations, November 27, 1945.

27. Standley's program and efforts are summarized in State Department 861.4061 Motion Pictures/40, March 31, 1943, and State Department 861.4061 Motion Pictures/45, April 7, 1943. For published portions of the March 31 message, see *FR*, 1943, III, pp. 642–643.

28. William H. Standley and Arthur A. Ageton, *Admiral Ambassador to Russia* (Chicago: Henry Regnery Company, 1955), p. 306.

29. State Department, 861.4061 Motion Pictures/15, Standley to Hull, August 23, 1942.

30. *Ibid.*

31. *Ibid.*

32. Standley, *Admiral Ambassador*, p. 306.

33. State Department 861.4061 Motion Pictures/15, Standley to Hull, August 23, 1942.

34. *Ibid.*, Department memorandum, August 27, 1943.

35. State Department, 861.406A Motion Pictures/45, Standley to Hull, April 7, 1942.

36. State Department, 811.4061 Motion Pictures/15, State Department to Embassy, Kuibyshev, September 15, 1942.

37. Standley, *Admiral Ambassador*, p. 306.

38. Solomon Abramovich Lozovsky, Assistant People's Commissar for Foreign Affairs and Georgy Nikolaevich Zarubin, Chief of the American Section of the Commissariat for Foreign Affairs.

39. Standley, *Admiral Ambassador*, p. 320.

40. *Ibid.* Those quotes are taken from Standley's later account, but his cables sent at the

time support their accuracy. See State Department, 861.4061 Motion Pictures/45, April 7, 1943, and, for a brief version of the same, *FR*, 1943, III, p. 644.

41. State Department, 861.4061 Motion Pictures/53, enclosure no. 1, "Gentlemen's Agreement between A.N. Andrievsky and John Young," May 31, 1943. As finally concluded the agreement gave each side the right to reject films that it considered unsuitable, but it was the United States, not the Soviet Union, that initially insisted upon this form of censorship. The draft agreement contained no such provision, and Washington ordered the correction. For draft agreement see State Department 861.4061 Motion Pictures/36, March 9, 1936; for Washington's correction, State Department 861.4061 Motion Pictures/43, April 23, 1943.

42. State Department, 861.4061 Motion Pictures/49, Standley to Hull, May 4, 1943.

43. State Department, 861.4061 Motion Pictures/72, "Proposal of Admiral Standley ... to American Motion Picture Industry through Mr. Hays," June 16, 1943. This memorandum has no file number, but is attached to the file here cited, dated December 29, 1943.

44. Standley, *Admiral Ambassador*, p. 424. The individual films are listed in State Department 861.4061 Motion Pictures/62A, August 31, 1943.

45. *FR*, 1943, III, pp. 691–694.

46. *Ibid.*, p. 718.

47. *Ibid.*, p. 721.

48. *Ibid.*, 1945, V, p. 880, n. 1.

49. *Ibid.*, 1944, IV, pp. 991, 998, 1028.

50. *State Department Bulletin*, XXVII (July 28, 1952), pp. 127–132.

51. *NYT*, October 25, 1945, p. 11; *Time*, XLVII (July 28, 1952), p. 128.

52. *State Department Bulletin*, XXVII (July 28, 1952), p. 128.

53. *FR*, 1945, V, pp. 880–881.

54. State Department, 811.42761/10-545, Benton to Kennan, October 5, 1945. Published in *FR*, 1945, V, pp. 893–894.

55. State Department, 811.42761/11-945, Byrnes to Harriman, November 9, 1945.

56. State Department, 811.42761/4-1646, Smith to Secretary of State, April 16, 1946. In this communication Smith was recounting some of the earlier efforts toward cultural contacts.

57. Minutes of this meeting were sent to several individuals and organizations, as indicated by cover letters, but the minutes themselves are not in the files. Subsequent communications, however, tell a great deal about the meeting.

58. State Department, 811.42761/3-2246, Herschell Brickell, Division of International Exchange of Persons, to Stephen P. Duggan, March 20, 1946.

59. *Ibid.*

60. State Department, 811.42761 SE/3-747, Lawrence Duggan to Benton, March 7, 1947.

61. *Ibid.*

NOTES TO CHAPTER VII

1. *FR*, 1943, III, 713.

2. Eric A. Johnston, "My Talk with Joseph Stalin," *Reader's Digest*, XLV (October, 1944), pp. 5, 10.

3. Barghoorn, *Image*, p. 231. For remarks by Standley and Harriman, see pp. 85, 88.

4. *Ibid.*, pp. 83, 235.

5. Alexander Werth, *Russia: The Postwar Years* (New York: Taplinger Publishing Company, 1971), p. 99.

6. SF-ARI Files, press releases, unmarked folder. See also State Department, 811. 42761/5-2345, Kennan to Secretary of State, no date.

7. For Stalin's remarks to Stassen, see *NYT*, May 4, 1947, pp. 1, 50; for remarks to Roosevelt, see Elliot Roosevelt, "A Personal Interview with Stalin," *Look*, II (February 4, 1947), pp. 21–25. The LICS Files are replete with statements such as that made by B.G.

Skramataev, member of the Soviet Purchasing Commission in the United States and director of the Central Institute for Industrial Building Research in Moscow, that it was imperative that the two nations achieve "mutual understanding between our peoples through the exchange of scientific works and through understanding of our mutual needs and achievements." Folder Organizations-General, 1944, LICS Files.

8. Andrei Gromyko speech, Folder Organizations-General, 1944, LICS Files.

9. Barghoorn, *Image*, p. 81; Magidoff, *In Anger and Pity*, pp. 223–235.

10. See p. 98.

11. State Department, 811.42761/9-1144, memorandum of conversation between Roy Harris and Charles A. Thomson, September 11, 1944. For OWI music shipment, see p. 69.

12. State Department, 811.42761/11-145, Shapley to Byrnes, November 1, 1945. By 1944 the Soviets were giving widespread publicity to Lend-Lease contributions. See *FR*, 1944, IV, pp. 1045–1057, 1094–1097. For Standley's complaints concerning earlier lack of acknowledgment, see *FR*, 1943, III, pp. 636–641, 647–648.

13. Standley, *Ambassador*, p. 394.

14. See p. 70.

15. State Department, 861.4061 Motion Pictures/11, Standley to Hull, July 10, 1942.

16. NCASF Newsletter, August 13, 1945, Folder NCASF, 1944–1946, LICS Files.

17. Magidoff, *In Anger and Pity*, pp. 223–235.

18. Barghoorn, *Image*, p. 244.

19. For references pertaining to the scientists' remarks, see p. 342, n. 80. For Menuhin's reception, see *NYT*, November 20, 1945, p. 19. Since he was a musician unencumbered by military, diplomatic or political importance, and since his arrival coincided with the "euphoric interlude between war and cold war, when happiness in victory and hope for peace seemed ... perfectly reasonable responses," Menuhin later wrote, he was received with "a warmth of affection" that outstripped his fondest hopes." Yehundi Menuhin, *Unfinished Journey* (New York: Alfred A. Knopf, 1977), p. 184.

20. Louie D. Newton, "An American Churchman in the Soviet Union." Booklet describing the ventures of the religious leaders in the USSR, Folder ARI 1, LICS Files.

21. *FR*, 1943, III, p. 715.

22. Eric Johnston, *We're All In It* (New York: E.P. Dutton and Company, 1950), p. 49. See also the same author's "My Talk with Joseph Stalin," and Harrison Salisbury, "Russia Beckons Big Business," *Collier's*, CXIV (September 2, 1944), p. 11.

23. Fleming speech, Folder FR/US, 1945, Organizations-General, LICS Files. For details and events surrounding both Fleming's and Wallace's trips, see *FR*, 1944, IV, pp. 964–965, 969–970, and 1020–1022.

24. *NYT*, January 18, 1947, p. 2.

25. The American-Russian Institutes in New York and San Francisco and the National Council of American-Soviet Friendship distributed large quantities of posters, pamphlets, films, etc., in the United States.

26. State Department, 811.42761 SE/8-2547, Scheele to Williams, August 25, 1947.

27. Press release of Simonov's speech, unmarked folder, SF-ARI Files. For Parin's speech, see *NYT*, July 7, 1946, p. 6.

28. State Department, 811.42761/5-2345, Kennan to Secretary of State. No date.

29. State Department, 811.42761/4-1646, Smith to Secretary of State, April 16, 1946. Though the minutes to this meeting are missing from the files, it is obvious from other references that the question of tuition scholarships was indeed a prime consideration.

30. Standley, *Admiral Ambassador*, p. 424.

31. *Ibid.*, p. 425.

32. *Ibid.*

33. *Ibid.*

34. Standley, *Admiral Ambassador*, p. 425.

35. State Department, 861.4061 Motion Pictures/2-1846, February 18, 1946.

36. *Ibid.*

37. *Ibid.*

38. State Department, 861.4061 Motion Pictures/11-645, Harriman to Secretary of State, November 6, 1945.

39. State Department, 861.4061 Motion Pictures/12-1445, Kennan to Secretry of State December, 14, 1945.

40. State Department, 861.4061 Motion Pictures/8-2544, Harriman to Secretary of State, August 25, 1944.

41. *Ibid.*

42. *Ibid.*

43. State Department, 861.4061 Motion Pictures/9-1144, Harriman to Secretary of State, September 11, 1944.

44. *Ibid.* For the agreement between Young and Zarubin, see p. 86.

45. *Ibid.*

46. *Ibid.*

47. State Department, 861.4061 Motion Pictures/9-1144. Hull to Embassy, Moscow, October 18, 1944; and State Department 861.4061 Motion Pictures/11-944, memorandum of meeting between Elbridge Durbrow and RKO executive John Whitaker, November 9, 1944.

48. State Department, 861.4061 Motion Pictures/11-2944, Department memorandum of conversation, November 29, 1944; State Department 861.4061 MP/2-145, Will Clayton to Ned E. Depinet, President, RKO, February 1, 1945; State Department 861.4061 MP/3-2145, Kennan to State Department, February 21, 1945; and State Department 861.4061 MP/4-1045, Tathoon to Clayton, April 10, 1945.

49. State Department, 861.4061/21. Lacy Kastner to John Begg, October 20, 1942. By 1946 the Embassy was, however, placing more emphasis on the use of films as propaganda; on the portrayal through motion pictures of a particular image of America and American life. See Kennan's outline for a motion picture program in State Department 861.4061 Motion Pictures/2-1846, Kennan to State Department, February 18, 1946.

50. State Department, 861.4061 Motion Pictures/11-944, memorandum of conversation between Durbrow and Whitaker, November 9, 1944. Text of agreement attached.

51. State Department, 861.4061 Motion Pictures/4-2546, April 25, 1946, and June 25, 1946.

52. State Department, 861.4061 Motion Pictures/11-645, Harriman to Secretary of State, November 6, 1945.

53. State Department, 861.4061 Motion Pictures/9-2645, Murray Silverstone, President, Twentieth Century Fox, to State Department, September 26, 1945.

54. The "Minister," the Embassy assumed, was Stalin. State Department 811.42761/2-547, Smith to Secretary of State, February 5, 1947; and State Department 861.4061 Motion Pictures/4-1147, Smith to Secretary of State, April 11, 1947.

55. State Department, 811.42761/2-547, Smith to Benton, February 5, 1947.

56. State Department, 861.4061 Motion Pictures/3-146, Kennan to Secretary of State, March 1, 1946.

57. *Ibid.*

58. State Department, 861.4061 Motion Pictures/3-946, Kennan to Secretary of State, March 9, 1946.

59. See pp. 70–71.

60. State Department, 811.42761/2-1146, Kennan to Secretary of State, February 11, 1946. See Kennan's attached letter to K. A. Mikhailov, Chief of American Division, VOKS.

61. *Ibid.*

62. State Department, 811.42761/3-1946, Kennan to Secretary of State, March 19, 1946. See enclosure no. 3, letter from Kennan to Mikhailov, dated March 13, 1946.

63. State Department, 811.42761/7-2546, Ruggles to Secretary of State, July 25, 1946.

64. State Department, 811.42761/10-2646, Ruggles to Secretary of State, October 26, 1946.

65. For Lenin Library refusal, see *Ibid.* For Library of Congress request, see State Department 811.42761/3-2147, Ruggles to Secretary of State, with attached letter to I. Kharmskii, Chief of American Division, VOKS, February 14, 1947.

66. State Department, 811.42761/3-2147, Kharmskii to Ruggles, no date.

67. *Ibid.*, Ruggles to Kharmskii, no date.

68. State Department, 811.42761/11-1947, Ruggles to Secretary of State, November 19, 1947.

69. *Ibid.*
70. State Department, 811.42761/8-546, Acheson to Embassy, Moscow, August 5, 1946.
71. State Department, 811.42761/9-946, Durbrow to Secretary of State, Sept. 9, 1946; and State Department 811.42761/9-446, State Department to Embassy, Moscow, Sept. 4, 1946.
72. State Department, 811.42761/9-746, Durbrow to Secretary of State, Sept. 7, 1946.
73. *Ibid.*
74. State Department, 811.42761/9-1346, Durbrow to Secretary of State, Sept. 13, 1946.
75. State Department, 811.42761/9-1446, Durbrow to Secretary of State, Sept. 14, 1946.
76. State Department, 811.42761/9-2046, Durbrow to Secretary of State, Sept. 20, 1946.
77. *Ibid.*
78. State Department, 811.42761/9-2646, Embassy to Secretary of State, Sept. 26, 1946.
79. *Ibid.*
80. *Ibid.*
81. *Ibid.*, Acheson to Embassy, Moscow, October 14, 1946.
82. State Department, 811.42761/10-1246, Durbrow to Secretary of State, Oct 12, 1946.
83. State Department, 811.42761/2-147, Embassy, Moscow, to State Department, February 1, 1947.
84. See pp. 113–114.
85. State Department, 811.42761/10-2346, Durbrow to Secretary of State, October 23, 1946; and *Ibid.*, State Department to Embassy, Moscow, October 24, 1946.
86. State Department, 811.42761/11-1646, Smith to Secretary of State, Nov. 16, 1946.
87. State Department, 811.42761/1846, Smith to Secretary of State, November 18, 1946; and State Department 811.42761/11-546, State Department to Embassy, Moscow, November 21, 1946.
88. State Department, 811.42761/11-1846, Acheson to Moscow Embassy, Nov. 26, 1946.
89. State Department, 811.42761/12-1446, Embassy to State Department, October 14, 1946; and 811.42761/12-2346, Embassy to State Department, December 23, 1946.
90. State Department, 811.42761/10-946, Aydolette to Colligan, October 9, 1946.
91. *Ibid.*, Embassy to State Department, October 18, 1946; and 811.42761/10-2246, Colligan to Aydolette, November 5, 1946.
92. See pp. 75, 82.
93. See p. 104.

Notes to Chapter VIII

1. Elliot Roosevelt, "A Personal Interview with Stalin," *Look*, II (February 4, 1947), pp. 21–25.
2. *State Department Bulletin*, XVI (March 2, 1947), p. 393.
3. State Department, 811.42761 SE/1549, Embassy, Moscow, to State Department, transmitting information not earlier forwarded, March 15, 1949, and State Department 811.42761 SE/5-2447, Smith to Secretary of State, May 24, 1947.
4. State Department, 811.42761 SE/3-1549, Embassy, Moscow, to State Department, March 15, 1949. See enclosure no. 2.
5. See above, pp. 141–142.
6. State Department, 811.42761/4-1646, Smith to Secretary of State, April 16, 1946.
7. State Department, 811.42761 SE/12-346, Acheson to Smith, December 3, 1946.
8. State Department, 811.42761 SE12-1146, Benton to Smith, January 2, 1947.
9. State Department, 811.42761 SE/1-847, Smith to Benton, January 8, 1947.
10. *NYT*, October 9, 1946, p. 30. The Foreign Agents Registration Act of 1938 required that "any person who acts or engages or agrees to act as a public relations counsel, publicity agent, or as agent, servant, representative, or attorney for a foreign principal ..." register as "an agent of a foreign principal." Diplomats, consular officials and certain persons acting in a private capacity were excluded from the requirement. *Foreign Agents Registration Act of 1938, Statutes at Large*, LII, sec. 1(d), p. 632 (1938).
11. *NYT*, October 11, 1946, p. 4. The *NYT* was quoting from a letter sent by the Justice Department to the delegates.

12. *Ibid.*

13. *Ibid.*, October 20, 1946, sec. 2, p. 7.

14. *Ibid.*, October 15, 1946, p. 27; and *Ibid.*, October 20, 1946, sec. 2, p. 7.

15. *Ibid.*, October 19, 1946, p. 9.

16. State Department, 811.42761 SE 12/1146, Smith to Benton, January 2, 1947.

17. State Department, 811.42761 SE/1-847, Smith to Benton, January 8, 1947; and *Ibid.*, Benton to Smith, January 15, 1947.

18. State Department, 811.42761 SE/4-747, Smith to Secretary of State, April 7, 1947. For exact wording, see State Department 811.42761/5-1147, Durbrow to Secretary of State, May 11, 1947.

19. State Department, 811.42761 SE/4-747, Smith to Secretary of State, April 7, 1947.

20. State Department, 811.42761 SE/12-1146, Smith to Secretary of State, December 11, 1946. For a list of specific fields and individual scholars as originally suggested by Smith, see State Department 811.42761 SE/11-2746, November 17, 1946.

21. State Department, 811.42761 SE/4-2947, Embassy to Secretary of State, enclosing copy of Vyshinsky's letter, April 29, 1947.

22. *Ibid.*

23. State Department, 811.42761 SE/4-747, Smith to Secretary of State, April 7, 1947.

24. As Simmons remarked to Soviet Vice-Minister of Foreign Affairs Jacob Malik while in Moscow in August, 1947. State Department, 811.42761 SE/8-2947, Smith to Secretary of State, enclosure no. 1, "Visit of Professor Ernest J. Simmons of Columbia University," August 29, 1947. NOTE: This dispatch from Smith, with enclosures, is a lengthy report on Smith's activities. It will be cited below as Smith to Secretary of State, August 29, 1947, with, when applicable, appropriate enclosure number.

25. Ernest J. Simmons, "Negotiating on Cultural Exchange," in Raymond Dennett and Joseph E. Johnston, eds., *Negotiating with the Russians* (Boston: World Peace Foundation, 1951), p. 254.

26. *Ibid.*

27. *Ibid.*

28. *Ibid.* For the complete proposals, see *Ibid.*, pp. 256-258.

29. Smith to Secretary of State, August 29, 1947.

30. *Ibid.*

31. *Ibid.*

32. *Ibid.* See also Simmons, "Negotiating," p. 255.

33. Smith to Secretary of State, August 29, 1947, enclosure no. 2.

34. *Ibid.*

35. *Ibid.*

36. *Ibid.*

37. *Ibid.* See also Simmons, "Negotiating," p. 258.

38. *Ibid.*

39. Simmons, "Negotiating," p. 259.

40. *Ibid.*

41. *Ibid.*

42. Smith to Secretary of State, August 19, 1947, enclosure no. 1; Simmons, "Negotiating," p. 259.

43. Smith to Secretary of State, August 29, 1947, enclosure no. 2.

44. *Ibid.*

45. Simmons, "Negotiating," p. 260.

46. Smith to Secretary of State, August 29, 1947; Simmons, "Negotiating," pp. 259–261.

47. *Ibid.*, enclosure no. 2.

48. *Ibid.*

49. *Ibid.*

50. *Ibid.*

51. Simmons, "Negotiating," p. 262.

52. Smith to Secretary of State, August 29, 1947, enclosure no. 1.

53. *Ibid.*

54. *Ibid.*

55. *Ibid.*
56. *Ibid.*
57. *Ibid.*
58. Simmons, "Negotiating," p. 260.
59. Smith to Secretary of State, August 29, 1947. See also enclosure no. 3.
60. See pp. 120–121.
61. Smith to Secretary of State, August 29, 1947.
62. *Ibid.*
63. Simmons, "Negotiating," pp. 268–269.

NOTES TO CHAPTER IX

1. *FR*,1947, IV, pp. 569–571.
2. *Ibid.*
3. Walter Bedell Smith, *My Three Years in Moscow* (New York: J.B. Lippincott Company, 1950), p. 104. Spaso House was the official residence of the American ambassador in Moscow.
4. *Ibid.*
5. Werth, *Russia: The Postwar Years,* p. 255.
6. *FR*, 1948, IV, pp. 798–800.
7. Salisbury, *Moscow Journal,* p. 87.
8. *State Department Bulletin,* XIX (October 24, 1948), p. 525.
9. Salisbury, *Moscow Journal,* p. 87.
10. *State Department Bulletin,* XXXII (January 31, 1955), p. 199.
11. Werth, *Russia: The Postwar Years,* p. 197.
12. Harold Swayze, *Political Control of Literature in the USSR, 1946–1959* (Cambridge: Harvard University Press, 1962), p. 36.
13. *Ibid.* See also Werth, *Russia: The Postwar Years,* pp. 107–215, and Andrei Zhdanov, *Essays on Literature, Philosophy and Music* (New York: International Publishers, 1950), pp. 15–44.
14. Swayze, *Political Control of Literature,* pp. 40–41.
15. *Ibid.,* p. 37.
16. Werth, *Russia: The Postwar Years,* p. 210.
17. *Ibid.,* p. 209; State Department, 861.4061/9-1246, Embassy to Secretary of State, transmitting article in *Moscow News* written by vice-chairman of the Committee on Arts, September 12, 1946; *NYT*, March 22, 1949, p. 16. Even the renowned film producer Eisenstein fell victim to the purges. Accusing him of "harmful deviationism," and "petit bourgeois Hollywood standards," censors destroyed many of his films before they were released, castigated his "Ivan the Terrible" for its portrayal of Ivan, and mutilated his classic, "Potemkin." His sudden and unexplained death put an end to the persecution. See Fueloep-Miller, *Mind and Face of Bolshevism,* p. 301.
18. State Department, 861.4061/5-2049, Kohler to Secretary of State, transmitting article in *Evening Moscow,* May 20, 1949.
19. *Ibid.*
20. State Department, 811.42761 SE/6-1147, Embassy to State Department, transmitting article in *Culture and Life,* by Kaftanov, June 11, 1947.
21. "Resolution of the Central Committee of the Communist Party of the Soviet Union on the Opera THE GREAT FRIENDSHIP," by Vano Muradell, printed in *Bolshevik,* February 10, 1948; contained in Folder FR/US, LICS Files, translated by Bernard Koten.
22. *Ibid.*
23. Werth, *Russia: The Postwar Years,* pp. 362–375.
24. G. Mikhailov, "A Soviet Expose of Our Musical Press," *Musical America,* LXX (January 15, 1950), pp. 6, 96–97.
25. *Ibid.,* p. 97.
26. Fueloep-Miller, *Mind and Face of Bolshevism,* p. 299.
27. *Ibid.*

28. State Department, 811.42761 SE/10-2547, Durbrow to Secretary of State, transmitting *Izvestia* review, October 25, 1947. The reference to the "Yellow Devil" stemmed from Gorki's characterization of the all-powerful dollar as the Yellow Devil in his *City of the Yellow Devil*, published after a trip to New York in 1906.

29. State Department, 811.42761 SE/11-1847, Embassy to Secretary of State, transmitting article in Literary Gazette, November 18, 1947.

30. State Department, 811.42761 SE/2-1248, Embassy to Secretary of State, transmitting article in *Literary Gazette*, February 12, 1948. The Soviet press likewise attacked Columbia University's Russian Institute as a school for spies, charging that its head, historian Geroid T. Robinson, was a "seasoned agent." See Magidoff, *In Anger and Pity*, p. 75.

31. State Department, 811.42761 SE/10-2547, Durbrow to Secretary of State, October 25, 1947.

32. *Ibid.*

33. Resolution by Central Committee of the Communist Party, "On the Repertoire of the Dramatic Theaters and Measures for Its Improvement," adopted August 26, 1946. Folder FR/US, LICS Files. See also Swayze, *Political Control of Literature*, p. 36.

34. State Department, 861.4061/4-447, Smith to State Department, April 4, 1947. The Embassy flooded the Department with reviews, comments, judgments, etc., regarding the various anti-American plays. The citation above and those below refer to only one of several dispatches concerning each production. For published material relevant to the plays, see Gleb Struve, "Anti-Westernism in Recent Soviet Literature," *Yale Review*, XXXIX (December, 1949), pp. 209–224; and Andrew Hanfman, "The American Villain on the Soviet Stage," *Russian Review*, IX–X (January, 1951), pp. 131–145.

35. State Department, 861.4061/9-949, Embassy to State Department, transmitting accounts and reviews of "The Mad Haberdasher," September 9, 1949. The following accounts and reviews are likewise taken from State Department records, and will be referred to by decimal file and date only. "Round the Ring," 861.4061/12-1249, December 12, 1949; "To the Rustling of Eyelashes," 861.4061/4-1849; "Conspiracy of the Doomed," 861.4061/3-3049; "The Voice of America," 861.4061/12-1549.

36. State Department, 861.4061/12-2249, Embassy to State Department, Dec. 22, 1949.

37. See p. 93.

38. "Court of Honor," State Department 861.4061/8-1648, August 16, 1948.

39. "An Alien Shadow," State Department 861.4061/5-2549, May 25, 1949.

40. See p. 122.

41. State Department, 811.42761 SE/8-2947, Smith to Secretary of State, August 29, 1947, enclosure no. 1.

42. See p. 79.

43. Thompson and Laves, *Cultural Relations and Foreign Policy*, pp. 57–69.

44. *Ibid.*

45. *Ibid.*

46. *Ibid.*, pp. 67–69.

47. *Ibid.*, p. 72.

48. *Ibid.*, p. 79.

49. Harry S Truman, "Fight False Propaganda with Truth," *State Department Bulletin*, XXII (May 1, 1950), pp. 669–672.

50. For a detailed account, see Edward W. Barrett, *Truth is Our Weapon* (New York: Funk and Wagnalls Company, 1953), pp. 72–100.

51. *Sixth Semiannual Report of the United States Advisory Commission on Information*, House Doc. No. 526, 82nd Cong., 2nd sess. (1952), p. 2.

52. *Fifth Semiannual Report on Education Exchange Activities*, House Doc. No. 108, 82nd Cong., 1st sess. (1951), p. 3.

53. *Ibid.*

54. *Ibid.* See also, *Supplemental Appropriations Bill for 1951*, House Hearings, p. 5; *Departments of State, Justice, Commerce and the Judiciary Appropriations*, 1952, Senate Hearings, 82nd Cong., 1st sess. (1951), Part 2, p. 1786.

55. *Overseas Information Program of the United States*, Senate Hearings, Part I, Committee on Foreign Relations, 82nd Cong., 1st sess. (1952), pp. 112, 195–196.

56. State Department, FW811.42761/2-2149, Department Memorandum, "Proposed Visit of Shostakovich and Others," prepared by Deputy Asst. Secretary of State Charles M. Hulten, March 1, 1949. For a list of the hundreds of sponsors of the conference, see *NYT*, March 24, 1949, p. 4.

57. *Ibid.*

58. *Ibid.*

59. *Ibid.*

60. State Department, 811.42761/13-1349, Fred Warner Neal to Charles M. Hulten, March 13, 1949.

61. U.S., Congress, House, 81st Cong., 1st sess., March 17, 1949, *Congressional Record*, XCV, p. 2736.

62. For the terms of Proviso Nine, see p. 186, no. 82.

63. State Department, 811.42761/2-2149, Department Memorandum by Charles M. Hulten, March 1, 1949.

64. *Ibid.* For published material relating to the matter, see *FR*, 1949, V, pp. 806–815. For the recommendation of the Advisory Committee on Educational Exchange, see *State Department Bulletin*, XIX (October 31, 1948), p. 560; for State Department reply, see *State Department Bulletin*, XIX (December 26, 1948), pp. 808–809.

65. *Ibid.*, Hulten Memorandum.

66. *NYT*, March 25, 1949, p. 1. On March 23, 1949, the Department released a 25 page study summarizing the American overtures and Soviet rejections in the postwar period. "The only conclusion that can be drawn from Soviet opposition to an exchange of students and professors and an expansion of publications exchange," the report stated, "is that the Soviet Government fears a free exchange of ideas because of a realization that thirty years of Communism have failed to provide the patient Soviet people with a living standard anywhere approximating that enjoyed by the workers in the United States ... have deprived the Soviet people of freedom of thought and action, freedom which once experienced through contact with American people or American books will make them ill-content with their life in the Soviet Union." Considering the difficulties some Americans were having with their own government over the issue of American-Soviet contacts, and considering the wars and devastation suffered in the USSR since the Revolution, some might conclude that the State Department analysis was not particularly balanced or objective. See U.S. Department of State, *Cultural Relations between the United States and the Soviet Union*, State Department Publication No. 3480, International Information and Cultural Series No. 4 (Washington, 1949), pp. 1–25.

67. *NYT*, March 24, 1949, p. 3.

68. *Ibid.*, March 26, 1949, p. 1; and *Ibid.*, March 25, 1949, p. 1.

69. *Ibid.*, March 28, 1949, p. 4.

70. *Ibid.*

71. "Shostakovich Visits America," *Musical America*, LXIX (April, 1949), pp. 4–5; Howard Marx, "Shostakovich in New York," *Music News*, XLI (May, 1949), p. 4.

72. *NYT*, March 30, 1949, p. 1; *Ibid.*, March 25, 1949, p. 17.

73. *Ibid.*, March 30, 1949, p. 1.

74. *Internal Security Act of 1950* (McCarran Act), *Statutes at Large*, LXIV, secs. 6–12, 22, pp. 993–997, 1006–1009 (1950). For an example of a Nobel Prize winning American scientist being denied a passport because the State Department suspected he was a communist, had heart reports that he had criticized the United States, and because it deemed his anticommunist statements insufficiently strong, see Linus Pauling, "My Efforts to Obtain a Passport," *Bulletin of the Atomic Scientists*, VIII (October, 1952), p. 253.

75. *Immigration and Nationality Act of 1952*, *Statutes at Large*, LXIV, sec. 212, p. 184 (1952). For a detailed comparison of the 1950 and 1952 restrictions, see *Bulletin of the Atomic Scientists*, VIII (October, 1952), p. 257.

76. For fingerprinting requirement, see *Ibid.*, sec. 221(b), p. 191. For the terms of Proviso Nine, see p. 186, n. 82.

77. *State Department Bulletin*, XXVI (March 24, 1952), p. 451.

78. *Ibid.*, XXXII (January 31, 1955), pp. 193–197.

79. *Ibid.*, p. 198.

80. *NYT*, November 12, 1952, p. 5. The matter became public when David Dallin, historian and contributing editor of the *New Leader*, by no means pro-Soviet, editorialized on his failure to receive expected copies of the Soviet publication *Bolshevik*. See "Post Office Folly," *New Leader*, October 20, 1952, p. 11.

81. *State Department Bulletin*, XXVII (July 28, 1952), pp. 127–132.

82. *Bulletin of the Atomic Scientists*, VIII (October, 1952), pp. 210–214. See also *FR*, 1950, I, pp. 896–904, "Impact of the Internal Security Act of 1950 upon the Conduct of United States Foreign Relations." Memorandum prepared by Jesse M. MacKnight.

83. Edward A. Shils, "America's Paper Curtain," *Bulletin of the Atomic Scientists*, VIII (October, 1952), p. 212.

84. *Ibid.*, p. 217

85. "Whom Shall We Welcome?" *Ibid.*, IX (February, 1953), pp. 17–20.

86. *NYT*, November 17, 1952, p. 24. See also "The Exchange of Scientific Information with the Soviet Union," *Bulletin of the Atomic Scientists*, IX (February, 1953), pp. 13–15.

87. Press release, May 12, 1948, Folder FR/US, Organizations – NCASF, 1948, LICS Files. Among the signers were five bishops of the Protestant Episcopal Church, a United States senator and numerous leaders from the academic and business professions.

88. State Department, 861.4061 MP/9-949, Kirk to Secretary of State, Sept. 9, 1949.

89. State Department, 811.42761/34, Graves to Kelley, February 5, 1934. See attached page concerning report of special agent Logan J. Lane.

90. *NYT*, February 19, 1947, p. 18; State Department, FW811.42761/5-2247, State Department to J. Edgar Hoover, enclosing letter from Russell McGill to Dean Acheson, May 22, 1947.

91. State Department, 811.42761 SE/2-347, State Department to FBI and Military Intelligence Division, enclosing letter from Pvt. Charles J. Halleck to State Department, March 12, 1947.

92. State Department, 811.42761 SE/1-2248, State Department to FBI, enclosing letter from John B. Stall to Jack D. Neal, February 2, 1948.

93. Clippings from *New York Journal American*, December 22, 1945. One of the "proofs" listed under "Objectives of the Campaign Underway to Sell Communism," was that the organizations intended to "use pressure and organize teachers to demand that Soviet history be added to college and high school curricula." Clippings contained in Folder ARI/NYU, NCASF, 44–45, LICS Files.

94. Press release, August 9, 1948, Folder FR/US, 1948, LICS Files.

95. "Survey of Activities of the ARI from January to December, 1947," Folder FR/US, ARI, LICS Files.

96. Tom C. Clark to Ernest C. Ropes, August 4, 1948, Folder FR/US, 1948, LICS Files.

97. *Annual Report of the American-Russian Institute, 1948*, and *Annual Report of the American-Russian Institute, 1949*, Folder FR/US, ARI, 1949, LICS Files.

98. *Ibid.*

99. *Ibid.*

100. Press release, September 19, 1950, Folder FR/US, 1949, LICS Files.

101. Richard Morford, "Not My Liberty But Ours," pamphlet located in Folder ARI/NYU, NCASF, 1944–1945, LICS Files. For details of the November rally, see p. 68.

102. Corliss Lamont to John S. Wood, Chairman, House Committee on Un-American Activities, December 9, 1945, Folder ARI/NYU, NCASF, 1944–1945, LICS Files.

103. "Notes on the Hearings of Corliss Lamont and Richard Morford before the House Un-American Activities Committee," Folder FR/US, U.S. Organizations, NCASF, 1946, LICS Files. Press releases from the same folder, dated March 23, 1946.

104. Morford, "Not My Liberty But Ours," LICS Files.

105. *Ibid.*

106. Transcript of Complaint for Injunction and Declaratory Judgment, U.S. District Court, District of Columbia, Folder ARI/NYU, NCASF, 1949–1952, LICS Files.

107. *Science*, CVIII (September 10, 1948), p. 279; *Science News Letter* LIV (August 7, 1948), p. 88. See also Walter Goodman, *The Committee: The Extraordinary Career of the House Committee on Un-American Activities* (New York: Farrar, Strauss and Giroux, 1968), pp. 232–239.

108. "The Case of the National Council of American-Soviet Friendship versus the Attorney General of the United States and the McCarran Act," pamphlet located in Folder ARI/NYU, NCASF, 1955–1956, LICS Files.

109. *Ibid.*

110. Newsletter from Richard A. Morford to NCASF members, June 23, 1955, Folder ARI/NYU, CCASF, 1955–1956, LICS Files.

111. Press release, February 8, 1956, Folder ARI/NYU, 1955–1956, LICS Files.

112. For example, the NCASF sponsored a "Festival of Soviet Culture," featuring exhibits on Soviet industry, dams, women, child care and other facets of Soviet life at Yugoslav Hall in November, 1951. Folder NCASF, 1949–1952, LICS Files.

113. Clipping from *Washington Post*, July 1, 1948, Folder ARI, FR/US, U.S. Organizations, NCASF, 1948, LICS Files.

NOTES TO CHAPTER X

1. *Life*, XXIV (April 20, 1953), p. 22.

2. For a general description of the increasing Soviet activity, see Frederick C. Barghoorn, *The Soviet Cultural Offensive* (Princeton: Princeton University Press, 1960). For more specific examples, see "Soviet Musical Offerings," Musical America, LXXV (January 1, 1955), p. 5; and "European Artists Visit Moscow," *Ibid.*, LXXIII (November 1, 1953), p. 9. One knowledgeable publication, quoting State Department sources, stated that the numbers of delegations entering and leaving the Soviet Union jumped 60% between 1950 and 1953, doubled the following year, and was still increasing in 1955. See "Soviet-American Cultural Exchanges: A Review Since 1917," *Institute of International Education News Bulletin*, XXXIII (October, 1956), p. 22.

3. Harrison Salisbury, *Moscow Journal: The End of Stalin* (Chicago: Chicago University Press, 1961), p. 368.

4. Ilya Ehrenberg, "Concerning the Writer's Work," Znamya, October, 1953, pp. 160–183, translated in *Current Digest of the Soviet Press*, Vol. V, No. 52, February 10, 1954, pp. 4–13. Cited hereafter as CDSP. Aram Khachaturian, "Concerning Creative Boldness and Imagination," *Sovetskaya Muzyka*, November, 1953, pp. 7–13, translated in *CDSP*, Vol. V, No. 46, December 30, 1953, pp. 3–6.

5. *Pravda*, November 27, 1953, p. 3, translated in *CDSP*, Vol. V, No. 52, February 10, 1954, p. 3.

6. Dmitri Shostakovich, "The Joy of Creative Search," *Sovetskaya Muzyka*, January, 1954, translated in *CDSP*, Vol. V, No. 52, February 10, 1954, p. 304.

7. For the twisted path of Soviet literary and artistic controls, see Marc Slonim, *Soviet Russian Literature: Writers and Problems, 1917–1977* (New York: Oxford University Press, 1977), pp. 321–418.

8. *NYT*, March 15, 1954, p. 5; *Ibid.*, November 1, 1954, p. 26; *Sovetskaya Kultura*, December 23, 1954, p. 4, translated in *CDSP*, Vol. VI, No. 52, February 9, 1955, p. 32. See also *NYT*, December 24, 1954, p. 7.

9. "Calling a Turn," *Musical America*, LXXIV (May, 1954), pp. 12–13.

10. Ilya Ehrenberg, "Yesterday and Today," *New Republic*, CXXXIV (June 11, 1956), pp. 53–55.

11. Suggested most fully by Barghoorn in his *Soviet Cultural Offensive*.

12. "No Weather Cold War," *Science News Letter*, LVI (October 22, 1949), p. 261. Concerning publications exchanges, see Reuben Peiss, "Problems in the Acquisition of Foreign Scientific Publications," *State Department Bulletin*, XII (January 30, 1950), pp. 151–155; "The Exchange of Scientific Information with the Soviet Union," *Bulletin of the Atomic Scientists*, IX (February, 1953), pp. 13–15; and "Russian Journals Now Easier to Obtain in the U.S.," *Science News Letter*, LXIII (February 28, 1953), p. 133.

13. G.K. Gresser, "I Went to Moscow," *Ladies Home Journal*, LXVII (October, 1950), pp. 48–49.

14. Oliver Vickery, "Capitalist on the Loose in Moscow," *Life*, XXXII (June 2, 1952), pp. 102–112.

15. "Iron Curtain: A Peek Behind It," *Newsweek*, XXXV (April 13, 1950), p. 35.

16. Dodee Wick, "Minnesota View of Life in the USSR," *Life*, XXXIV (April 20, 1953), pp. 21–25.

17. "College Reporters Interview the USSR," *Life*, XXXX (October 19, 1953), pp. 40–43.

18. "Russia's Wintry Look," *Life*, XXXVI (April 26, 1954), pp. 104–109.

19. Marshall MacDuffie, "Russia Uncensored," *Colliers*, CXXXIII (March 5, 1954), pp. 90–101. Among the Congressmen who went were Senator Margaret Chase Smith of Maine, Representative Victor Wickersham of Oklahoma and Representative Laurie C. Battle of Alabama. For examples of comments and reports, see *NYT*, November 8, 1955, p. 4; *Ibid.*, November 18, 1955, p. 3; and *Ibid.*, October 9, 1955, pp. 4, 6.

20. *Saturday Review*, XXXVII (May 15, 1954), pp. 29–31.

21. Emmet John Hughes, "A Perceptive Reporter in a Changing Russia," *Life*, XXXVI (February 8, 1954), pp. 114–120; Clifton Daniel, "First Surprises for the Moscow Visitor," *New York Times Magazine*, December 5, 1954, pp. 10–11.

22. Darryl Zanuck to Sherman Adams, April 20, 1953, Official File, Box 889, Folder 225-1, 1952–1953, USSR. Dwight D. Eisenhower Library, Abilene, Kansas. Cited hereafter as OF, Box 889, 225-1, 1952–1953, USSR, Eisenhower Library.

23. Transcript of Pearson broadcast, January 24, 1954, OF, Box 889, 225-1954, Eisenhower Library.

24. Pearson to Adams, January 25, 1954, *Ibid.*

25. Adams to Zanuck, May 4, 1953 and May 15, 1953, OF, Box 889, 225-1, 1952–1953, USSR, Eisenhower Library.

26. Adams to Pearson, February 4, 1954, OF, Box 889, 225-1954, Eisenhower Library.

27. Smith to Pearson, January 28, 1954, *Ibid.*

28. Transcript of Pearson broadcast, February 14, 1954, *Ibid.*

29. *NYT*, May 2, 1953, p. 20; *Ibid.*, May 3, 1953, p. 13; *Ibid.*, June 8, 1953, p. 35.

30. *Ibid.*, July 1, 1953, p. 16.

31. *Ibid.*, July 9, 1953, p. 1.

32. *Ibid.*, July 10, 1953, p. 1.

33. *Ibid.*, July 13, 1953, p. 12.

34. *NYT*, February 17, 1954, p. 36; *Ibid.*, February 19, 1954, p. 30; *Ibid.*, February 26, 1954, p. 26; *Ibid.*, October 30, 1954, p. 19; and *Ibid.*, October 29, 1954, p. 1. "Are the Doors Opening?" *Institute of International Education News Bulletin*, XXXI (October, 1955), p. 36; *State Department Bulletin*, XXXIII (November 14, 1955), p. 785; "Medicine in Russia," *Newsweek*, XLVI (September 26, 1955), pp. 104–105; Samuel Reshevsky, "Chess is Another Soviet Gambit," *New York Times Magazine*, June 13, 1954, pp. 18–19.

35. "Goodwill Gambit," *Newsweek*, XLIII (June 28, 1954), p. 54.

36. *NYT*, March 11, 1955, p. 4; *Pravda*, March 12, 1955, p. 4, translated in *CDSP*, Vol. VII, No. 10, April 20, 1955, p. 20; and *Pravda*, March 18, 1955, p. 4, translated in *CDSP*, Vol. VII, No. 11, April 27, 1955, p. 19.

37. "How Soviet 'Big Shots' Look to an American," *U.S. News and World Report*, XXXVIII (March 11, 1955), pp. 84–91; "Hearst in Moscow," *Nation*, CLXXX (March 12, 1955), pp. 211–212; and William O. Douglas, *Russian Journey* (Garden City, New York: Doubleday and Company, 1956). For Kennedy's comments and reactions regarding the trip, see Arthur M. Schlesinger, Jr., *Robert Kennedy and His Times* (New York: Ballantine Books, 1978), pp. 130–140; and *U.S. News and World Report*, XXXVIII (October 21, 1955), p. 62.

38. *NYT*, April 10, 1955, p. 15; "Medicine in Russia," pp. 104–105; *State Department Bulletin*, XXXIII (November 14, 1955), pp. 785–786. For text of the official agreement, see U.S. Department of State, *United States Treaties and Other International Agreements*, Vol. VI, pt. 3. "Exchange of Medical Films," TIAS No. 3409, September 5, 1955, pp. 3969–3970. See also "Are the Doors Opening?" p. 36.

39. "How Soviet 'Big Shots' Look to an American," p. 89.

40. *State Department Bulletin*, XXXII (March 21, 1955), p. 487. See also "Soviet Student Editors to Visit U.S.," *Institute of International Education News Bulletin*, XXX (April, 1955), p. 4–6.

41. "The Soviet Editors' Projected Visit," *Institute of International Education News Bulletin*, XXX (May, 1955), pp. 4–6.

42. Thye to Eisenhower, March 11, 1955, OF, Box 889, 225–1955, Eisenhower Library.

43. *NYT*, March 11, 1955, p. 24.

44. "The Soviet Editors' Projected Visit," p. 6.

45. *Ibid*.

46. *State Department Bulletin*, XXXIII (April 25, 1955), p. 695; *NYT*, April 16, 1955, p. 3. For the Soviet position, see *Pravda*, April 17, 1955, p. 2, translated in *CDSP*, Vol. VII, No. 16, June 1, 1955, p. 19.

47. *State Department Bulletin*, XXXIII (July 18, 1955), p. 104; *NYT*, April 16, 1955, p. 3.

48. *NYT*, April 18, 1955, p. 4; *Ibid.*, April 24, 1955, p. 53; *Ibid.*, May 8, 1955, p. 45.

49. *Pravda*, February 3, 1955, pp. 1–5, translated in *CDSP*, Vol. VII, No. 6, March 23, 1955, pp. 3–12.

50. Lauren Soth, "If Russians Want More Meat," *Des Moines Register*, February 10, 1955, p. 10.

51. *Selskoye Khozyaistvo*, March 1, p. 3, translated in *CDSP*, Vol. VII, No. 9, April 13, 1955, pp. 28–29.

52. Lauren Soth, "Let the Russians Come to Iowa," *Des Moines Register*, March 2, 1955, p. 8.

53. *NYT*, March 3, 1955, p. 9; U.S., President, *Public Papers of the Presidents of the United States* (Washington, D.C.: Office of the Federal Register, National Archives and Records Service, 1960–1961), Dwight D. Eisenhower, 1955, pp. 305–306.

54. *Business Week*, March 12, 1955, p. 196.

55. *Newsweek*, XLV (March 14, 1955), p. 250.

56. *Nation*, CLXXX (March 26, 1955), p. 10.

57. *Ibid*.

58. *Wall Street Journal*, March 14, 1955, p. 10.

59. *NYT*, March 4, 1955, p. 22.

60. "Cancelled Trip," *Commonweal*, LXII (April 29, 1955), pp. 92–93.

61. *NYT*, March 11, 1955, p. 4. See also *State Department Bulletin*, XXXII (June 6, 1955), p. 933.

62. *NYT*, March 11, 1955, p. 4.

63. Reproduced in *NYT*, May 7, 1955, p. 1. Original in *Pravda*, May 1, 1955, p. 1.

64. *State Department Bulletin*, XXXII (June 6, 1955), pp. 932–933. See also *NYT*, May 8, 1955, p. 45, and *NYT*, May 12, 1955, p. 7.

65. *State Department Bulletin*, XXXII (June 13, 1955), p. 970.

66. For travel schedules, names of delegates, etc., see *State Department Bulletin*, XXXIII (July 25, 1955), pp. 151–152.

67. *New York Times Index*, 1955, pp. 25–27.

68. Clifton Daniel, "Soviet Lets Its Farmers Read What Visiting U.S. Group Says," *NYT*, August 7, 1955, p. 2. For a specific example of American comments, see *Pravda*, August 21, 1955, p. 4, translated in *CDSP*, Vol. VII, No. 34, October 5, 1955, pp. 14–16. For other comments, see *CDSP*, Vol. VII, No. 31, pp. 14–16; *Ibid.*, No. 32, p. 15; and *Ibid.*, No. 33, pp. 18–19.

69. *NYT*, August 3, 1955, p. 7; *Ibid.*, August 8, 1955, p. 6; *Ibid.*, July 30, 1955, p. 15.

70. *Ibid.*, July 25, 1955, p. 5. See also "The Common Coin of Peace," *Colliers*, CXXXVI (September 2, 1955), pp. 82–83.

71. *NYT*, July 19, 1955, p. 3; and *Ibid.*, August 7, 1955, p. 2. For more regarding Matskevich and the Soviet delegates by the person chosen by the State Department to accompany them in the United States, see John Strohm, "The Truth about the Russian Visitors," *Farm Journal*, September, 1955, pp. 43–45.

72. "Common Coin of Peace," p. 83.

73. *Ibid*.

NOTES TO CHAPTER XI

1. U.S., Department of State, *The Geneva Conference of Heads of Government, July 18–23, 1955*, Pubn. No. 6046 (1955), pp. 18–22.

2. *Ibid.*, pp. 63–64.

3. *Ibid.*

4. For President Truman's proclamation extending the list of goods embargoed to Soviet bloc countries, see *NYT*, March 27, 1948, pp. 1–2. For the Commerce Department's "catalogue" of goods which those countries could purchase in the U.S., see *Ibid.*, May 13, 1948, p. 37.

5. *Mutual Defense Assistance Control Act of 1951* (Battle Act), Statutes at Large, LXV, secs. 101–105, 201–203, pp. 644–646 (1951). Other acts, particularly the Export Control Act, Trading with the Enemy Act, and Munitions Control Act, provided even more controls. For an informative article by the Deputy Director for Mutual Defense Assistance Control, see Walter S. Delany, "East-West Trade Controls," *State Department Bulletin*, XXXIII (December 5, 1955), pp. 918–924.

6. *Geneva Conference of Heads of Government*, pp. 67–68.

7. U.S., Department of State, *The Geneva Meeting of Foreign Ministers, October 27–November 16, 1955*, Pubn. No. 6156 (1955), p. 235.

8. *Ibid.*, pp. 237–238.

9. *Ibid.*, pp. 239–240.

10. *Ibid.*, p. 242.

11. *Ibid.*, p. 243.

12. *Ibid.*, p. 244.

13. *Ibid.*, pp. 242–248.

14. *Ibid.*, p. 248.

15. U.S., Department of State, *American Foreign Policy: 1950–1955: Basic Documents*, II, General Foreign Policy Series Pubn. No. 6446 (1957), p. 2021, n. 3.

16. *Geneva Meeting of Foreign Ministers*, pp. 266–267, 269–270.

17. Even the press releases at the Eisenhower Library are silent on the meetings. The releases provide a great deal of information to Saturday, November 12th, but skip from that day to Wednesday, November 16th. During those days the matter of East-West contact was discussed. McCardle Papers, Box 3, "Mr. Suydham's Briefings, Geneva — October, November, 1955," Eisenhower Library.

18. *Geneva Meeting of Foreign Ministers*, p. 249.

19. *Ibid.*

20. *Ibid.*, pp. 257–258, 270–272.

21. *Ibid.*, p. 272.

22. *Ibid.*, p. 271.

23. *Ibid.*

24. *Ibid.*, pp. 272–277; see also pp. 253–255.

25. *Ibid.*

26. *Ibid.*, p. 275.

27. *Ibid.*, p. 274.

28. *Ibid.*, p. 272.

29. *Ibid.*, pp. 277–278.

30. *Ibid.*, p. 278.

NOTES TO CHAPTER XII

1. For the housing specialists, see *Newsweek*, XLVI (October 17, 1955), p. 84; and *Time*, LXVI (November 21, 1955), p. 16; and for an article critical of the Soviet newsman and their presence by the person assigned by the State Department to accompany them in the U.S., Frank L. Kluckhohn, "Around the U.S. with Seven Reds," *Reader's Digest*, LXVIII (May, 1956), pp. 57–61. For the engineers, see *Science*, CXXII (December 16, 1955), p. 1180. For examples of Soviet visitors in the United States in early 1956, see Harrison Brown, "After Geneva," *Saturday Review*, XXXIX (June 23, 1956), p. 20; "USSR Seeks Polio Fighting Know-How," *Science News Letter*, CXIX (January 28, 1956), p. 57, and "Russian and U.S. Churchmen Talk," *Christian Century*, LXXIII (June 20, 1956), p. 751. See also *NYT*, December 4, 1956, p. 1.

2. The Soviet performances were heavily reported. For some examples, see *NYT*, August 7, 1955, sec. 2, p. 9; "Russian Virtuoso," *Musical America*, LXXV (November 1, 1955), p. 41, and "Russians and Records," *Newsweek*, XLVII (January 30, 1956), p. 92.

3. "Russians, Music and Us," *Musical America*, LXXV (December 15, 1955), p. 4.

4. *NYT*, December 4, 1956, p. 1.

5. *Time*, LXVI (September 19, 1955), p. 21. For views of some of the Congressmen who made the journey, see "What We Found Inside Russia: Interviews with Thirteen Congressmen," *U.S. News and World Report*, XXXIX (October 21, 1955), pp. 100–113.

6. W.S. Hall, "A Recent Visit to Moscow," *Publishers' Weekly*, CLXVIII (December 10, 1955), pp. 2342–2346; "Russian, U.S. Libraries to Expand Publications Exchange," *Ibid.* (November 5, 1955), pp. 1973–1974; and *NYT*, October 28, 1955, p. 1.

7. "Porgy and Bess Hailed in Moscow," *Musical America*, CXXV (January 15, 1956), p. 29. For a report by an accompanying writer, see Truman Capote, "Onward and Upward with the Arts: Porgy and Bess in Russia," *New Yorker*, XXXII (October 20–27, 1956), pp. 38–40, 41–42; and for the Soviet reaction as expressed by a person from the Soviet Embassy in Washington, Innoketny Popov, "Russian Report: Porgy and Bess," *Musical Courier*, CLIII (March 1, 1956), p. 7.

8. *Life*, XL (January 9, 1956), pp. 17–23. An official of the Soviet Ministry of Culture told *Variety* reporter Irving R. Levine that there would be no generalizations of an unfavorable sort that could endanger the cause of contacts between the two countries, and an examination of the reviews in the *CDSP* bears out the official's remark. See Irving R. Levine, "ussr May Cite 'Porgy' as Evidence there's No Iron Curtain for Arts," *Variety*, CCI (December 29, 1955), p. 1.

9. For Isaac Stern, see "A Violinist Looks at Russia," *NYT*, July 8, 1956, sec. 2, p. 7; "Isaac Stern Reports on Russian Tour," *Musical America*, LXXV (July, 1956), p. 21; Irving R. Levine, "Isaac Stern's Rock Soviet Tour Raises Reds' Opinion of U.S. Cultural Standing," *Variety*, CCII (May 30, 1956), p. 60. For Jan Peerce, see *NYT*, July 29, 1956, sec. 2, p. 7; M.J. Matz, "Soviet Gesture: An Interview with Jan Peerce," *Opera News*, XXI (November 19, 1956), pp. 16–19.

10. *NYT*, September 16, 1956, sec. 4, p. 4; "Boston in Russia," *Time*, LXVIII (September 17, 1956), p. 86. For an example of a Soviet review, see *CDSP*, Vol. VIII, no. 36, pp. 6–7.

11. *Public Papers of the Presidents*, Eisenhower, 1956, p. 713.

12. *Ibid.*, p. 751.

13. *NYT*, December 4, 1956, p. 1. See also David Dallin's comments in *Ibid.*, December 16, 1956, sec. 4, p. 8.

14. *Variety*, CC (October 5, 1955), p. 68; *Ibid.* (October 12, 1955), pp. 75–76; *NYT*, September 24, 1955, p. 3; *NYT*, June 23, 1957, p. 32; *NYT*, June 28, 1957, p. 30; *NYT*, April 7, 1957, sec. 2, p. 9.

15. *Variety*, CCII (May 15, 1956), p. 60; *Ibid.* (April 4, 1956), p. 60; *NYT*, March 6, 1956, p. 26.

16. *Variety*, CCI (December 28, 1955), p. 3; *NYT*, March 6, 1956, p. 26; *NYT*, August 27, 1956, p. 14.

17. *NYT*, April 13, 1956, p. 1; Popov, "Porgy and Bess," p. 7.

18. *NYT*, June 8, 1956, p. 2.

19. *Ibid.*, pp. 1, 6.

20. Paul E. Zinner, *Documents on American Foreign Relations, 1956* (New York: Harper and Brothers, 1957), pp. 219–220.

21. *Ibid.*, pp. 215–216.

22. *NYT*, April 27, 1956, pp. 1, 3; *Ibid.*, May 20, 1956, pp. 2, 3; *Ibid.*, October 12, 1956, p. 1; *Ibid.*, October 14, 1956, p. 11.

23. McCardle Papers, Box 7, 1955 Press Conferences, October 18, 1955, Eisenhower Library.

24. McCardle Papers, Box 7, 1956 Secretary's Press Conferences (1), April 24, 1956, Eisenhower Library.

25. *State Department Bulletin*, XXXIV (May 7, 1956), p. 752.

26. *NYT*, November 11, 1955, p. 1; *Ibid.*, November 12, 1955, p. 3; *Business Week*, November 19, 1955, p. 74.

27. Chester Bowles, "What Are We Afraid Of?" *Saturday Review*, XL (August 24, 1957), pp. 12–13; *NYT*, June 20, 1957, p. 4.

28. White to Adams, July 9, 1956, OF Box 889, 225, 1956–1, Eisenhower Library. See also "Dr. White Goes to Russia," *Science News Letter*, LXIX (August 4, 1956), p. 70.

29. *Variety*, CC (October 26, 1955), p. 55; *Ibid.*, CCI (December 28, 1955), p. 1; *Ibid.*, CCII (April 4, 1956), p. 60.

30. *Musical America*, LXXV (December 15, 1955), p. 4; *Variety*, CCII (May 16, 1956), p. 60.

31. Jackson to Cabot, March 5, 1956, C.D. Jackson Papers, Time, Inc. Files, Box 30, BSO, 53–56, Eisenhower Library. "The thing that gives me pain really is that we have fallen into the same pattern of behavior," Cabot replied three days later. True enough, he wrote, they "might bring in under cover of a bass viol some sort of a spy but they can get the spies in anyway. The general attitude of fear and suspicion which has been created in this country merely builds more fear and suspicion in Russia. Someday, somehow, somewhere, the vicious cycle needs to be broken." Cabot to Jackson, March 8, 1956, as cited above.

32. *Public Papers of the Presidents*, Eisenhower, 1956, p. 472; *State Department Bulletin*, XXXV (July 9, 1956), pp. 54–55.

33. *NYT*, June 13, 1957, p. 30.

34. *State Department Bulletin*, XXXVII (July 1, 1957), p. 13.

35. *Ibid.*, XXXIV (January 2, 1956), pp. 18–19.

36. *New York Times Magazine*, July 29, 1956, pp. 8–9.

37. According to *Time*, thirteen American publishers refused to print the Soviet publication before the State Department persuaded Manhattan's small Hemisphere Press to do so. *Time*, LXVIII (July 30, 1956), p. 50.

38. *State Department Bulletin*, XXXV (October 8, 1956), p. 550. For the Soviet reply, see *Ibid.*, (October 15, 1956), p. 582.

39. *Ibid.*, (October 29, 1956), p. 665; "Were Those Election Observers Really Spies?" *Saturday Evening Post*, CCXXIX (December 15, 1956), p. 10.

40. Dulles speech before Philadelphia Bulletin Forum, Philadelphia, February 26, 1956, in Zinner, *Documents, 1956*, pp. 196–198.

41. From May 15, 1956, news conference, *Ibid.*, p. 204.

42. *Ibid.*, pp. 203–204.

43. *State Department Bulletin*, XXXVII (August 5, 1957), pp. 228–229. In the shake-up to which Dulles referred, Malenkov, Kaganovich, Molotov and Shepilov were branded an anti-Party group and removed from their posts in the Presidium and Central Committee. For translation of resolution on anti-Party group by Central Committee as printed in *Pravda*, July 4, 1956, see *CDSP*, Vol. I, no. 23, July 17, 1957, pp. 5–7.

44. *State Department Bulletin*, XXXVII (August 5, 1957), pp. 228–229.

45. Robert R. Bowie, "Tasks Ahead for the Free World," *Ibid.*, XXXVI (May 27, 1957), p. 838.

46. Khrushchev made the point at a meeting with a group of American governors in 1959. What, he asked, did American officials want from his country? "If it is what we think you want, you will not achieve it, I will tell you...," he answered his own question, "if it is the hope that through various exchanges, the sale of American newspapers, the Soviet people can be turned from Communism to private enterprise, that is impossible." Moreover, he stated later during the discussion in reference to the 1959 exhibit, according to his intelligence reports and State Department documents, some in Washington believed that the exhibit "would so captivate the Russian people, they would immediately overthrow the government." That, the Soviet leader told his guests in an angry tone, was a severe misunderstanding. "Interview with Premier Khrushchev at the Kremlin, Moscow, July 7, 1959," OF, Box 891, 225-1959-2, Eisenhower Library. See also *NYT*, June 3, 1957, p. 6, for Khrushchev's remarks on American television concerning the matter.

47. *NYT*, June 20, 1957, p. 4.

48. *Ibid.*, June 23, 1957, p. 32; *Ibid.*, June 28, 1957, p. 30; *Musical America*, LXXVII (July, 1957), p. 17.

49. *NYT*, June 28, 1957, p. 30.

50. *Ibid.*, June 3, 1957, p. 6.

51. *Ibid.*, June 7, 1957, p. 4; *Ibid.*, June 20, 1957, p. 4; *Variety*, CCVII (June 19, 1957), p. 2.

52. Text of Eisenhower news conference, *NYT*, June 6, 1957, p. 14; *State Department Bulletin*, XXXVII (July 1, 1957), p. 13.

53. Text of speech in *Congressional Record*, CIII, June 10, 1957, pp. 8576–8577.

54. For a sampling of the Senators' remarks and editorial comments, see *Ibid.*, pp. 8577–8579; 8791–8792; 8892–8894; 8929–8930; 8982–8984; 9311; A4671–A4672; A4758; A5425–A5427; A5487; A5863.

55. *Ibid.*, p. A4758.

56. *State Department Bulletin*, XXXVII (July 15, 1957), p. 119.

57. *NYT*, June 28, 1957, p. 1.

58. Text of Soviet note in *Ibid.*, July 28, 1957, p. 4.

59. *Ibid.*

60. See, for instance, comments of three top Soviet leaders pertaining to fingerprinting at a reception attended by Isaac Stern, *NYT*, June 1, 1956, p. 1.

61. Earl Voss, "Should We Fingerprint Foreign Visitors?" *Washington Star*, July 21, 1957, as printed in *Congressional Record*, CIII, August 5, 1957, pp. 13598–13599; Ernest K. Lindley, "Why Fingerprinting?" *Newsweek*, L (August 19, 1957), p. 32.

62. Zinner, *Documents*, 1956, pp. 81–82, and *Documents*, 1957, p. 69.

63. *NYT*, July 21, 1957, p. 1.

64. U.S., Congress, Senate, Senator Jacob Javits introducing Senate Concurrent Resolution 44 and Senate Bill 2704, 85th Cong., 1st sess., August 5, 1957, *Congressional Record*, CIII, p. 13598.

65. *State Department Bulletin*, XXXVII (October 28, 1957), p. 682.

66. U.S., Department of State, *American Foreign Policy: Current Documents, 1957*, General Foreign Policy Series Pubn. No. 7101 (1961), pp. 738–740.

67. *State Department Bulletin*, XXXVII (November 18, 1957), pp. 801–803.

68. William S.B. Lacy interview, Oral History Research Office, Columbia University, June 14, 1972, Eisenhower Library.

69. *Ibid.*

70. U.S., Department of State, *United States Treaties and Other International Agreements*, Vol. IX, "Agreement Between the United States of America and the Union of Soviet Socialist Republics on Exchanges in the Cultural, Technical, and Educational Fields," TIAS No. 3975, January 27, 1958, pp. 13–25.

71. *Ibid.*, p. 14.

72. *Ibid.*, pp. 14, 25.

NOTES TO CHAPTER XIII

1. U.S., Congress, Senate, Committee on Foreign Relations, *United States Exchange Programs with the Soviet Union, Poland, Czechoslovakia, Rumania and Hungary*, Committee Print, 86th Cong., 1st sess., August 20, 1959, pp. 1–3.

2. *Ibid.*, pp. 1, 4.

3. *Ibid.*, p. 1. For negotiating specific arrangements and showing the first films under the agreement, see *State Department Bulletin*, XXXIX (November 3, 1958), pp. 697–698; and *State Department Bulletin*, XLI (November 9, 1959), p. 671. For an informative article concerning film exchanges, see Jack Valenti, "The Motion Picture Bridge Between East and West," *Saturday Review*, L (December 23, 1967), pp. 8–10. For text of agreement between the science academies, see *State Department Bulletin*, XLI (September 7, 1959), pp. 350–353.

4. *United States Exchange Programs with the Soviet Union, Poland, Czechoslovakia, Rumania and Hungary*, p. 4.

5. Bob Hope, "I Found the Russians Can Laugh Too," *Look*, XXII (June 10, 1958), pp. 22–26; "End Play by the Arts," *Christian Century*, LXXV (April 30, 1958), p. 524.

6. For Van Cliburn see Chris Nelson, "Van Cliburn: Young Man with a Mission," *Musical Courier*, CLVII–CLVIII (September, 1958), p. 2; for the Philadelphia Symphony, *Ibid.*, (July, 1958), p. 18; and for Leopold Stokowski, *Ibid.*, (June, 1958), p. 4.

7. Harold C. McClellan, "The American National Exhibition in Moscow," OF, Box 722, 139-B-5(5), Eisenhower Library. This lengthy report written by the general manager of the Moscow Fair contains a great deal of interesting and useful information concerning the staging of that extravaganza. Representative Francis E. Walter, Chairman of the House Un American Activities Committee, decided that at least half the artists represented at the Fair had communist connections, and demanded that some of the paintings be removed. Eisenhower refused, but did agree to add more works to make the exhibit more "American." For Walter's published accusations see Francis E. Walter, "Our Art Exhibition in Moscow," *American Mercury*, LXXXIX (September, 1959), pp. 98–104. The two most important communications between Walter and Eisenhower on the matter were Walter to Eisenhower, July 8, 1959, and Eisenhower to Walter, July 16, 1959, contained in OF, Box 722, 139-B-5(3), Eisenhower Library. See also Frank Getlein, "Politicians as Art Critics: Thoughts on the U.S. Exhibition in Moscow," *New Republic*, CXLI (July 27, 1959), pp 11–14, and the same author's "Pictures at an Exhibition: Russia's Reaction to U.S. Show in Moscow," *Ibid.*, CXLI (August 24, 1959), pp. 12–15.

8. McClellan, "The American National Exhibition in Moscow," p. 40.

9. See "Americans There, Russians Here: Biz Terrific," *Life*, XLIV (April 28, 1958), pp. 28–35; "Moscow's Hit Show in the U.S.," *New York Times Magazine*, May 11, 1958, pp. 16–17; and "Direct from Moscow: Russia's Best," *Newsweek*, LIII (April 13, 1959), pp. 111–115.

10. "Direct from Moscow: Russia's Best," p. 113.

11. For Shostakovich's return, see *Musical America*, LXXIX (December 1, 1958), pp. 3–8; for the Soviet Exhibit, see *Architectural Record*, CXXVI (August, 1959), pp. 24–25.

12. Clifton Daniel, "First Surprises for the Moscow Visitor," *New York Times Magazine*, December 5, 1954, pp. 10–11.

13. For examples, see Emmet John Hughes, "A Perceptive Reporter in a Changing Russia," *Life*, XXXVI (February 8, 1954), pp. 114–120; Charles W. Thayer, "I Found Russia Changed," *Saturday Evening Post*, CCXXVIII (December 10, 1955), p. 1.

14. Merle Fainsod, "What Russian Students Think," *Atlantic Monthly*, CXCIX (February, 1957), p. 33.

15. "What We Found Inside Russia: Interviews with Thirteen Congressmen," *U.S. News and World Report*, XXXIX (October 21, 1955), p. 100.

16. *Ibid.*, pp. 106, 108. See also remarks of Catholic priest James A Magner in *Commonweal*, LXV (November 23, 1956), pp. 204–206; Paul B. Anderson in "Churchmen Visit Russia: A Report of the National Council of Churches Deputation to Moscow," *Christian Century*, LXXIII (April 18, 1956), pp. 480–483; and the editor of the *Arizona Daily Star* in *Saturday Review*, LXXXVII (May 15, 1954), pp. 29–31.

17. Hughes, "Perceptive Reporter," p. 115.

18. "The Quakers Meet the Russians," *Saturday Review*, XXXIX (September 8, 1956), p. 16.

19. Daniels, "First Surprises," p. 10.

20. Frederick L. Schuman, "Russia Revisited: Moscow, Symbol of Change," *Nation*, CLXXXIII (July 19, 1956), p. 51.

21. "That Cultural Curtain," *Nation*, CLXXXII (February 4, 1956), p. 83. For Chandler's nine part series on the Soviet trip as printed in the *Los Angeles Times*, November 6–15, 1955, see reprint in *Congressional Record*, CCII, January 9, 1956, pp. A108–A114.

Selected Bibliography

Unpublished Material

This study is based largely on unpublished sources. The Diplomatic Branch of the National Archives in Washington afforded basic information concerning Washington's official cultural contacts with Moscow as well as valuable information and leads relating to nonofficial contacts. The records and correspondence of the New York American-Russian Institute, held by the Library for Intercultural Studies located in the Bobst Library on the New York University campus yielded extensive material on the Institute's activities as well as those of its predecessor, the Society for Cultural Relations with Russia. The currently functioning San Francisco American-Russian Institute generously provided access to similar information concerning its activities. A limited amount of material pertaining to early contacts was found in the Hoover Institution on War, Revolution and Peace at Palo Alto, California, and the Eisenhower Library, Abilene, Kansas, yielded random but useful material on contacts during the fifties.

Official Documents

An Act to Exclude from the United States Aliens Who Are Members of Anarchistic and Similar Classes. Statutes at Large, Vol. XL (1918).
Dennet, Raymond and Turner, Robert, eds. *Documents on American Foreign Relations*, Vol. IX–XIII. Princeton, New Jersey: Princeton University Press, 1949–1953.
Foreign Agents Registration Act of 1938. Statutes at Large, Vol. LIII (1938).
Immigration Act of 1917. Statutes at Large, Vol. XXXIX (1917).
Immigration and Nationality Act of 1952. Statutes at Large, Vol. LXVI (1952).
Internal Security Act of 1950 (McCarran Act). *Statutes at Large*, Vol. LXIV (1950).
Mutual Defense Assistance Control Act of 1951 (Battle Act). *Statutes at Large*, Vol. LXV (1951).
U.S., Congress. *Congressional Record*, 79th through 85th Congresses, Vols. XCI–CIV, 1945–1948.
U.S., Congress. House. *Fifth Semiannual Report on Educational Exchange Activities*. H. Doc. 108, 82nd Cong., 1st sess., 1951.
U.S., Congress. House. *Sixth Semiannual Report on the United States Advisory Commission on Information*. H. Doc. 526, 82nd Cong., 2nd sess., 1952.

217

U.S., Senate. Committee on Foreign Relations. *United States Exchange Programs with the Soviet Union, Poland, Czechoslovakia, Rumania and Hungary.* Committee Print, 86th Cong., 1st sess., 1952.

U.S., Congress. Senate. *Departments of State, Justice, Commerce and the Judiciary, Appropriations for 1952.* Senate Hearings, Part II, 82nd Cong., 1st sess., 1951.

U.S., Senate. Committee on Foreign Relations. *Overseas Information Program of the United States.* Senate Hearings, Part II, 82nd Cong., 1st sess., 1951.

U.S., Department of State. *Department of State Bulletin.* Vols. I–XLI (1939–1959).

U.S., Department of State. *Foreign Relations of the United States: Annual Volumes, 1918–1950.* Washington, D.C., 1931–1978.

U.S., Department of State. *Foreign Relations of the United States: The Soviet Union, 1933–1939.* Washington, D.C., 1952.

U.S., Department of State. *The Geneva Conference of Heads of Government, July 18–25, 1955.* Pubn. No. 6046 (1955).

U.S., Department of State. *The Geneva Meeting of Foreign Ministers, October 27–November 16, 1955.* Pubn. No. 6156 (1955).

U.S., Department of State. *United States Treaties and Other International Agreements,* Vol. IX. "Agreement Between the United States of America and the Union of Soviet Socialist Republics on Exchanges in the Cultural, Educational and Technical Fields," TIAS No. 3975, January 27, 1958.

U.S., Department of State. *United States Treaties and Other International Agreements,* Vol. VI, part 2. "Exchange of Medical Films," TIAS No. 3409, September 5, 1955.

U.S., Department of State. *American Foreign Policy: Current Documents, 1950–1955.* General Foreign Policy Series Pubn. No. 7101 (1961).

U.S., President. *Public Papers of the Presidents of the United States.* Washington, D.C.: Office of the *Federal Register,* National Archives and Records Service, 1950–1961. Dwight D. Eisenhower, 1956–1958.

Zinner, Paul E., ed. *Documents on American Foreign Relations, 1955–1959.* New York: Harper and Brothers, 1956–1960.

Newspapers and Miscellaneous

Current Digest of the Soviet Press, 1950–1958.
New York Times, 1918–1958.
Wall Street Journal, 1955–1958.

Articles in Magazines and Journals

"Aid to Russian Scientists." *Science,* LVI (November 3, 1922), 503–505.

Alexandrova, Vera. "America and Americans in Soviet Literature." *Russian Review,* II (Spring, 1943), 19–26.

Allison, Brent Dow. "From the Cultural Front in Russia." *Dial,* LXXXV (September, 1928), 239–245.

"American Assistance for Russian Educational Institutions." *Science,* XLIX (June 27, 1919), 613–614.

"American Books Presented for Soviet Libraries." *Publishers Weekly,* CXLV (January 15, 1944), 207.

"American Committee to Aid Russian Scientists with Scientific Literature." *Science*, LV (June 23, 1922), 667–668.

"American-Soviet Architects Committee." *Magazine of Art*, XXXVII (May, 1944), 195–196.

"American-Soviet Building Conference." *Architectural Record*, XCVII (June, 1945), 20.

"An Appeal from Russian Intellectuals." *Living Age*, CCCV (June 12, 1920), 650–651.

Anderson, Paul B. "Churchmen Visit Russia: A Report of the National Council of Churches Deputation to Moscow." *Christian Century*, LXXIII (April 18, 1956), 480–483.

"Architects' Committee for American-Soviet Friendship." *Journal of American Institute of Architects*, I–II (May, 1944), 250–252.

"Architecture Exhibit Presented to Russia." *Architectural Record*, XCVIII (December, 1945), 134.

"Are the Doors Opening?" *Institute of International Education News Bulletin*, XXXI (October, 1955), 36–38.

"Art Supplies for Russia." *Magazine of Art*, XXXVII (February, 1944), 69.

"Artists Seek Closer Relations." *Soviet Russia Today*, (September, 1945), 25.

"As They See Us in Russia." *Modern Music*, XX (May–June, 1943), 268–270.

Barnes, Joseph. "Cultural Recognition of Russia." *Nation*, CXXXVI (May 18, 1932), 565.

Barnes, Kathleen. "Intensive Study of the Russian Language." *Institute of International Education News Bulletin*, XIII (February 1, 1938), 6–9.

Bird, Carol. "The Philosophy of Russian Dancing." *Theatre Magazine*, XXXV (January, 1922), 22.

Blake, Peter. "The Soviet Architectural Purge." *Architectural Record*, CVI (September, 1949), 127–129.

Blum, R. "Letter from Leningrad." *New Yorker*, XXXVIII (July 14, 1962), 81–82.

"Books Sought for Soviet Libraries." *Publishers Weekly*, CXLIV (November 6, 1943), 1789–1790.

Bowles, Chester. "What Are We Afraid Of?" *Saturday Review*, XL (August 24, 1957), 12–13.

Brasch, Frederick E. "History and Activities of the USSR Academy of Sciences During the Past Twenty-Five Years," *Science*, XCIX (June 1, 1944), 439–444.

Brickman, William W. "John Dewey's Foreign Reputation as an Educator." *School and Society*, LXX (October 22, 1949), 257–265.

Brown, Harrison. "After Geneva." *Saturday Review*, XXXIX (June 23, 1956), 2.

Burgi, Richard T. "Russian Virtuoso." *Musical America*, LXXV (November 1, 1955), 9–10.

Burk, Dean. "A Scientist in Moscow." *Scientific Monthly*, XLVII (September, 1938), 227–231.

Byrnes, Robert F. "The Academic Labor Market: Where Do We Go from Here?" *Slavic Review*, (June, 1977), 286–291.

"Calling a Turn." *Musical America*, LXXIV (May, 1954), 13–14.

"Cancelled Trip." *Commonweal*, LXII (April 29, 1955), 92–93.

"Chaliapin—Another Thrill." *Literary Digest*, LXXI (December 31, 1921), 24–25.

Chamberlin, Henry. "Missionaries of American Technique in Russia." *Asia*, XXXII (July, 1932), 422–427.

Cockerell, T.D.A. "A Journey in Siberia." *Scientific Monthly*, XIX (October, 1924), 415–433.

Cole, Toby. "A Library on the Soviet Union." *Library Journal*, LXX (May 15, 1945), 476–479.

"College Reporters Interview the USSR." *Life*, XXXV (October, 1953), 40–43.

"Cultural Relations with the Soviet Union." *Nation*, CXX (January 14, 1925), 53.

Dallin, David. "Post Office Folly." *New Leader* (October 20, 1952), 11.

Daniel, Clifton. "First Surprises for the Moscow Visitor." *New York Times Magazine*, (December 5, 1954), 10–11.

Delany, Walter S. "East-West Trade Controls." *Department of State Bulletin*, XXXIII (December 5, 1955), 918–924.

Dewey, John. "Impressions of Soviet Russia." *New Republic*, LVI (November 14, 1928), 343–344; LVII (November 21–December 19, 1928), 11–14, 38–42, 64–67, 91–94, 134–137.

Dimand, M.S. "Exhibition of Russian Icons." *Parnassus*, III (February, 1931), 35 36.

"Dr. White Goes to Russia." *Science News Letter*, LXIX (August 4, 1956), 70.

Duggan, Stephen P. "Cultural Cooperation with the USSR." *Institute of International Education News Bulletin*, IX (December, 1933), 3–5.

Dunn, L.C. "Scientific Interchange Between the United States and Soviet Russia." *Science*, XCI (February 23, 1945), 200–201.

Dvoichenko-Markov, Eufrosina. "Benjamin Franklin, the American Philosophical Society and the Russian Academy of Sciences." *Proceedings of the American Philosophical Society*, XCI (1947), 250–257.

_____. "The American Philosophical Society and Early Russian-American Relations." *Proceedings of the American Philosophical Society*, XCIV (December, 1950), 549–610.

Eddy, Harriet G. "Beginning of United Library Service in USSR." *Library Journal*, LVII (January 15, 1932), 61–67.

Ehrenberg, Ilya. "Of Love and Hate." *Soviet Russia Today*, (June, 1946), 8.

_____. "Yesterday and Today." *New Republic*, CXXXIV (June 11, 1956), 53–55.

"Eisenstein in Hollywood." *New Republic*, LXVIII (November 4, 1931), 320–322.

Eisenstein, Serge Mikhailovich. "Mass Movies." *Nation*, CXXV (November 9, 1927), 507–508.

"Exhibit for the USSR." *Architectural Forum*, LXXXI (September, 1944), 194.

Fainsod, Merle. "What Russian Students Think." *Atlantic Monthly*, CXCIX (February, 1957), 31–36.

Fischer, Louis. "What They Read in Soviet Russia." *Nation*, CXXI (November 11, 1925), 538–539.

Feuer, Lewis S. "American Travelers to the Soviet Union, 1917–1932: The Formation of a Component of New Deal Ideology." *American Quarterly*, XIV (Summer, 1962), 118–149.

Ford, Henry. "Why I Am Helping Russian Industry." *Nation's Business*, XVIII (June, 1930), 20–23.

Fuller, Donald. "New York, '42; Soviet Tribute." *Modern Music*, XX (November–December, 1942), 37–38.

Gannett, Lewis S. "Americans in Russia." *Nation*, CXIII (Aug. 17, 1921), 167–168.

Getlein, Frank. "Politicans as Art Critics: Thoughts on the U.S. Exhibition in Moscow." *New Republic*, CXLI (July 27, 1959), 11–14.

_____. "Pictures at an Exhibition: Russia's Reaction to the U.S. Show in Moscow." *New Republic*, CXLI (August 24, 1959), 12–15.

Gresser, G.K. "I Went to Moscow." *Ladies Home Journal*, LXVII (October, 1950), 48–49.

Hanfman, Andrew M. "The American Villain on the Soviet Stage." *Russian Review*, IX–X (January, 1951), 131–145.

Hanser, Richard. "Okay, Comrades, Let's Jazz it Up." *Saturday Review*, XXXIX (June 16, 1956), 36–37.

Hanson, Haldore. "Two-Way Traffic to Moscow." *New Republic*, CXXXIII (November 7, 1955), 6–8.

Hastings. A. Baird and Shimkin, Michael B. "Medical Research Mission to the Soviet Union." *Science*, CIII (May 17–May 24, 1946), 605–609; 637–644.

Hindus, Maurice G. "American Authors in Russia." *Saturday Review of Literature*, I (August 16, 1924), 50–51.

_____. "Ford Conquers Russia." *Outlook*, CXLVI (June 29, 1927), 280–283.

_____. "Pinch-Hitter for the Soviets." *American Magazine*, CXIII (April, 1932), 31–33.

"How Soviet 'Big Shots' Look to an American." *U.S. News and World Report*, XXXVIII (March 11, 1958), 84–91.

Hughes, Emmet John. "A Perceptive Reporter in a Changing Russia." *Life*, XXXVI (February 8, 1954), 114–120.

Huntington, W. Chapin. "The Russian Translation Project of the American Council of Learned Societies." *Russian Review*, IV (Spring, 1945), 40–48.

_____. "The Russian Translation Project Three Years Later. Russian Review, VII (Spring, 1948), 76–87.

"Isaac Stern Reports on Recent Russian Tour." *Musical America*, LXXV (July, 1956), 21.

Jennings, Amy S. "How to Travel in Soviet Russia." *Nation*, CXXXVI (May 10, 1933), 528–530.

Johnston, Eric A. "To Bridge the Gulf Between the U.S. and Russia." *Reader's Digest*, XLV (August, 1944), 33–36.

_____. "My Talk with Joseph Stalin." *Reader's Digest*, XLV (Oct., 1944), 1–10.

Jones, Dorsey D. and Meltzer, Sol. "Colleges Need Russian History." *Journal of Higher Education*, IV (October, 1933), 358–359.

Josephson, Matthew. "From a Russian Notebook." *Travel*, LXIV (November, 1934), 16–19.

Karmashov, V. "Non-Ferrous Metal Industry in Soviet Russia." *Engineers and Mining Journal*, CXXX (July 24, 1930), 67–68.

Kellog, Vernon B. "The Present Status of University Men in Russia." *Science*, LIV (November 25, 1921), 510–511.

Kennel, Ruth Epperson. "Kuzbas in 1924." *Nation*, CXIX (November 26, 1924), 566–568.

_____. "Kuzbas Tells Its Own Story." *Nation*, CXVII (August 8, 1923), 145–147.

Kluckhohn, Frank L. "Around the U.S. with Seven Reds: Close-Up of Soviet 'Journalists' in Action." *Reader's Digest*, LXVIII (May, 1956), 57–61.

Koten, Bernard. "Library for Soviet Research." *Library Journal*, LXXXII (November 15, 1957), 2874–2875.

_____. "Our G.I.'s Learn about Russia." *Soviet Russia Today* (July, 1946), 16–18.

"KR Dissolves Cancer?" *Science Digest*, XXI (January, 1947), 33.

"KR for Cancer." *Time*, XLVIII (July 8, 1946), 63–64.

Krutch, Joseph Wood. "The Season in Moscow: Eisenstein and Lunacharsky." *Nation*, CXXVI (June 27, 1928), 716–717.

LaFollette, Robert M. "What I Saw in Europe." *LaFollette's Magazine*, XVI (January, 1924), 4–6.

Langmuir, Irving. "Science and Incentives in Russia." *Scientific Monthly*, LXIII (August, 1946), 85–92.

"Libraries in Soviet Russia." *Literary Digest*, XCIII (April 9, 1927), 28.

Littell, Robert. "Soviet Arts and Handicrafts." *New Republic*, LVIII (February 20, 1929), 18–19.

Magidoff, Robert. "American Literature in Russia." *Saturday Review of Literature*, XXI (November 2, 1946), 9–12.

Marx, Howard. "Shostakovich in New York." *Music News*, XLI (May, 1949), 4.

McNab, Tansey. "The Soviet Invasion of America." *Nation*, CXXV (November 9, 1927), 528–530.

"Medical Aid for Russia." *Nation*, CXV (November 1, 1922), 470.

"Medicine in Russia." *Newsweek*, XLVI (September 26, 1955), 104–105.

Mikhailov, G. "A Soviet Exposé of Our Musical Press." *Musical America*, LXX (January 15, 1950), 6.

Moseley, Philip E. "The Russian Institute of Columbia University." *Proceedings of the American Philosophical Society*, XC (January, 1955), 36–39.

Mudd, Stuart. "Cultural Interchange Between the United States and the Soviet Union." *Science*, C (December 1, 1944), 486–487.

————. "Recent Observations on Progress for Medicine and National Health in the USSR." *Proceedings of the American Philosophical Society*, XCI (April, 1947), 181–188.

Muller, H.J. "Observations of Biological Sciences in Russia." *Scientific Monthly*, XVI (January–June, 1923), 539–542.

Narodny, Ivan. "American Jazz and Russian Ballet: The Rhythmic Reformers of Russia and America." *Theatre Magazine*, XLII (October, 1925), 12.

"No Weather Cold War." *Science News Letter*, LVI (October 22, 1949), 262.

O'Hara, Eliot. "Russia Today as a Field for Painters." *American Magazine of Art*, XXI (April, 1930), 214–218.

Parry, Albert. "Soviet Writers View America." *Bookman*, LXXIII (August, 1930), 576–583.

Pauling, Linus. "My Efforts to Obtain a Passport." *Bulletin of the Atomic Scientists*, VII (October, 1952), 252–253.

Peiss, Reuben. "Problems in the Acquisition of Foreign Scientific Publications." *Department of State Bulletin*, XXII (January 30, 1950), 151–155.

Pope, Arthur Upham. "Scientists are Public Heroes." *Soviet Russia Today* (September, 1945), 9–11.

"Porgy and Bess in Moscow." *Musical America*, LXXV (January 15, 1956), 29.

Posin, J.A. "Russian Studies in American Colleges." *Russian Review*, VII–VIII (Spring, 1948), 62–68.

Powell, Lyman P. "A Clergyman Looks at Russia." *Review of Reviews*, XC (October, 1934), 62–63.

Prokofiev, Serge. "My Cinderella." *Modern Music*, XXI (Jan.–Feb., 1944), 67–69.

Reshevsky, Samuel. "Chess is Another Soviet Gambit." *New York Times Magazine* (June 13, 1954), 18–19.

Richman, Alfred. "Serge M. Eisenstein." *Dial*, LXXXVI (April, 1929), 311–314.

Rickard, Edgar. "Engineers Work Through the Relief Administration." *Mining and Metallurgy*, III (November, 1922), 35–37.

Rodis, Themistocles Clayton. "Russo-American Contacts During the Hoover Administration." *South Atlantic Quarterly*, LI (April, 1952), 235–245.

Robinson, Reid. "A CIO Report on the USSR." *Soviet Russia Today* (January, 1946), 13.

Roosevelt, Elliot. "A Personal Interview with Stalin." *Look*, II (Feb. 4, 1947), 21–25.

Rothschild, John. "The Intelligent Traveler: Tours to the Soviet Union." *Nation*, CXXXVII (May 9, 1934), 536–537.

"Russia Bids for the Tourist Trade." *Review of Reviews*, LXXXIV (August, 1931), 94–96.

"Russia Expects Many Tourists." *Literary Digest*, CXVII (June 9, 1934), 45.

"Russian and American Season." *Modern Music*, XXII (May–June, 1945), 254–255.

"Russian and U.S. Churchmen Talk." *Christian Century*, LXXIII (June 20, 1956), 751.

"Russians and Records." *Newsweek*, XLVII (January 30, 1956), 92.

"Russians, Music and Us." *Musical America*, LXXV (December 15, 1955), 4.

"Russia's Wintry Look." *Life*, XXX (April 26, 1954), 104–109.

Salisbury, Harrison. "Russia Beckons Big Business." *Colliers*, CXIV (Sept. 3, 1944), 11.

Sayler, Oliver M. "Europe's Premier Playhouse in the Offing: The Noted Moscow Art Theatre and Its Plans for an American Tour." *Theatre Magazine*, XXXVI (October, 1922), 215–217.

_____. "The Lyric Daughter of the Sober Russians." *Theatre Magazine*, XLII (September, 1925), 12–14.

Schuman, Frederick L. "Russia Revisited." *Nation*, CLXXXIII (July 14, 1956), 51–53.

Schwartz, Harry. "The Cold War on Russia's Stage." *New York Times Magazine* (November 27, 1949), 28–29.

"Scientific Interchange Between the United States and Soviet Russia." *Science*, CI (February 23, 1945), 200–201.

"Seeing Red—Russia Attracts Many Students." *Review of Reviews*, XCII (June 9, 1934), 70–71.

Shapley, Harlow. "Stars over Russia." *Soviet Russia Today* (September, 1945), 11.

"Shostakovich Visits America." *Musical America*, LXIX (April, 1949), 4–5.

Simonson, Lee. "Exhibition of Russian Icons." *Metropolitan Museum Bulletin*, XXVI (January, 1931), 2–6.

Soth, Lauren, K. "Exchanges in Perspective." *Institute of International Education News Bulletin*, XXXI (November, 1955), 2–5.

"Soviet-American Exchanges: A Review Since 1917." *Institute of International Education News Bulletin*, XXXII (October, 1956), 16–25.

"Soviet Art Rejoicing in New-Found Freedom." *Literary Digest*, C (February 23, 1929), 22–23.

Steinbeck, John and Capa, Robert. "The USSR." *Ladies Home Journal*, LXV (February, 1948), 45–49.

Strohm, John. "Ivan Looks at Iowa." *Reader's Digest*, LXVIII (January, 1956), 173–177.

Struve, Gleb. "Anti-Westernism in Recent Soviet Literature." *Yale Review*, XXXIX (December, 1949), 208–224.

Suchkov, Z. "Soviet Industry and the U.S." *Review of the Soviet Union* (February 2, 1934), 45.

Taylor, J.F. "Russian Actors under Soviet Rule." *Theatre Magazine*, XXX (May, 1922), 298.

Talberg, Ina. "Heroes and Villains in Soviet Drama." *American Sociological Review*, IX (June, 1944), 308–311.

Thayer, Charles W. "I Found Russia Changed." *Saturday Evening Post*, CCXXVIII (March 31–April 14, 1956), 26; 31; 42.

"The Exchange of Scientific Information with the Soviet Union." *Bulletin of the Atomic Scientists*, IX (February, 1953), 13–15.

"The Fifteenth International Congress of Physiology: The Congress and Russian Physiology." *Science*, LXXXII (September 13, 1935), 240–243.

"The Genetic Furor in the USSR." *Journal of Heredity*, VIII (February, 1937), 57.

"The Quakers Meet the Russians." *Saturday Review*, XXXIX (Sept. 8, 1956), 15–18.

"The Soviet Editors Projected Visit." *Institute of International Education News Bulletin*, XXX (May, 1955), 4–6.

"The YMCA Expelled from Russia." *Literary Digest*, XCI (November 20, 1926), 37.

"Those Amazing Moscow Players." *Literary Digest*, LXXIX (Dec. 22, 1923), 26–28.

Truman, Harry S. "Fight False Propaganda with Truth." *State Department Bulletin*, XXII (May 1, 1950), 669–672.

"Two Self-Portraits: Russian and American." *New York Times Magazine* (July 29, 1956), 8–9.

"USSR Seeks U.S. Polio Fighting Know-How." *Science News Letter*, LXIX (January 28, 1956), 57.

Vickery, Oliver. "Capitalist on the Loose in Moscow." *Life*, XXXII (June 2, 1952), 102–112.

Villard, Oswald Garrison. "Russian from a Car-Window." *Nation*, CXXIX (November 6, 1933), 555–557.

"What We Found Inside Russia—Interviews with Thirteen Congressmen." *U.S. News and World Report*, XXXIX (October 21, 1955), 100–113.

Wick, Dodee. "Minnesota View of Life in the USSR." *Life*, XXXIV (April 20, 1953), 21–25.

Woody, Thomas. "Faults and Futures in American-Soviet Cultural Relations." *School and Society*, LXIV (September 28, 1946), 209–213.

Wilson, Edmund. "Eisenstein in Hollywood." *New Republic*, LXVII (November 4, 1921), 320–322.

———. "The Moscow Players." *Dial*, LXXIV (March, 1923), 319–320.

Wright, Frank Lloyd. "Architecture and Life in the USSR." *Architectural Record*, LXXXVII (October, 1937), 57–63.

Young, Edward L. "An American Surgeon on Soviet Medicine." *Soviet Russia Today* (October, 1946), 12–13.

Books

Anderson, Marian. *My Lord, What a Morning: An Autobiography*. New York: Viking Press, 1956.

Babkin, B.P. *Pavlov: A Biography*. Chicago: University of Chicago Press, 1949.

Bailey, Thomas A. *America Faces Russia: Russian-American Relations from Early Times to Our Day*. New York: Cornell University Press, 1950.

Barghoorn, Frederic C. *The Soviet Cultural Offensive*. Princeton: Princeton University Press, 1960.

———. *The Soviet Image of the United States: A Study in Distortion*. Port Washington, New York: Kennikat Press, 1969.

Barrett, Edward W. *Truth Is Our Weapon*. New York: Funk and Wagnalls, 1953.

Bechet, Sidney. *Treat It Gentle*. New York: Hill and Wang, 1960.

Bertensson, Sergei and Leyda, Jay. *Sergei Rachmaninoff: A Lifetime in Music*. New York: New York University Press, 1956.

Bolkhovitinov, Nikolai N. *The Beginning of Russian-American Relations 1775–1815*. Translated by Eleneva Levin. Cambridge: Harvard University Press, 1975.

Bourman, Anatole. *The Tragedy of Nijinsky*. Westport, Connecticut: Greenwood Press, 1970.

Bullitt, Orville H., editor. *For the President, Personal and Secret: Correspondence between Franklin D. Roosevelt and William C. Bullitt*. Boston: Houghton-Mifflin Company, 1972.

Cannon, Walter Bradford. *The Way of an Investigator: A Scientist's Experiences in Medical Research*. New York: W.W. Norton Company, 1945.

Chaliapine, Feodor Ivanovitch. *Pages from My Life: An Autobiography*. Translated by H.M. Buck. New York: Harper and Brothers, 1927.

Conant, James B. *My Several Lives: Memoirs of a Social Inventor*. New York: Harper and Row, 1970.

Day, Donald. *Will Rogers: A Biography*. New York: David McKay, 1962.

Dewey, John. *Impressions of Soviet Russia and the Revolutionary World*. New York: New Republic, Inc., 1929.

Douglas, William O. *Russian Journey*. Garden City, New York: Doubleday, 1956.

Dreiser, Theodore. *Dreiser Looks at Russia*. New York: Horace Liverwright, 1928.

Duggan, Stephen P. *A Professor at Large*. New York: Macmillan Press, 1943.

Duncan, Isadora. *My Life*. New York: Horace Liverwright, 1927.

Farnsworth, Beatrice. *William C. Bullitt and the Soviet Union*. Bloomington: Indiana University Press, 1967.

Filene, Peter G. *Americans and the Soviet Experiment, 1917–1933*. Cambridge: Harvard University Press, 1967.

Fisher, H.H. *The Famine in Soviet Russia, 1919–1923: The Operation of the American Relief Administration*. New York : The Macmillan Company, 1927.

Fuelop-Miller, Rene. *The Mind and Face of Bolshevism: An Examination of Cultural Life in the Soviet Union*. Translated by F.S. Flint and D.F. Tait. New York: Harper and Row, 1965.

Geduld, Harry and Gottesman, Ronald. *Sergei Eisenstein and Upton Sinclair: The Making and Unmaking of "Que Viva Mexico."* Bloomington: Indiana University Press, 1970.

Grigoriev, S.L. *The Diaghilev Ballet, 1909–1927*. Translated by Vera Bowen. New York: Dance Horizons, 1953.

Hamilton, Virginia. *Paul Robeson: The Life and Times of a Free Black Man*. New York: Harper and Row, 1974.

Hammer, Armand. *The Quest of the Romanoff Treasure*. New York: Payson, 1932.

Harper, Paul V., editor. *The Russia I Believe in: The Memoirs of Samuel N. Harper*. Chicago: University of Chicago Press, 1945.

Hurok, Sol. *Impresario*. Westport, Connecticut: Greenwood Press, 1946.

_____. *Sol Hurok Presents: A Memoir of the Dance World*. New York: Hermitage House, 1953.

Jelagin, Juri. *Taming of the Arts*. Translated by Nicholas Wreden. New York: E.P. Dutton and Company, 1951.

Johnston, Eric. *We're All In It*. New York: E.P. Dutton and Company, 1950.

Kennell, Ruth Epperson. *Theodore Dreiser and the Soviet Union: A First-Hand Chronicle*. New York: International Publishers, 1969.

Lamont, Corliss and Margaret. *Russia Day by Day: A Travel Diary*. New York: Covici-Friede, 1933.

Laves, Walter C. and Thompson, Charles A. *Cultural Relations and U.S. Foreign Policy*. Bloomington: Indiana University Press, 1963.

Littlepage, John D. and Bess, Demaree. *In Search of Soviet Gold*. New York: Harcourt, Brace and Company, 1937.

Ludwig, Emil. *Nine Etched from Life*. New York: Robert M. McBride, 1934.

Lyons, Eugene. *Assignment in Utopia*. New York: Harcourt, Brace and World, 1937.

_____. *Six Soviet Plays*. New York: Houghton-Mifflin Company, 1934.

Magidoff, Robert M. *In Anger and Pity: A Report on Russia*. Garden City, New York: Doubleday and Doubleday, Inc., 1949.

Menuhin, Yehudi. *Unfinished Journey*. New York: Alfred A. Knopf, 1977.

Murray, Robert K. *The Red Scare: A Study in National Hysteria, 1919-1920*. New York: McGraw Hill Book Company, 1964.

Nelson, George. *Industrial Architecture of Albert Kahn, Inc*. New York: Architectural Book Publishing Company, 1939.

Nevins, Allan and Hill, Frank Ernest. *Ford: Expansion and Challenge, 1915-1933*. New York: Charles Scribner's Sons, 1957.

Reiss, Clare R. *Composers, Conductors and Critics*. New York: Oxford University Press, 1961.

Sayler, Oliver M. *Inside the Moscow Art Theatre*. Westport, Connecticut: Greenwood Press Publishers, 1970.

Seroff, Victor. *Sergei Prokofiev: A Soviet Tragedy*. London: Leslie Frewin, 1969.

Simmons, Ernest J. "Negotiating on Cultural Exchange," in Raymond Dennet and Joseph E. Johnston, *Negotiating with the Russians*. Boston: World Peace Foundation, 1951.

Slonim, Marc. *Russian Theatre from the Empire to the Soviets*. New York: Collier Books, 1962.

_____. *Soviet Russian Literature: Writers and Problems, 1917-1977*. New York: Oxford University Press, 1977.

Smith, Walder Bedell. *My Three Years in Moscow*. New York: J.B. Lippincott Company, 1950.

Stalin, Joseph. *Foundations of Leninism*. Moscow: Foreign Languages Publishing House, 1954.

_____. *Voprosy Leninisma*. Moscow, 1945.

Standley, William H. and Ageton, Arthur A. *Admiral Ambassador to Russia*. Chicago: Henry Regnery Company, 1955.

Stanislavsky, Constantin. *My Life in Art*. Translated by J.J. Robbins. New York: Theatre Art Books, 1948.

Steiger, Andrew. *American Engineers in the Soviet Union*. New York, 1942.

Sutton, Anthony C. *Western Technology and Soviet Economic Development*. 3 Vols. Stanford: Stanford University Press, 1968-1973.

Swallow, Norman. *Eisenstein: A Documentary Portrait*. London: George Allen and Unwin, 1976.

Swayze, Harold. *Political Control of Literature in the USSR, 1946-1959*. Cambridge: Harvard University Press, 1962.

Thayer, Charles W. *Bears in the Caviar*. Philadelphia: Lippincott Company, 1951.

Wald, Lillian. *Windows on Henry Street*. Boston: Little, Brown, 1934.

Weissman, Benjamin M. *Herbert Hoover and Famine Relief to Russia, 1921-1923*. Stanford: Hoover Institution Press, 1974.

Werth, Alexander. *Russia: The Post-War Years*. New York: Taplinger Publishing Company, 1971.

Wilson, Joan Hoff. *Ideology and Economics: U.S. Relations with the Soviet Union, 1918-1933*. Columbia, Missouri: University of Missouri Press, 1974.

Zhdanov, Andrei. *Essays on Literature, Philosophy and Music*. New York: International Publishers, 1950.

Index